TANK RIDER

EVGENI BESSONOV

TANK RIDER

INTO THE REICH
WITH THE RED ARMY

Evgeni Bessonov
Translated by Bair Irincheev

CASEMATE
Philadelphia

This Edition of Tank Rider: Into the Reich with the Red Army
Published in 2005 by
CASEMATE

© Evgeni Bessonov 2003

Edited by Sergei Anisimov
Translated by Bair Irincheev

Publication made possible by the 'I Remember' website (www.iremember.ru)

ISBN 1-932033-48-3

Cataloging-in-Publication data available
from the Library of Congress

Also published in the United Kingdom by
Greenhill Books, Lionel Leventhal Limited,
Park House, 1 Russell Gardens,
London NW11 9NN
www.greenhillbooks.com
ISBN 1-85367-671-3

Typeset by Palindrome
Manufactured in the United States of America

CONTENTS

LIST OF ILLUSTRATIONS AND MAPS

PLATES

MAPS

FOREWORD

Many of my comrades told me that I should write my memoirs but it is actually a difficult thing to do. After all, I'm not a professional writer – if the truth be known, I'm very far from that. But I can tell the story of my family, my childhood and my youth, and relate to you my experiences during the years of the Great Patriotic War.

Human memory is an amazing thing and life erodes away many experiences and events. With all the burdens and cares of daily life I had no time to indulge myself in my memories. I was not a government official or a politician, but a simple individual just like millions of others in our country. My memoirs will concern themselves with events that I saw take place or with those events which had an impact on me and those around me during the War. I do not claim to have a full and objective reflection of events – human memory isn't perfect – but I will try my best. Similarly, I will try not to be too critical in my judgement of others. Things that are described in the memoirs are my personal point of view, my personal judgement and my perception of life. These memoirs are a look back at the life of a typical member of the Red Army, a career officer, who served 35 years of his life in the military – from 1941 to 1976. I entered service when I was 18 and retired at the age of 53 as a Colonel.

Of course, my memoirs will focus almost exclusively on the war years. There are fewer and fewer veterans left and those who are still alive are old. I myself turned 80 in 2003. The Great Patriotic War took a tremendous toll on the peoples of the Soviet Union but, regardless of how hard it was, the common people stood up to the test, despite heavy losses, and despite it being very hard both at the front and behind the lines. My aim is to show the War through the eyes of a participant in those events – not through the eyes of a Marshal or a writer, but of a platoon leader and company commander of tank riders, the motor rifle battalion of a mechanized brigade in the 4th Guards Tank Army. I fought for two years in the 4th Guards, from 1943 to 1945, and I covered around 3,800 kilometres with this unit. Such was my wartime voyage, and it was tough every step of the way. I participated in infantry assaults and rode into battle on tanks attacking the enemy positions. Intuition, experience of battle and knowledge of enemy tactics saved my life many times, but I think that I mostly survived by pure luck. Luck was vital at the front, and I can't over-emphasize its importance for any soldier.

EVGENI BESSONOV 2003

CHRONOLOGY

1941

22 June   Germany invades the Soviet Union
16 July   The Germans reach Smolensk
9 August   Drafted into Red Army, to Chebarkulski military
                 camp
16 November   Transferred to Kamyshlov military infantry
                 academy

1942

July   Assigned to 365th Reserve Rifle Brigade at Surok
                 station
19 November   The Soviet counteroffensive at Stalingrad begins

1943

31 January   The Germans surrender at Stalingrad
Late May   Transferred to personnel section, Moscow
5 July   The battle of Kursk begins
July   Assigned to Bryansk front
August   Joined 4th Tank Army, assigned to 6th Guards
                 Mechanized Corps, 49th Mechanized Brigade, 1st
                 Motor Rifle Battalion, appointed 2nd platoon
                 leader
September   Fighting in the Orel offensive
October–December Into reserve at Karachev
6 November   Kiev is recaptured

1944

January   4th Tank Army transferred to Kiev
February   Transported by train to Polonnoe, marched to

	Shepetovka, by truck to Slavuta
4 March	Spring offensive is launched in the Ukraine
March–April	Fighting in the Kamenets-Podolsk campaign (brigade awarded title of 49th Mechanized Kamenets-Podolsk Brigade)
May–June	Into reserve at Kopychintsy
July–September	Fighting in the Lvov-Sandomir operation
October–November	Into reserve at Sandomir
December–January	Fighting in the Vistula-Oder operation, through Poland to the German border

1945

February	Fighting to the Neisse bridgehead
March–April	Into reserve at Oberau
April	The march on Berlin, wounded in action
30 April	Hitler commits suicide
2 May	Berlin surrenders to the Red Army
8 May	Keitel signs German surrender at Zhukhov's Headquarters
9 May	Prague falls to the Red Army
May	Discharged from hospital, rejoined battalion at Prague; end of the Great Patriotic War

TANK RIDER

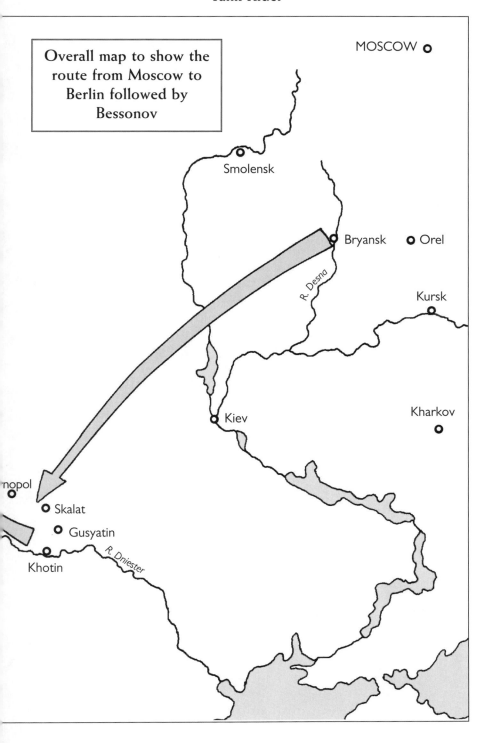

Overall map to show the route from Moscow to Berlin followed by Bessonov

MOSCOW ○

Smolensk

Bryansk ○ Orel

R. Desna

Kursk

Kiev

Kharkov

rnopol

Skalat

Gusyatin

Khotin

R. Dniester

YEARS OF CHILDHOOD
AND YOUTH

I was born in Moscow on 20 July, 1923, in no. 77 Friedrich Engels street, formerly known as Irininskaya. My father, Ivan Vasilievich Bessonov, moved to Moscow from a village in 1908 at the age of fifteen. Although he had almost no education, he managed to get a job in a small store and after a while become a *prikazchik* (salesman) and later senior salesman. In 1915 he married my mother, Olga Pavlovna, a native of Moscow. They had a daughter Elena (we called her Lelya) in 1916 and that same year my father was drafted into the army. He served in the army until the February revolution and retired in 1917. After the Great October Revolution my father worked in trade before retiring in 1960. My mother studied at a school for tailors in Moscow but didn't like to recall that period of her life. As she put it, it was pure drudgery. They had to get up at 5 or 6 o'clock in the morning, start the oven, cook tea for the foremen, wash dishes after their meal and clean the rooms and the workshop. Such apprentices would only start their professional training several years later, as it was profitable for the master to have several minor servants almost free of charge. After she completed her professional training and became a tailor, my mother got a job in a more prestigious tailor's shop at Kuznetski bridge and had a decent salary for that time – 37–40 roubles in 1913. After she married my father she had four children and became a housewife.

In early 1917 my parents were renting an apartment in the building where I was to be born. It was a typical Moscow yard, surrounded by a high fence. There were many small yards like this in the street, and they were named after the landlords: Krushinski, Reshetkin, Maslov, Petrusinski and so on.

There were three wooden buildings in our yard, two of them were available for a rather high rent, and the landlady with her family occupied the third one. A carriage shed with stables was adjacent to the landlady's building. All the buildings were one storey high, heated by stoves, without running water or plumbing, so we had to get water in the street from a water pump. The landlady had a fruit garden in the yard with apple and cherry trees, raspberry and gooseberry bushes.

After the October Revolution they took all three houses from the landlady and father started to pay significantly less for the two twelve-square-metre rooms that we occupied. We had to share our kitchen with neighbours, who also had two rooms. A Russian stove heated our two rooms and one of the neighbour's rooms. In wintertime the temperature would drop to 13–15 degrees Celsius by morning.

Dinner, or food in general, was heated on kerosene heaters and Primus stoves; we also used these devices to boil water for tea, as the main stove and the oven were only stoked once a day. They only installed gas in the building after the Great Patriotic War and the wood oven was only then replaced by a gas oven. Other conveniences, or rather inconveniences, remained the same.

I should say that they only installed electric lights in our street in 1935 or 1936 and that the street had been illuminated by gas lamps until then. Every evening a special worker would walk around the street and light the lamps and put them out in the morning. He carried a special ladder with him for this purpose, and the lamp-posts had a special crossbar to rest it on.

Until the mid-1930s our neighbourhood was a haunt for thieves and hooligans and we even had famous thieves living in our yard. Between 1936 and 1938 measures were taken, they all went to jail and our neighbourhood became quiet.

Recalling our life before 1941, I think that our family had a modest life. We had a Singer sewing machine, and our mother made all our clothes for us with the help of this machine. Clothes were passed on from one sister to another, and even I received some things adapted from my sisters' clothes. Our furniture was quite simple, for besides the sewing machine we had a wall clock, a chest of drawers, an old wardrobe, two metallic beds, two chests that we children used as beds, chairs and a bookshelf with some books.

It was cramped: sometimes I had a hard time finding somewhere to do my homework. For some time my sister Lelya even had to sleep on the table, which was, fortunately quite large.

In every room in the place of honour there were three icons with lampstands; grandmother lit them up quite frequently. After Lelya and Galya entered *Komsomol* (the common name for VLKSM, the All-Union Lenin's Communistic Union of Youth) in 1933, my father took the icons down and hid them, leaving just one icon in the kitchen for our grandmother.

On holidays, sometimes on Sundays, we would bake *pirogi*, pastries, jam patties, and sometimes a *pirog* with a jam or meat filling *(pirogi are small pies, a* pirog *here refers to a large one for the whole family — translator's comment)*. For New Year our father would buy a New Year tree, decorate it with toys, candles which we lit in the evening and sweets if we had them. At Easter, my mother and grandmother baked two Easter cakes; sometimes they went to the church to sanctify them; they would leave early and then stay there for a very long time. My father rarely invited guests — his friends with their wives, sometimes with children. Mother's friend, aunt Shura, her former classmate, would come to visit her sometimes.

Before leaving for school for the first shift (as there was a lack of schools, some of them had to organize teaching in two shifts — the first one in the morning and the second one in the evening), we had tea and bread with butter if we had it; we did not have any hot meal. After coming back from school we had soup or *schi (traditional Russian soup; the main ingredient is cabbage — translator's comment)* for the first course; for the second course we had potatoes, pasta, millet porridge or buckwheat porridge, sometimes we had fried cutlets or fish. In the evenings we had tea with bread, very rarely we had sausage. We had free breakfasts at school.

On Sundays we went with friends to watch films for children at a cinema or to the Markov club or the '3rd International' cinema next to Bumanskaya Metro station. The Markov club was next to the school where I studied, on Bolshaya Pochtovaya street.

I went to the parades on Red Square on a regular basis on 1 May and 7 November, together with our school or with the workers from the factory where our neighbour Sergei Glazkov, a highly professional turner, worked. I liked going to parades — it was fun, people were dressed in festive clothes, sang songs, danced, orchestras played music everywhere and children received gifts from the factories (sweets, cookies and soft drinks).

Until the age of 13 or 14 I was a sickly and thin child. I would fall sick very often, I had scarlet fever, measles, pneumonia and inflammation of my middle ear. I was shy, I was often lost when I had to answer in class, I could not always express my thoughts properly. First I had trouble with mathematics, then I got it sorted out, but I never learned to write properly – my writing has always been full of mistakes. In order to improve my health I started to do sports: athletics, cross-country skiing, soccer and volleyball. We had high jump and long jump competitions. For two years I was in the wrestling section at Lokomotiv stadium, at the same place where I lifted weights in order to strengthen my muscles. In the school we boys jumped over the vaulting horse and did some exercises on the horizontal bar. Sports did me good, for I became stronger physically and illness left me alone. In the 10th grade I was the school's best high jumper, together with my classmates Fakin and Zolotukhin. I took part in the district-level ski race, but did not achieve any outstanding success, the same with wrestling. When I was called up to the army in September 1941, I was 180 cm high and weighted 70 kilograms, which was a normal combination for an 18 year old boy. Sports helped me to take the physical stress in army life and at the front. Later, in the army, I discovered a talent for shooting small-arms, especially pistols.

I was not too brave and so I got into fights very rarely; not only because I did not know how to fight, but also because of my character – I felt bad hitting someone in the face, especially a friend. I was never angry with anyone, unlike some other boys. A couple of times I was hit and just could not bring myself to hit back.

I think I was the last one in our class to join Komsomol. That was as late as 1939. I was a Pioneer in junior classes, so I had my red tie before I entered (the Young Pioneers was a youth organization for 10- to 15-year-olds, highly ideological in character with aims of educating children about the Soviet state, the history of the Communist party, etc. – translator's comment).

When our 341st school joined the trade school in December 1940 we were transferred to the 350th school on Bolshaya Pochtovaya street, the Komsomol organization elected me the chairman of voluntary Osoviakhim society (renamed DOSAAF after the war) *(this was the Society for the Promotion of Aviation and Defence against Chemicals. It was an educational organization in the USSR in the 1930s, providing a basic military education along with training in defence against chemicals – translator's comment).* I would not say that this organization did a lot of activities in the school, but there were sometimes shooting competitions, which were especially important; we arranged hiking trips in gas-masks; sometimes even classes and other activities were done in gas-masks. My best friends in the street at that time were Vladimir Dolmatov, Petr Hromyshev, Lev Kolyhalov (killed in 1942) and Yevgeni Bogolyubski (missing in action). Later my best friends in my class were Alexander Fokin (killed in 1943) and Andrey Otryganiev (became a Lieutenant Colonel and died in 1957 at the age of 35). We all lived close to our school, we had common views and areas of interest, we were all tall and athletic guys and attained similar results in our studies.

Unfortunately, in the last quarter of the 1941 school year we stopped all sports activities – we had to prepare for graduation exams. After a long discussion, several guys from my class, including me, decided to apply for the Sevastopol Navy Academy, but I did not pass the medical commission – they said I had colour-blindness, rather insignificant, though. Nevertheless, the commission found me unfit for service in the Navy and Air Force (I also tried to enter a pilot club). We schoolmates did not think of war, believing that war would take place on the enemy's territory, and we were light-hearted then. I passed all my graduation exams with distinction, except for Russian literature composition. The graduation party took place on 17 June and we received our 'Maturity certificates'. The war started five days later.

THE WAR BEGINS

I first heard that the war had broken out while I was in the city, where I had gone with Vladimir Grivnin, my classmate – we had plans to go to a retro film theatre, which was at Nikitski Gate. We young boys took the news quite calmly, we thought that the Nazi invaders were about to be thrown back from the country's borders. But exactly the opposite happened. This conflict, the harshest of all wars, would last 1,418 days for us, or 3 years, 10 months and 17 days.

On 25 or 26 June, 1941, I, along with other Komsomol members, was invited to the Baumanski district committee of Komsomol. There they suggested that we go to the Bryansk region to build fortifications. On the evening of the same day we were loaded on to a train with some personal belongings and food; we travelled westwards to build fortifications. We started to work at Kirov city in the Bryansk region. We worked twelve hours a day, and as we were not used to physical labour, we were really exhausted. We fell asleep as soon as our heads touched our 'beds' of hay or straw, which were made mostly in barns. We dug anti-tank ditches, dug around the riverbanks, dug trenches and set barbed-wire obstacles. In some cases we had to repair the railways destroyed during air raids and clear them from the debris of destroyed goods trains. However, our main job was to dig anti-tank ditches. The food was poor, it was not enough for us and the village population was not very kind to us. Our foreman, who arrived with us from Moscow, had to talk to the locals, mostly to leaders of the *kolkhos* (collective farm) or village, if they had not been drafted into the army, and persuade them to give us some food, at least potatoes. Such talks helped, but quite rarely. The German air force bombed us several times: scared, we ran in all directions like rabbits. We were young and healthy and could run fast. We did not suffer any losses, especially as the bombs exploded far away from us, but as we had not seen fire, we were quaking in our boots. We worked there for 45 days, until 8 August, 1941, and then were urgently loaded on a train and in the morning of 9 August we were back in Moscow, at Kiev station. College students were drafted in the army on the spot and were sent to different units.

When we, five to seven young men, walked into a metro train, passengers started to pay attention to us. We were dirty and ragged, in patched-up shirts and trousers, our hair grown long and dirty and tangled. However, women came up to us and started to ask us who we were where we were from. When they learnt that we were from the labour front, they, just like all mothers, started to ask us about their children, but we had not known or seen anyone that they were asking about. When I came home, there was already an official paper that said that I had been drafted into the Red Army and had to show up at the assembly point in school in Takmakov lane by 11 August. That was the assembly point for the Baumanski district military commissariat of Moscow. Some neighbours in the street and classmates also received similar call-up notes.

During the night of 12 August we were loaded on to a train, taking our places in freight wagons (for 40 men or 8 horses) and we rolled eastwards. On the way individual cars were taken away as the men were sent to different military academies. Alexander Fokin left our company this way. In the vicinity of Chelyabinsk we were quartered in tents at the Chebarkulski military camp, where army units of the Urals Military District stayed during the summer. Before the cold weather set in, we lived in that camp, mostly doing drill. We still had civilian clothes. With the arrival of cold weather we were transferred to the summer film theatre of the Chelyabinsk park of culture. Moscow also had similar summer film theatres before the war. The autumn in the Urals was cold: we were freezing in the film theatre, some were falling sick and the shoes of some men fell apart, plus the food was very bad, and some men turned to theft. After that some top brass decided to get rid of this large, unmanageable and motley crew (we were at least 500), the majority of whom went into the city in the morning searching for food. They started to send the men out to different places of service. My friends Turanov, Tvorogov and Silvanovich left. I met them only after the war in Moscow. They all went through the war and survived, although Silvanovich was crippled after being wounded. In October a strange Sergeant Major picked us, some twenty men, and together with him we went to a *kolkhoz* to harvest potatoes, which the locals had not managed to harvest before the first frosts. They put us in an unheated room, we were freezing at night, but we were getting so tired during the day that we did not notice the cold. That was in Urals region, and it was already mid- or late October. The villagers did not help us at all, did not give us either food or firewood, we did not even have a pot to boil potatoes in. We were constantly hungry, besides that, many of us, including me, caught cold. Our superior also did not take proper care of us; it was good that they made a decision to move us back to Chelyabinsk. I can to some extent understand the words of one woman from a village where we had been digging anti-tank trenches, who refused to give us food saying: 'What am I going to feed the Germans with, when they come?' But that was in Bryansk region, not in the Urals, which was far away from the Germans. Never again in my life did I meet such people — they really deserve their name *choldons (a name for Russians living in Siberia; however, normally the name does not have any negative connotation — translator's comment)*. We only encountered such attitudes in the Western Ukraine, but those were Bandera's areas *(Bandera was a famous Ukrainian anti-Soviet resistance leader — translator's comment)*, which only became part of USSR in 1940.

We never returned to the summer film theatre in Chelyabinsk. We were moved from one barracks to another, but the good thing was that they were at least warm. They fed us really badly: boiled root beets in hot water, and that was it. Instead of dishes we had a clean small wash-tub. It is hard to explain such poverty, it was only the fourth month of the war. We saw plenty of soldiers drafted from the reserve. They were gloomy, untidy, a set of doomed 40-year-old men, who looked much older. I never met such backward men at the front. It was amazing that they were Siberian! In early November 1941 some 400 of us were loaded on to a train in Chelyabinsk. We were all sent to Kamyshlov military infantry academy. We suffered a lot from hunger on the way to Kamyshlov. As usual, they appointed a crook as the senior man of our team; he received the food for the whole group, gave out a ration for one day and disappeared with the rest of the food – we never saw him again. Stealing was widespread in the early days of the war, while thieves were hard to catch. Hungry boys literally turned over food kiosks at railway stations, taking everything they could find. After several similar attacks they started to make stops only in open fields and not at railway stations or villages. I received some food from the guys that I knew, mostly bread.

They unloaded us in the town of Kamyshlov in the Sverdlovsk region, some 180 km to the east of Sverdlovsk (now Yekaterinburg). The ones that arrived on that train were distributed among four companies – the 13th, 14th, 15th and 16th, which formed the fourth battalion. I ended up in the 15th company. Those who stubbornly and consistently refused to study, as well as some former criminals, were sent into army units that were in process of formation for the front in the Urals region.

We were sworn in at the academy on 16 November, 1941, and we were all officially accepted as cadets. First we received boots with puttees instead of jack-boots. We had a hard time with them – you try to wrap it around your leg and all of a sudden it slips out of your hand, and you have to start all over again. During that period almost all soldiers of the Red Army had boots with puttees, especially the infantry. They issued winter uniforms to us in the academy (that was when puttees were replaced by jack-boots): cotton foot-cloths, woollen tunics and padded trousers, a padded jacket to be worn under the greatcoat and mittens. We did not have winter hats, though, and we had to walk around in garrison caps. Some put a towel under a garrison cap when the temperatures dropped to minus 20–25 degrees Celsius. That winter frosts in the Urals region were sharp, we saw sparrows freezing to death in mid-flight – I am not making this up. We received winter hats as late as January 1942. We lived on the first floor of a huge two-storey barrack. We slept on two-level metallic beds. We ourselves stuffed mattresses and pillows with hay in the administration platoon of the academy. We were issued two sheets and a cotton blanket. There were two large Ural-style wood stoves in the opposite corners of the barrack. Every floor housed two companies of 120 men each. Companies were separated by a wide corridor, where we would all fall in for a morning inspection (form no. 20 – the code for a lice check) and an evening inspection. In the ends of the barrack building there were a storage room, officers' room, a rifle park (or, more accurately, a rifle pyramid), bathroom and toilets. Classes lasted from 10 to 12 hours, including individual study time. The reveille was at 6:00 or 6:30, I do not remember exactly, taps were at 23:00. We would get very tired during the day, as we only had classes outdoors, so we were always hungry and sleepy. They fed us quite well. They gave us some 750 grams of bread a day, sugar at breakfast and dinner for our tea. Breakfast as a rule included porridge, a piece of butter (20 grams), tea and bread. For lunch we had soup or *schi* based on meat bouillon, mashed potatoes or porridge with meat for the second course, stewed fruit and bread. Dinner was quite poor – beetroot salad or a piece of boiled fish (sometimes herring) with potatoes, tea, bread and sugar. Cadets had even better food than commanders *(in 1941 and 1942 officers in Red Army were still officially referred to as commanders – translator's comment)* in their own canteen. However, we were using a lot of energy and spending all the daytime in the frost outside, so our young bodies required more food and sleep. The sleeping time was insufficient for us, although we had a rest time after lunch. Some cadets could not take such physical stress and grew noticeably weaker and thinner, the others, not used to such strong frosts, had their feet frost-bitten.

Our company commander was Senior Lieutenant Suleimenov, a Kazakh, physically strong and an excellent training officer. The company had four platoons, 30 cadets in each platoon. The academy had a total of 20 companies (5 battalions). Lieutenant Khrapovitski was leader of my platoon, the 1st, and Lieutenant Ilyin led the 2nd platoon. I forget the names of the other two platoon leaders. The majority of cadets in the 1st and the 2nd platoons were Muscovites, while the 3rd and the 4th platoons mostly had local men from the Urals and adjacent areas.

The head of the academy was the *kombrig (pre-war and early war Red Army rank that corresponds to Major-General – translator's comment)* (he had one diamond on his collar tab), though the army had already introduced general ranks. We saw him quite rarely, mostly during parades, which we only had two or three times during our stay in the academy. They said that he was just recently released from jail. He had been arrested as a former officer of the Tsar's Army, as had happened with Rokossovski, Marshal of Soviet Union, and General Gorbatov.

In mid-December, 1941, our company was sent to a winter camp outside the city, where we lived in dugouts and slept on two-level plank-beds. There was no running water there, we had to wash ourselves with snow after the physical exercises, which we had to do outside in any frost, and by morning temperatures dropped to as low as minus 30–35 degrees Celsius! We skied 18 kilometres to *banya* three times a month *(a* banya *is a traditional Russian steam bath – translator's note)*. We also studied drill and ceremonies: ceremonial step, turning to left, right, around and saluting (at that time they called it greeting each other and the commanders). We studied weapons, service and field manuals. We also studied tactics – we rehearsed attacks on the enemy, as well as platoon and company action in defence. Sometimes we had range practice. After a month or a month and a half we returned to barracks in the city.

We were forbidden to leave the military area and go to town, but there was nothing to do there anyway. We had a post office, a store with all kinds of small things that a soldier might need, such as threads and needles. There was also a club with a cinema and a library. On Sundays (we cadets had a day off as well) I went to the library and read newspapers there, usually *Pravda*; I borrowed fiction, took it to the barracks and managed to find time to read it there. We marched in formation to see movies; normally that was during the morning before lunch. I only remember one film – *The Destruction of German forces at Moscow*. During the other films I would fall asleep, just like so many other cadets, even though the heating of the hall was very poor. When we were on duty in the company – a cadet on duty and three orderlies – we ran to the station cafe at the time of arrival of a train from Moscow to get some wheat porridge – it was not millet, but wheat porridge. There was nothing else in the cafe. We normally had it poured into the fire bucket. Several pieces of bread were also given with the porridge. We would finish the bucket of porridge during the night, and if we had porridge left, we woke up a couple of our friends. By morning the bucket was to be cleaned and hung on the fire-fighting stand again. There were different cadets in the academy – honest, responsive, helping each other, sharing food parcels with close friends according to the cadets' rule of thumb. Others were dishonest and did not respect even the elementary requirements of discipline. The cadets themselves dealt with thieves. In any case, the older cadets did not abuse the younger ones, or if they did, we did not know anything about it. It was easy for me to overcome the difficulties of military service, the same with the frosts. I was the third tallest cadet in the company. The tallest was Anatoly Pavlovich Zlobin − an outstanding writer after the war; he died in 2000. We were drafted from Moscow together. He was a mortar-battery commander at the front. I had good relations with all the men in the company, while in the platoon we were all good friends − we were all Muscovites from the same neighbourhood and graduated from neighbouring schools, we even had common acquaintances. We had nothing to fight about. Physically I was no worse than the other cadets in the platoon and the company. I was not outstanding, but I stood up for myself. I did not flatter anyone and didn't tell tales. The company commander was somehow distant from us, we did not see him every day. In the evenings we had classes with assistant platoon leaders; as a rule these were older cadets, not the former schoolboys, but cadets that had entered the academy earlier than ourselves. Some men had a hard time with the studies, and two cadets could not take it. One local man, Lisitsyn, shot himself in a dugout during his company guard duty. The second guy, Vischnevski, a native of Moscow, escaped. They looked for him for a long time, but never found him. Both incidents were emergency cases for the company. Later there was a rumour that a letter came from Vishnevski, in which he wrote that he was at the front and asked not to be considered a deserter. However, the letter was not officially read to us − probably so that other cadets would not follow his example.

We had to learn in six months what we would have studied for two years in the pre-war military academy. The front needed officers for platoon-company level, as these were being killed the fastest at the front. We studied field manuals and had to learn in practice, as they say in the army *Infantry Field Manual* of 1936, from the actions of individual soldiers to the responsibilities of a company commander in defence and attack. This manual was abolished in 1942 and replaced by a revised manual which was based on the experience gained in the first year of war. We were also supposed to know the army manual, internal service manual, guard duty manual and drill manual by heart. Besides that we studied technical manuals, we were supposed to know the weapons, assembling and disassembling weapons, employment, failures and repair, principles of its work. We studied the Mosin rifle Model 1892/1930, the Simonov automatic rifle, the Degtyarev light machine-gun (RPD or DP) and the Maxim heavy machine-gun – the difficulty with that was in assembling and disassembling its bolt or rather lock, which was intricate. This machine-gun, just like the Mosin rifle, dated back to the First World War and the Russian Civil War, and was used until the end of the Great Patriotic War. Besides those weapons, we studied mortars: the 37 mm company mortar (later withdrawn from service), the 50 mm and the 82 mm mortars, their technical data and employment, firing conditions and preparation for firing. I should say that the level of training was poor, as the teachers did not understand the subject themselves. In general, during the war our mortar crews were really bad shooters. Of course, artillery units – mortar battalions and even regiments – were very well trained, but the infantry mortars were not that successful. Indeed, they almost killed me once! German mortar teams were very good and well trained, while their artillery was just average.

Along with all the other things we were also trained in the language of command (in comparison with other subjects I achieved outstanding success in this field) and also had political classes. Political classes were confined to lectures given by a teacher; exhausted cadets could hardly take them, and some fell asleep. I can remember it myself – I was always dozing off at those lectures, and nothing remains in my memory from them. But in general most of the time in the academy we spent on military subjects, training was intensive and we became quite exhausted. We never completed the course of preparation of fire data for the 82 mm mortar and we had to learn this in our units at the front. But I stayed in infantry and besides me at least 30 men were not sent to mortar units. We never fired live ammo from those mortars, which was wise given that apparently our platoon leaders and company commander themselves did not really know how to operate them. Except for the company commander they were all graduates of the same Kamyshlov infantry academy and had not had mortar or artillery courses during their studies, as they would have had in artillery academies. They studied the theory of shooting a mortar together with us and could not give us any decent knowledge, while we cadets did not take that mortar course seriously.

Our course was over, and in early May 1942 the cadets received their military ranks, some became Lieutenants and some Junior

Lieutenants; to my great dismay, I was among the latter. I was upset, but gradually I calmed down – what was the difference, we all had to go to the front as platoon leaders anyway. 480 officers (4 companies) graduated. The graduation was passed unnoticed, just like another day – it was wartime. The barracks were empty, new cadets had yet to arrive. We said good-bye to everyone – to many of them for good. I was not even 19 years old, and we now had to lead other people, soldiers, who were older than us. The burden of responsibility that the war put on our young shoulders was especially heavy. We, young men, almost boys, had to lead at least 100 mature and experienced men; we were responsible for their lives, for orders; we had to solve moral problems, but we, the young ones, did not bend and did not break. That's the way it was.

Some commanders – we were no longer cadets – some 25 to 30 men, including me, stayed in the academy. They told us that we were supposed to undergo training as tank-hunter platoon leaders in the anti-tank rifle platoon. No one really knew what this might involve. Afterwards we received an explanation in the form of a manual. It stated that in every rifle battalion, first a platoon and then an anti-tank rifle company were to be formed to engage the enemy's tanks. The academy received two anti-tank rifles – the first one a Degtyarev model and the second a Simonov, the semi-automatic one, as well as anti-tank grenades. We rarely fired the rifles, as we had to spare the ammo, and threw dummy grenades instead of live ones. Then, in early July 1942, we were sent to an army unit.

We did not go straight to the front but ended up in the 365th Reserve Rifle Regiment of the 46th Reserve Rifle Brigade at Surok station in the Mariiskaya region. They trained replacements for the units at the front in that regiment. Red Army soldiers did basic military training, mostly shooting and tactics – the usual actions of an individual soldier in squad and platoon. Lieutenant Zhukov, a man from our academy and a Muscovite, and I were sent to a sniper company. A 40-year-old, Junior Lieutenant Chudakov, who was called up from reserve, was the company commander. I became platoon leader; I had 30 men as my subordinates. They were all of different ages and nationalities, and many of them had already lived a long life. At first I was a bit uncomfortable giving orders to older men and I felt frustrated, but later it all seemed normal. The platoon leader's wage was 600 roubles a month; 50 roubles were deducted as a military tax and we got 550 roubles in cash, but we did not have anything to spend the money on, as there were no shops in the regiment. Outside the regiment there was a rationing system, and market prices were very high: a loaf of bread was 200–250 roubles; half a litre of vodka or moonshine was 250–300 roubles – that was all we could get for our wage.

Besides shooting and studying weapons in the sniper company we taught the men to dig in with a small entrenching tool, camouflage in terrain, advance in short rushes, throw grenades, mostly RGD-33s, and to charge with the bayonet. They sent younger men who were enthusiastic about marksmanship to the sniper company, and they tried to reach my level of skill, but there were very few men in the regiment who could shoot better than me. Although we did not have real combat experience, we taught our subordinates to do the things that we knew and could do after graduation from the military academy. The training period for snipers was extended in comparison with the training period of a private from an infantry company. After two or three months of training, or sometimes even less, men were sent as replacements to the combat units, but the regiment's officers, or more correctly commanders, were rarely sent to the front. For example, I spent at least one year in the regiment (from June 1942 to April or May 1943). During the summer and autumn of 1942 I was twice sent as an escorting officer for marching companies to the combat units, first to Mozhaisk area, and the second time to Voronezh area. The task of the escorting officer was to deliver the company without losses in personnel (there were cases of escapes). Sometimes the political officer of the company accompanied the company commander. Marching companies were normally brought to the divisional or regimental HQ, where men were distributed among units. Officers also started to leave for the front from the 365th Reserve Regiment; officers that came *to* the regiment were from hospitals, where they had been recovering after wounds, sometimes serious ones. It was time for me to leave the regiment. I had been stuck in that regiment for a long time, but I obtained experience of leading men and received advanced knowledge of military science, and I also became an excellent shooter. I did not have any good friends left in the regiment – many of them had left already, and I was happy to leave the reserve regiment.

In late May 1943 I was sent to the personnel section of the Moscow Military District. They sent me and other officers to a battalion of the officer reserve in Kuchino, in the vicinity of Moscow, where the battalion was stationed. I did not stay there for long, just around a month. We did almost nothing there and tried to get sent to the front as quickly as possible. In late July 1943 we, around 100 officers, were sent to the Bryansk front. We started our journey from Moscow by train, then we hitchhiked and then even had to walk. That was the time of the Kursk battle – one of the largest battles of the war. Our counter-offensive started successfully, but because of bloody fighting in defence and then in attack units suffered heavy losses both in men and officers. This is why the units of the Bryansk Front desperately needed replacements.

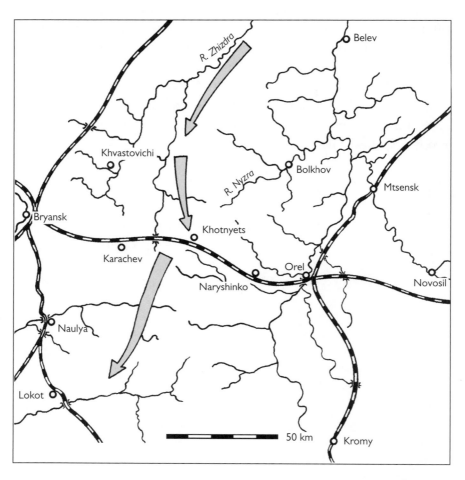

Map to show the Bryansk front and the Orel offensive, 26 July 1943 to 20 August 1943.

BAPTISM OF FIRE:
THE OREL OFFENSIVE

We arrived at the HQ of the Bryansk front on 2 or 3 August, 1943, and were distributed among different armies of the front. Along with several other officers I was sent to the 4th Tank Army, which launched its attack on 26 July and was engaged in fighting, overcoming enemy resistance and advancing towards Orel. On around 8 or 9 August we arrived at the HQ of the 4th Army, which were located in a ravine with all the necessary camouflage against the enemy's air force. During that period the army commander was Lieutenant-General V. M. Badanov. After a brief discussion with the chief of the army's personnel section I was sent along with several other officers to the 6th Guards Mechanized Corps under the command of Major-General A. I. Akimov. From the personnel section of the Corps staff we were sent to different brigades; by that time I was only accompanied by five to seven officers from the 100 that departed from Moscow. Some were sent to the 16th Guards Mechanized Brigade, the others to the 17th Guards, while I was the only officer who was sent to the 49th Mechanized Brigade (it had not yet been awarded with the Guards title); the Brigade was commanded by Lieutenant-Colonel Petr Nikitich Turkin. After some hesitation, on 13 or 14 August the head of the personnel section of the Brigade decided to send me to the 1st motor rifle battalion as a replacement. The commander of the battalion at that time was Senior Lieutenant Terenti Grigorievich Kozienko; he became Captain as late as October 1943. They sent a runner from the battalion, so that I did not have to wander around the ravines looking for the battalion HQ. With the runner I reported my arrival for further service to the battalion chief of staff Captain S. P. Mazurov. The 1st battalion had just disengaged the enemy and the men were putting themselves in order. This brief pause in the fighting was a great help for me – I was able to get to know the personnel quickly outside active operations, during a half-day break. I was appointed the platoon leader of the 2nd platoon in the first company, which was under the command of Junior Lieutenant Petr Ivanovich Titov. I fought the whole war as the 2nd platoon leader and only in September–October of 1945 was I officially appointed the commander of the 1st company.

Petr Sergeevich Shakulo was the leader of the 1st platoon, while the leader of the 3rd platoon was Lieutenant Gavrilov (I forget his first name). The machine-gun platoon leader was not there – he was in hospital after receiving a serious wound. The company's Sergeant-Major was Vasily Blokhin, former seaman of the Pacific Navy. The company had medic Safronov, company clerk Barakovski, as well as a sniper – a big Kazakh called Jambul. The deputy battalion commander for political affairs or *zampolit* was Abram Efimovich Gerstein and the deputy battalion commander (personnel section) was Senior Lieutenant Maxim Tarasovich Burkov, who was killed on 16 January, 1945. The 2nd motor rifle company was under Lieutenant Afanasi Nikitovich Gulik, while the 3rd was under Lieutenant Yuri Alexeevich Grigoriev, who became the battalion's chief of staff in May 1944.

Sergeant Major Blokhin introduced me to the assistant platoon leader Senior Sergeant Sabaev and the orderly in the company. On the evening of the same day we moved forward to our attack position in order to assault the Germans in the morning. During the night we three officers of the company were summoned by company commander Titov, who gave us our combat objectives for the attack. I did not recognize the platoon leaders in the darkness; they did not recognize me either. At dawn the company formed a line and together with two other companies of the battalion walked with a rapid step towards the hill, having no idea if the enemy was defending it. That was my baptism of fire. This was no longer training, it was war, and the enemy was in front of us. The enemy first opened up with machine-gun fire from the hill and then launched a concentrated mortar barrage on us. Just as I had in training, I ordered the soldiers: 'Forward run', and ran forward myself – just as I had in training. All of a sudden my soldiers were no longer in front of me. I heard voices from the side, from a ravine, where the soldiers from the company and from my platoon had already taken cover. They started to dig in. I did not even have an entrenching tool, let alone weapons – neither a pistol nor a submachine-gun; I only received weapons a couple of days later. To the right of me there was a soldier who had already dug his skirmisher's trench, so I asked for an entrenching tool from him. I dug in and made a breastwork. I gave the entrenching tool back to the red-headed man and asked who he was. He answered that he was platoon leader from the 1st company, Lieutenant Petr Shakulo. I had only seen him once in the night and did not recognize him in daylight. This is how Petr Shakulo became my best friend for the whole war. Our friendship lasted until his very death in 1988.

After darkness fell, we left the ravine and dug in at an open spot right in front of the hill, trying our best to camouflage our narrow foxholes from the enemy's air force and from observation. During the night we received an order to repeat the assault on the enemy forces defending the hill. A night assault is a special type of combat, it is complicated and requires the close co-operation of all battalion units, even between the individual soldiers of the company; it also requires bravery and fearlessness.

The assault began well until we reached a barbed wire entanglement and the company had to lie down in front of it. How could we overcome the obstacle? We did not have wirecutters. It might well be that several soldiers could sneak under the entanglement together with me. But what about the rest? Would they follow? It was impossible to see in the darkness. Would they help me or would I help them – that's the main thing in night combat. I did not know what to do and I sneaked out to look for Shakulo and Gavrilov, the two other platoon leaders of the company. The Germans were lighting up the area intensively with missiles, and I managed to find them. Lieutenant Nikolai Konstantinovich Chernyshov, platoon leader from the 2nd company, was also there with them. We all decided to withdraw to our starting positions.

We reported that we had failed to complete the mission and received a repeated order to seize the enemy's trench. To give spoken orders meant making myself and other soldiers a target for the Germans. Even without any noise from our side the Germans were delivering horrible flanking machine-gun fire with tracer bullets that shone brightly in the darkness. We prepared our soldiers for the new assault and discussed with the other platoon leaders how we could best fulfil the order. I noticed that two Kazakh soldiers from the platoon did not join the platoon during the assault and stayed in their foxhole. I warned them strictly that they could be severely punished for cowardice. Incidentally, during the daytime assault my assistant platoon leader Sabaev also fell behind, saying that he had stomach-ache. That was the only time in my life when I told another person: 'If this happens again, I'll shoot you.' Sabaev got the message, and in the second night assault I ordered him to check the foxholes, see if anyone had stayed behind and then join the assaulting line with those that he found. He fulfilled the order and no longer had stomach-ache.

The second assault was also unsuccessful. However, the Germans only spotted us when we got right under the entanglement. They tossed hand-grenades at us and opened machine-gun fire. A hand-grenade went off next to me, but in the heat of the battle I did not pay attention to it. After that the Germans opened fire with mortars, even though they knew they might hit their own troops. Again we had to withdraw with losses. My garrison cap was torn and I found out that I was wounded in my head by grenade splinters. Sabaev bandaged my head.

In daytime, after an unimpressive artillery preparation and with the support of three T-34 tanks, we again assaulted the enemy's trench and were again thrown back. The tanks were knocked out because of the failure of the crews: they had abandoned the tanks before they were knocked out and so the tanks kept on rolling empty towards the enemy. This really happened, I did not make it up and I never again saw such a shameful episode in the whole war.

During the night we assaulted twice more, and again it was in vain. To add trouble to our misery, a platoon of sixteen men led by a Lieutenant went missing in the 2nd company of the battalion during the night. They were looking for the platoon for several days, mostly at night, but never found them. Men just disappeared and no one knew where they went. These things also happen in war, war is always war.

I should say that the 2nd and 3rd battalions of the brigade also failed to advance during their attacks; their attacks were repelled with heavy losses in personnel. The enemy firmly held on to the dominant hill. The next day he sent his air force against us. From dawn till dusk, all day long, in wave after wave, German bombers dropped their bomb load on us. Soviet fighters were nowhere to be seen, so the German air force had every possible chance. Anti-aircraft guns tried to repel the air raid, but were also suppressed by the bombers. Besides bombing, the enemy opened artillery and mortar fire on us. We had the impression that the Germans were preparing for an attack, but it never came. Apparently, the enemy had been given the task of inflicting casualties on us to try and stop our attempts to capture the hill. And that is exactly what happened. That was my first experience of such a heavy air raid. It was pure hell; it is hard to find a comparison for it. You are just lying in your foxhole and waiting for death, bombs are exploding all around, the ground is shaking and you are shaking. I was frightened to death and wanted to run away from that hell, but I was a commander and had to stay with my soldiers. One has to know how to overcome fear. There are no fearless men, fear is natural, but some people are able to overcome it; others shiver but remember their responsibilities and get over it. The third type of people grows numb with fear and they literally lose their minds. Such people run anywhere just to hide, creating panic among others. These people are especially horrified by the enemy's air force.

The twilight of that horrible day set in. The sun was setting and the enemy's air force ceased its air raids; the artillery and mortar fire had stopped even earlier; it probably lasted just around one hour, or maybe even less. Time goes by slowly in such hell. One by one, the soldiers started to crawl out of their foxholes. Sabaev and I got out of the trench to check the soldiers in the platoon. I also spoke to the other platoon leaders and we counted our losses. To my surprise, the losses were lower than one might think considering the condition of our positions. Both mine and the other platoons in the company had insignificant losses. The 2nd and the 3rd companies of the battalion were the worst hit. The ground around our trenches was churned up with bomb craters, some foxholes collapsed and buried the soldiers that were in them, but they survived. My assistant platoon leader Sabaev had left a bag-pack and a helmet lying on the breastwork, which were hit with splinters – the helmet was pierced in several places. We were all thirsty, during the whole day we did not have a droplet of water. We were summoned to company commander Titov; his trench was some 150–200 metres from the front, on a ravine slope. We had some water at his place and asked to bring water to the front, to the soldiers. Titov cursed violently us for failing to complete the task and informed us that we were to retire from the sector and the brigade was transferred to another sector of the front.

We reported our losses from the air raid to Titov. I think we did not have anyone killed, but ten to twelve men were wounded and shell-shocked. Before dawn, still in darkness, the company quietly abandoned its positions. We marched for some 5 or 6 kilometres and stopped for a break in a ravine. A field kitchen drove up, we were fed and went to sleep. The day passed by. Battalion commander Kozienko summoned the officers in the evening and scolded us for not being able to capture the German trench and to overcome the barbed wire fence. However, he added: 'There was no barbed wire entanglement. You just thought it up.' The company commanders unanimously reported that there was an entanglement, but the battalion commander insisted on his version.

After our fruitless attempts to capture the hill we tried to launch attacks along different sectors of the front, but all those attempts failed and sometimes we pretended to launch the attack in order to distract the enemy's reserves.

It was unbearably hot on those August days of 1943 in the Orel area, and we mostly moved on trucks during the night. There was a huge amount of dust on the roads, our feet sank into it as if it were cotton. By morning we were all covered with thick layer of dust. In an attempt to turn the area around Orel into a wilderness, the enemy burnt entire villages during his retreat, putting everything that he could to the torch. Just chimneys remained after the fire – a horrible, depressing view. Surviving civilians had to come back to those ashes. The Germans blew up railways and broke sleepers with a special machine, snapping them in two. Before their retreat the Germans, as a rule, would set village houses on fire. From the black pillars of smoke that rose from the burning houses we knew that the Germans were about to retreat and we could advance without resistance from their side, capturing the village as it burned. On 13 September, 1943, on the order of the front, the entire personnel of the Brigade, except for the officers, were transferred to other units to replace losses. Our company had just the sergeant–major, clerk, medic and company commander's orderly, as well as my assistant platoon leader Sabaev. However, we continued to move along the front on trucks at night, sometimes with lights on, as late as 15 or 18 September. It was explained to us that this was done to deceive the enemy. During those days all units of the 4th Tank Army disengaged and went into reserve, concentrating in the thick forests around Bryansk in the vicinity of Karachev.

TRAINING FOR
A NEW OFFENSIVE

After the end of the Orel operation the battalion had just 28 or 30 officers left, among them five company commanders, ten platoon leaders and thirteen staff officers – the remaining sixteen were either dead or wounded. The signal platoon leader – chief of communications of the battalion – was among the wounded staff officers. Only ten out of 22 platoon leaders were left. Just six of these ten lived to see Victory Day, and I was among those six. Just three company commanders survived the war. At that time we were all young: the platoon leaders were 20 or 21 years old. Company commanders were 26 to 27 years old, the battalion commander was 29. Most of the officers were young men in their twenties.

The autumn was dry and warm, which allowed us to build dugouts for the incoming replacements and ourselves before the cold weather set in. We found metal barrels to make stoves and metal pipes for chimneys; however, we could not find doors for the dugouts, and we had to cover them with rain-proof capes. Officers and enlisted men started to arrive. The battalion commander in person distributed them among the companies. Lieutenant Kolosov arrived at our company as a machine-gun platoon leader. Young soldiers arrived at the company, born in 1925, just boys and middle-aged Azeri men, older than 30 or 35 years. They could not speak very good Russian and could hardly understand an order, but after some time started to understand orders without a translator. The Azeri men fought well and I had no complaints about them. Sergeant Major Vasili Blokhin left for the 3rd company, assistant platoon leader Sabaev was appointed Sergeant Major of the 2nd company on my recommendation. Mikhail Karpovich Bratchenko, machine-gun crew leader from the battalion's machine-gun company, became the company's

Sergeant Major. We fought almost till the end of the war together with him.

An intensive training period started after the arrival of replacements. The personnel arrived from the replacement regiment; they were not from civil life and had some skills, but we had to teach them many things, especially firing the PPSh submachine-gun and the RPD (sometimes called DP) light machine-gun. We never had rifles in the battalion, just submachine-guns. After the cold weather set in, we were issued winter uniforms – *valenki* (felt boots), *vatnik* (padded jackets) and trousers, winter hats, woollen helmet liners and tarpaulin mittens with three fingers, warm underwear, woollen foot cloths. Officers were issued sweatshirts, fur vests and sheepskin coats. I did not take the sheepskin coat – the Germans knew that officers were dressed in sheepskin coats and tried to kill them first. Besides that, I was warm enough in a padded jacket. I did not wear the helmet liner and felt boots either. As ill luck would have it, the supply unit personnel could not get the winter hat for me and I had to wear a civilian hat of my size, of a reddish colour.

We had all kinds of training for the personnel. After the first snowfalls we even learnt to ski, although many did not know the first thing about skiing. I was reasonably demanding in my relationship with the soldiers, I tried to be just and did not try to find small faults, I treated every soldier as an individual. Most of the soldiers were 18 years old in 1943. They were not strong physically, mostly small and frail youngsters, so I tried to adjust the training programme to meet their physical and health capacity. Day and night we trained them for the future battles. We taught them things that they would need in combat at the front. We knitted the units together in tactical training, trying to cultivate a sense of comradeship. Soldiers had to adjust to each other; they had to understand how a platoon or company attacked in order to assist each other. That was the main thing. We had to build a core, to have a team, not a group of individual soldiers. We paid most attention to training at the platoon-company level. We had political classes as well – conversations and political information.

We considered that removing 'tank fear' and training soldiers to knock tanks out with hand grenades was a crucial point in the training. We did a 'tank test-drive' for that purpose. Soldiers would sit in trenches, while a T-34 would roll over the trenches once or twice.

Boys were happy to see that it was not that scary and they were happy to see how brave they were. We had a little combat training with live ammo in attack and defence. I would often tell them about life at the front, sharing my combat experience. I went through the war all the way to Berlin with some soldiers from that replacement of 1943.

We all felt that our combat training was about to end. By then the soldiers had learnt skills, such as handling weapons, and grew stronger; I could see bravery and confidence in their eyes. Some of them were appointed squad leaders or even assistant platoon leaders. A short period of time passed – just two and a half months, and one could see the military bearing in them, the young boys had transformed into soldiers that I could lead into battle.

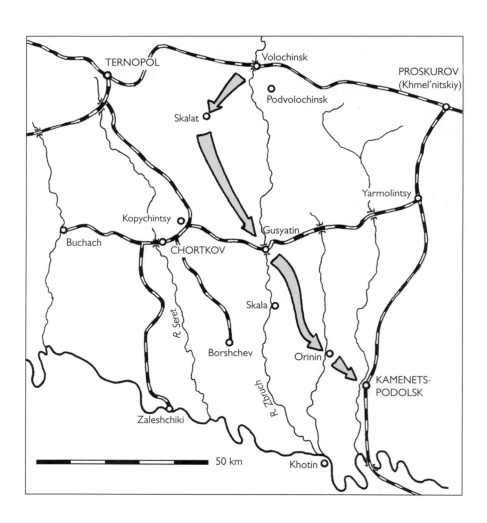

Map to show the Kamenets-Podolsk offensive, July to August 1944.

THE KAMENETS–PODOLSK
OPERATION

In early January, 1944, following the order of Stavka, the 4th Tank Army was transferred to the Kiev area from the Bryansk forests. Our battalion and the tank regiment travelled to Bravary station near Kiev in one train. After this we crossed the Dnieper river by means of a temporary bridge, drove into Kiev's outskirts and stayed in the buildings of a former technical college not far from Klavdievo station. That was in late January. We stayed there for a long time. I remember that the supply units fell behind us on the march and for some time we had awfully poor food – rye flour boiled in water without salt. We were constantly hungry. It was impossible to buy food for money, one could only exchange things for food, but we had nothing to offer for exchange. Officers had to put up with it, but soldiers were soldiers, they had to get good food – one could kick the bucket with that rye flour. Food was finally arranged by the efforts of the battalion commander and the *zampolit*; after a week we started to receive decent rations. In mid-February 1944 we were again loaded on to a train, and even received 100 grams of vodka before getting on it *(veterans usually refer to 'grams' of vodka – translator's note)*. That was the first and the last time that we received vodka – we never received it later. It was already late February when we got off the train at Polonnoe station. These rail journeys, both from the Bryansk forest area to Kiev and from Kiev to this station, took ages; especially long was the journey to Kiev, as it took about two weeks. The military trains were following each other at short distances, so we had to unload quickly, as the next train was about to arrive. The sky was cloudy; that is probably why the enemy's air force was not present. We unloaded in darkness at Polonnoe station and marched on foot to Shepetovka, walking in dirt the whole night with short breaks for rest. We walked some 30 kilometres in the night and reached Shepetovka, where we went into houses and immediately fell asleep, even refusing to eat. We were so tired and exhausted that we did not even pay attention to the enemy's artillery strikes that fell on the city.

At noon the battalion loaded on to Studebaker trucks and arrived in Slavuta. After a brief rest and meal we received an order to attack. That happened on 27 or 28 February, or perhaps even in early March. At first our battalion did not encounter any resistance from the enemy. The Germans were quickly abandoning their positions. In some places they would leave some outposts, but we would quickly defeat them. The terrain was open, without trees, cut by ravines and with a large number of settlements. That year spring came early to the Ukraine, and spring rain showers washed away the earth roads, making them hardly passable even for tanks, not to mention the wheeled vehicles. We had to walk on foot. That was where soldiers and officers suffered hellish pain – heavy mud stuck to our boots and we could barely drag our feet out of the sticky quagmire. Many soldiers carried machine-guns, boxes with ammo, mortars and mines. It was at least good that the battalion commander had ordered that the gas masks be left behind and appointed an officer who was to turn them over to the Brigade's warehouse. Seemingly, a gas mask did not weigh much, but if one had to march on foot from dawn till dusk or even till midnight or next dawn, doing some 16 hours of marching, even a needle would seem heavy. Besides that, we could not always have a normal meal – the battalion kitchen was stuck in the dirt somewhere and could not catch up with us. It was impossible to find a dry spot during breaks, we had to sit down right in the dirt and immediately fell asleep for 10 or 15 minutes. Some soldiers even fell asleep while walking from exhaustion. One should not forget that most of the soldiers were just 18 years old.

We only survived on food provided by the population of the villages that we liberated from the Germans. At night and very rarely during the day we would make one-and-a-half- or two-hour stops in those villages to have a snack with what God had in store for us. The population welcomed us warmly, regardless of how hard it was for them to provide food to soldiers; they always found some nice treats – some villagers boiled chicken, others boiled potatoes and cut lard (soldiers dubbed this kind of catering 'a grandmother's ration'). However, such attitudes were common only in the Eastern Ukraine. As soon as we entered the Western Ukraine, that had passed to the Soviet Union from Poland in 1940, the attitude of the population was quite different – people hid from us in their houses, as they disliked and feared the Muscovites and *Kastaps (a disparaging name for Russians in Ukraine – translator's comment)*. Besides that, those places were Bandera areas, where the nationalistic movement was quite strong. They were not very eager to give us food and they could hardly 'find' food for us: usually it was millet and potatoes. As a rule, they would say in Ukrainian: 'We do not have anything, the Germans took it all.' In some cases I had to act severely and took tough measures on the villagers in order to feed five or seven soldiers. I had a German hand-grenade with a long handle without a fuse; if the house owners refused to feed the soldiers, I would say something like this: 'The Germans (Schwabs) destroyed our field kitchen, if you do not boil potatoes, the grenade explodes in an hour (or half an hour).' This argument helped a lot! Of course, now this behaviour does not look very humane, but I did not have any other choice. From my point of view this was the 'middle way' – we did not loot the villages, but on the other hand, soldiers did not starve.

However, the main problem was not exhaustion, not hard conditions, not even the absence of regular food (the battalion kitchen never showed up), but the fact that the battalion went into action with almost no ammo and grenades. This was a tragedy for us. Most of the ammo and grenades we spent in heavy fighting for Voitovtsy, Podvolochinsk and Volochinsk. A rifle without ammo is just a stick. It was the only time during the war, when I screwed up and my platoon was left without ammo – I never allowed this to happen again.

I still carried the PPSh submachine-gun in the Orel and Kamenets-Podolsk operations, but I got tired of carrying it around. In the battles that followed, my weapon was a German Walther pistol that I found in Kamenets-Podolsk; sometimes I carried a second pistol as well – of smaller calibre. I had to run around a lot. A soldier is a soldier, no one wants to die, and so he might lie down and hide, while my task was to get him up. It was easier to run around with a Walther. I was not supposed to fire; after all, it was the soldiers' job to fire, while my job was to organize them. I loved my Walther. I did not like the Parabellum, as the lock was unreliable. The Walther was a good gun, fired well and precisely, and there was plenty of ammo for it. I would not have the gun in my hand during the battle; I would run around with a small entrenching tool in my hand. I had to use the tool both for its intended purpose, and sometimes to tap the butts of 'too-long-on-the-ground' soldiers. Besides that, I always carried a couple of excellent Russian F-1 hand grenades. We did not like the German grenades − one was the size of a chicken's egg, the other one, with a long handle, was very inconvenient to carry, and both of them were weak. I also had a Finnish knife, but I lost it later.

In action I tried to keep close to the first platoon leader Petr Shakulo and he tried to stick close to me. Normally it was us two who solved the problems in the course of battle. We rarely saw company leader Titov, even more rarely battalion commander Kozienko. I do not recall a single case when we had lunch together with Titov or even had a talk during lunch. I will be honest and say that those battles before 20 March, that is until we reached Skalat, have not remained clear in my memory. Sixty years have passed, and of course I have forgotten many things, but some events are still firmly entrenched in my mind.

From the company commander I received a mission to capture a village − a *kolkhoz* named after Voroshilov, which was on some high ground. The platoon assaulted the village by crossing a ploughed field, and our feet sank into the soaked soil, we could barely move our feet. We tried to run under fire, but got exhausted very quickly − an overwhelming feeling of indifference set in, an awful apathy; we walked towards the Germans, paying no attention to their fire. We walked silently, but stubbornly − a kind of 'psychological' assault. The enemy could not stand this and fled. When we reached the village, there were no traces of Germans. We stayed in that village for several days. For some reason, I do not remember why, I was the only one from the company to stay in the village with my platoon. I had to feed the soldiers, and I talked to the village elder, who used to be the chairman of the *kolkhoz* before the war. I requested him to provide houses where the soldiers could stay, and food. At first he did not 'get' me and brought only potatoes, so I had to 'explain' to him that besides potatoes soldiers needed other staples – meat, lard, cereals, sugar (that village had a lot of it). As I stayed with my orderly in the man's hut, I also warned him that I was to receive better food than the soldiers, not just some soup. Everything was done in the best possible way and the soldiers were fed well.

Well, food and accommodation were taken care of, but I did not forget that we were at war, so I had a defensive position built, just in case, in order to be ready to repel possible enemy attacks. We had little ammo though; for example, I had only some twenty rounds in my submachine-gun, my soldiers had even less, but we had a Maxim heavy machine-gun from Lieutenant Kolosov's platoon with a full ammo belt (250 rounds). We relied on the machine-gun and anti-tank rifles from the anti-tank rifle platoon of our battalion that stayed next to us.

On a quiet and sunny day we saw an attacking line of soldiers approaching us. We quickly prepared for action and occupied the trenches. The assaulting infantry opened fire, but did not inflict losses on us. I ordered the soldiers to hold their fire and let them come closer, but when they charged shouting 'Hurrah', we realized that these were fellow Soviet warriors. Soldiers of my platoon jumped out of the trenches, also shouted 'Hurrah', and waved their hands. The assaulting soldiers realized that we were not Germans, ceased fire, folded the line and walked up to us. We got acquainted and had a smoke together. It was some infantry company, not from our 4th Tank Army. Incidentally, we managed to get some ammo from them.

After a day or two, fresh and rested, we left this hospitable village and continued our march in the same dirt and mud. Our offensive was almost 24 hours a day. During short night rests we could not always recover, and the catering during the offensive was quite bad. The local population in the Eastern Ukraine was not rich, bread was especially scarce, but as I have mentioned, they were very well disposed towards us. Once our battalion passed a village and stopped for a short rest at a more or less dry spot not far from the village. Apparently, there were no Germans in the village. We saw peasants coming form the village, mostly women. A local priest headed the procession; people carried banners and other church paraphernalia. We all stood up, honouring them. Women ran up to us, weeping,

Tank Rider

kissing and hugging us. The priest addressed the battalion commander Kozienko and on behalf of the villagers invited us to the village to celebrate the joy of liberation from the Germans. Kozienko thanked him for the invitation and said that we had no time to party – we had to move on, chasing the Germans further – not only from their village, but also from other villages and from our land. We thanked all the villagers and the battalion marched on. In another place, when we were really hungry, we encountered a column of former partisans, who had fresh bread and lard. The partisans shared these riches with us, and all the personnel were fed – it became a nicer walk.

Despite all difficulties, the battalion stubbornly pressed forward, mostly on foot. The 2nd and 3rd battalions of the Brigade were somewhere on their own missions, while the tank regiment had not caught up with us yet – it was delayed during unloading at Polonnoe railway station. Trucks and tanks arrived later and the speed of our advance increased. Our battalion liberated Podvolochinsk, and then Volochinsk, the 2nd battalion with the tank regiment captured Manachin and Golshintsy on 5 March, while the 3rd battalion occupied Voitovtsy. Heavy fighting took place for those settlements; the young soldiers did an excellent job in these battles. At first I doubted the abilities of some of the soldiers because of their shortness; I considered them not fit for war, but they turned out to be able to take hard physical pressures and go into battle right after a march. They turned out to be the right kind of soldier – fast, smart and brave, skilful in handling their weapons. I relied on them and they relied on me, as they knew that there would be no unnecessary losses among them. The main thing for a soldier is to trust his commander, be provided with all necesseties and know what he is fighting for. That is it!

Artillery, armour and trucks – mostly Studebaker trucks that had been stuck on the roads – gradually caught up with us, and for some time the battalion had an opportunity to advance on Studebaker trucks. These trucks replaced our Soviet-made ZIS-5 trucks, which had been the main truck of the country before the war and were already somewhat obsolete. We had a break from the unceasing marching on foot.

THE BATTLES FOR
THE TOWN OF SKALAT

On 14 or 15 March, 1944, we approached the town of Skalat through rocky hills and started fighting for its liberation. The arrival of our battalion was quite unexpected for the German forces. They did not expect us to travel such a distance so quickly. However, the leadership of the Brigade for some reason did not use this element of surprise. As a result, all three battalions of the Brigade were stuck in street fighting. When our battalion arrived at the city in daytime, we – Shakulo, Kolosov and I (Gavrilov was wounded) – received an order from company commander Titov to advance along the left side of the road and go as deep as possible into the city. We did not encounter enemy resistance on the outskirts and advanced from house to house. The enemy was nowhere to be seen. We got a bit braver and realized that either there were no Germans in the city or they were retreating without a fight. Probably we were right. All of a sudden an orderly ran up to us with the order from the company commander to go back. We came back and reported that there were no Germans, but the company commander Titov told us that the sector where we were in was not our area of responsibility, it belonged to another unit and we were given the sector to the right side of the road. Other companies were also stopped. There was some confusion, we had not received the order to advance before darkness. We found a small house, abandoned by the occupiers, and the company occupied it. While the commanders were consulting, we laid down for a nap.

I was summoned to the battalion commander in the night. I entered the hut, where, in addition to battalion commander Kozienko, there were head of brigade staff Grigori Vasilievich Starovoit and some other staff officers. The mission that I was given was to advance forward on the road and locate the enemy – identifying in which buildings he had set up a defence, whether he had armour and what type of armour it was. I stated that I had already been in the city together with Shakulo's platoon the day before and had not seen any enemy, not to mention tanks. Nevertheless, I was ordered to check the city one more time. I woke my platoon up, explained the mission to the soldiers, and briefed the squad leaders separately. We quietly started our advance to the town centre along the road. In front of the platoon, at some distance, I had a squad in the vanguard for security and reconnaissance – I did everything by the book. Quite soon, on their signal, we halted and lay down on the road. It turned out that we had run into soldiers from the Brigade's scout company. They did not meet the enemy, did not see any tanks, but had heard voices from the building in front of us, and even said that they had seen a lit cigarette. When we reached the building at the crossroads of the two streets, I ordered a quiet search of the building. There was no enemy in the building; the scouts had made a mistake. It was war, it happened a lot. We did not advance any further, as the soldiers drew my attention to the sound of engines, and we recognized that tanks were advancing towards us, in fact, two Tiger tanks, which must have arrived shortly before to reinforce the infantry. Upon my return, I reported exactly what I saw – that the enemy had no infantry, even if he had, it was stationed in isolated strongpoints in some buildings (later this turned out to be true), as well as two tanks, which had not been in the city the day before. The commanders did not tell me anything and let me go to rest. I thought that I completed my mission. I do not know if they believed me after the report from the scout company. However, I can only say that if we had attacked the enemy in the city on the first day, we would not have suffered such unnecessary losses, being stuck in street fighting for almost a week from 14 to 20 March.

At dawn the battalions formed an attacking line in front of the city, in an open field, just as if it were a training session. The enemy was silent and did not open fire on us, although we were like sitting ducks for them. Why did we have to lie in the field? The battalion commander summoned us all for briefing. We, a group of officers, gathered in a group at the roadside, which did not even have ditches – not to mention any shelters, and all this was in the war! In the meantime, at least ten or twelve enemy aircraft appeared. They first dropped bombs on the tank regiment, which immediately suffered losses in tanks and personnel. After this the planes flew towards our battalion and opened fire on the soldiers, who had no time to dig in and were lying in the open. We were rescued by the fact that the planes had already dropped their bombs on the tank regiment.

Officers, before they could be briefed, dispersed in all directions, seeking cover. I also tried to find a shelter, but it was an open field, there was nowhere to hide. The battalion commander and several other officers dived into a drainpipe under the road surface. I couldn't think of anything better than running back to my foxhole. A German pilot noticed me and opened fire on me. Bullets were kicking up spurts of mud all around me. The pilot dived five times, trying to kill me. He opened the cockpit and I saw the bastard laughing at me. Still, I made it safely to my foxhole, his bullets missed. I jumped into my foxhole, and the pilot ceased fire. Planes strafed the battalion several more times, firing at people, then gathered in a formation and left. Some guy in desperation opened fire from an anti-tank rifle, but quickly stopped firing, there was no point – it was not an anti-aircraft gun, after all.

The losses of the battalion were insignificant: several soldiers were wounded, as well as company commander Lieutenant Yu. A. Grigoriev and Sergeant-major Vasily Blokhin, formerly Sergeant Major in our company, of the 3rd company. After the air strike we were briefed and quickly advanced forward. The Germans opened fire only after we went into the city and captured several buildings. Our tanks tried to support us, but after the Germans knocked out three T-34 tanks, with their crews being burnt alive, the rest of our armour did not advance any further and hid behind the buildings. It was two Tigers that delivered most of the fire on our infantry and tanks; they had a very convenient firing position behind the buildings, where they could not be seen. Shakulo and I advanced forward with our platoons, hiding behind the buildings. We had to drive the Germans out of some buildings, while other buildings they abandoned without a fight. Advancing in this way, we captured the building in front of the square with a church, ending up in the centre of the town on the right side of the street. However, by the wall of that building there was a German tank. It fired for some time but ceased fire soon – apparently to conserve ammo. We did not have petrol bombs or anti-tank grenades to knock it out, we were running out of ammo ourselves. The battalion's ammo depot had not arrived yet, and it would not arrive till the very end of Kamenets-Podolsk operation.

Twilight set in and firing ceased from both sides. It was just about time to get some food. War was war, but we were hungry anyway. Soldiers were sent out to look for food and they found a small warehouse with supplies and vodka. We had a nice meal: we had a little vodka and finished off all the canned food. Shortly before morning a liaison arrived from company commander Titov with a note. In the note he gave us an order to move along the left side of the street and to join the third platoon of the company, which was leaderless, as Gavrilov was wounded. An order was order, and under cover of darkness Shakulo and I crossed the street and joined the third platoon. The machine-gun platoon of the company accompanied us, under Lieutenant Kolosov. Soldiers from Gavrilov's platoon were distributed between our two companies on the order of the company commander. We tried to advance during the night, but in the dark we ran into the area of responsibility of the 2nd company of our battalion, so we had to move to the side of them. We ran into some Germans in the process, and the leader of the vanguard squad was wounded in the stomach. Our advance halted. It was good that the whole thing happened in darkness and the enemy could not deliver well-directed fire. However, we suffered casualties and were forced to stop and consolidate our lines. We did not dare to attack further – a German tank arrived and opened fire with machine-guns.

In the morning an orderly soldier passed on the order from the company commander to abandon the area, make way for the 2nd company, consolidate defences at the previous position and to continue attacking under cover of darkness, advancing to the outskirts of the town. It was a hard day for us – a Tiger was methodically firing its main gun at the building where we were stationed.

German snipers arrived on the scene. My soldiers tracked down one of them – he was firing from a window of a high house. Shakulo's platoon had a Soviet-made sniper rifle. I got a commission to get the guy (I used to train snipers in both male and female companies). I was looking out for him for a long time and when his head popped up in the window, fired a round. Soldiers, who were observing our duel through binoculars, told me that I got him. The German never popped up again.

Besides this, the Germans tried to counterattack, but were thrown back with casualties from machine-gun fire. During the night Shakulo and I bypassed the church square without encountering the enemy and consolidated our positions in wooden barns and huts in the outskirts. In the morning the Germans spotted us and opened machine-gun fire. Snipers were also there, setting the huts with soldiers on fire. We had to move to a safer place. In the daytime the enemy tried to attack again, but our riflemen repelled that assault as well. As twilight descended, we left the charred ruins and took up position in a strong brick building, also in the town's outskirts. As we learned later, *Gestapo* secret police had been stationed in that building during the occupation. In the cellar of the building we found honey, spirits and some other food staples.

During the day the enemy tried to attack again, not from the city, but from the opposite direction, from the open field. Our soldiers prepared to fire from windows. The Germans arrived on three or four trucks, dismounted and formed an attacking line some 600 to 800 metres from us. It was good that they had no tanks with them. We allowed them to approach us and wiped them off the face of the earth, using two Maxim heavy machine-guns. The fire strike on them was unexpected, heavy, but short – we were saving ammo. At the same time the Germans started to run across the street, concentrating for an attack from the centre of the city, not far from our building. There was a soldier with a sniper rifle in Shakulo's platoon and he opened fire on the running German soldiers. He was quite successful, the distance was less than 100 metres, and he got so many of them that the Germans first stopped running and then totally abandoned the area. A single sniper destroyed the attack.

In the evening an orderly came running from Titov with a written order. In his note the company commander ordered us to return to the former position and occupy that house 'with a Tiger by the wall'. We fulfilled the order, and Shakulo went to see the company commander to report the situation on Kolosov's and my behalf. At that time, as we learnt later, four more Tigers entered the city. Lieutenant Shakulo reported everything to Titov, as well as informing him that to the right of the main street there was only our company, while to the left there were two full companies of the battalion, as well as the entire 2nd battalion of the Brigade. If our company departed, the Germans would be able to occupy the houses to the right of the road and end up in the Brigade's rear. Titov left us alone and did not bother us any more.

In general, I think he should have arrived at the battlefield and seen the situation for himself instead of just sending notes to us. On the other hand, I should mention Titov's personal bravery. One sunny day a German tank rolled down the main street past our house, moving into our rear. It did not make it far – the company commander, Senior Lieutenant Petr Ivanovich Titov, blew it up. He burnt the tank with a single petrol bomb, which he threw from behind a house corner. For this heroic deed Titov was awarded with Order of Great Patriotic War 2nd Degree.

Blocks on our side of the street were practically freed from the enemy. The Germans only put up resistance to the left of the main road, where brigade units were still in action. Suddenly an orderly, who was going to our company commander, reported that in the rear of our company, behind our house there were three or four Tiger tanks. Apparently, they had driven through another street and arrived in our rear, controlling the main street. Quite a nasty surprise! It was good that they had no infantry with them. We sent the runner to the other street to report to the company commander and ask what to do. An order came – to stay where we were. So we did.

Of course, it was mostly the enemy's armour that prevented us from seizing the town of Skalat, although they had just some eight or ten tanks. The brigade had almost no weapons that would be effective against heavy tanks: we did not have anti-tank grenades, although they were anyway inefficient against the Tigers; we had very few petrol bombs that could be used. The Tigers grew so bold that they drove around town like chickens hanging around in a village, and only after Titov had burnt one Tiger did they become more cautious and stopped acting so boldly.

After a day or two some of our tanks from another unit arrived, accompanied by the regiment of Katyushas (BM-13), which had been able to overcome the mud on the roads. That regiment inflicted casualties on our Brigade. The regiment showered its fire not only on the enemy, but also on the 2nd battalion and the 3rd company of our battalion, which for some reason was in trenches in the field, outside the city, unlike our company. Apparently, they could not break through into the city, while Shakulo and I were lucky. A single salvo killed 30 to 35 soldiers. In one month of fighting we did not have such high casualties, as from one Katyusha salvo! It was painful to see the dead soldiers – young, healthy and needed for further battles. It hurt even more that they died from friendly fire, because of the carelessness of some commanders for the lives of soldiers, and their incompetence and lack of leadership skills. The worst part was that none of the commanders that allowed this to happen were punished. This salvo could have helped the Germans, who could have mounted an attack after it. However, the arrival of Katyushas and tanks forced the enemy to leave the town at night and on 20 March, 1944, the town of Skalat was fully liberated.

The brigade had suffered significant losses in personnel and hardware in fighting for Skalat. The 3rd company commander, Senior Lieutenant Grigoriev, was wounded; platoon leaders Lieutenant Kravtsov (he was burnt by petrol from a petrol bomb that broke at his feet), Gavrilov and someone else, as well as Sergeant Major Vasya Blokhin, my friend from Siberia, were wounded. The commander of the second company, Senior Lieutenant Gulik, the commander of the submachine-gun company, Lieutenant Kolomiitsev, and some other officers were killed. In front of my eyes a sniper killed a leader of a machine-gun platoon from the machine-gun company, a tall, slim and cheerful Bashkirian Lieutenant. He was supporting our two platoons, mine and Shakulo's, with his machine-gun platoon. We buried him in the garden of a house. I am sorry that I cannot remember his name, or the names of soldiers from my platoon who were killed in Skalat.

We were young, did not have any experience in life, and cared very little about our lives and the lives of others; sometimes we were even indifferent. In Skalat the soldiers arranged a game with death. Quite a brilliant idea they had: they ran from one side of the street to another under machine-gun fire from a German tank. They had a competition – who could run across the street fastest and not be hit. Normally Fritz would be late and open fire on an empty spot. Some soldiers ran across the street several times and even I dared to run across the street once, so that I would not look like a coward in the eyes of my subordinates. Luckily, no one was hit. I think that the Germans did not quite understand our game and thought that we were mounting an attack and were leaving several important buildings without a fight. Such things happened. Everything could happen in the war, and we considered such things normal.

After the end of battles for Skalat, when our company marched on the central street, I noticed the façade of a house, which looked more like a sieve – it was all battered by shells. I asked the soldiers whose house it was and how defenders could have stayed there. The men laughed and said that it was *our* house, the house where we had stayed for several days. I came up to company leader Titov; *zampolit* Gerstein was also there. I pointed at the building, told him about the conditions that we had had to fight in. Titov also remarked to the *zampolit* of the battalion that it was amazing how the company could hold such a battered building and repel German attacks, closing their access to the rear of the battalion. 'Was it hard?' Gerstein asked. What could I answer? I said: 'It was OK.'

THE BATTLE FOR GUSYATIN

From 20 March, 1944, onwards the Brigade received a new order: to advance towards the south and south-east to the towns of Gusyatin and Kamenets-Podolsk. *Tridtsatchetverkas* arrived, and our company left as tank riders with the Brigade's vanguard, as we had had fewer casualties in the previous battles (tridtsatchetverka *is a nick-name for T-34 tanks – translator's comment)*. It was also because the 2nd and 3rd companies, as well as the anti-tank rifle platoon, had lost their company commanders and platoon leader. These three companies only had one platoon leader each – Lieutenant Chernyshov in the 2nd company, Junior Lieutenant Belyakov in the 3rd company and Junior Lieutenant Drogovoz in the anti-tank rifle company. A five-day march to Kamenets-Podolsk started, with the objective to liberate it and encircle the enemy. At that time Kamenets-Podolsk was the centre of a province. We advanced on Studebaker trucks. Those trucks were real beasts! Sometimes they would rumble on the mud roads like tanks. We would travel on T-34 tanks even more often. The offensive was almost round the clock – during day and night, often we would make a long halt, hiding from the enemy's air force, which inflicted high losses on us, both in personnel and even tanks.

We continued to survive on 'grandmother's rations' – that is, on the food provided by the villagers. After the town of Skalat the brigade left the Western Ukraine and again marched in the eastern part of Ukraine, where the local population was happy to see us, often meeting us with tears of joy in their eyes. If we rushed through a village without stopping, villagers would throw loaves of bread and lard to us; we always shared this food with the tank crews. Several times in good weather we were bombed, but all worked out fine: in such cases we would quickly jump down from the tanks, scattering in all directions from the road. Tanks would also leave the road, trying to find some natural shelter – in a ravine, a depression, even stopping in the shade of a tree, as it was harder to be spotted under a tree. In daytime, during short halts, we normally parked tanks in the shade of a house or a barn. We camouflaged not only the tanks, but also trucks and other vehicles, and soldiers tried not to wander too much around the village. Sometimes we even asked the villagers not to stoke their stoves, as smoke from chimneys could draw the attention of the German air force. Germans had an all-weather scout plane that we called a 'frame' *(this is the German Focke Wulf FW 189 artillery observer's and scout plane; some Russians also called it a 'crutch' – translator's note)*. It was a two-fuselage aircraft, which would normally fly at high altitudes and had good optics. When a frame appeared, every activity froze on our territory, otherwise, if the frame spotted anything, the bombers of the enemy arrived. Soviet fighters would rarely engage the frame, because at its altitude and with its speed the frame would quickly disappear.

Our Tank Army, including our 49th Mechanized Brigade, was deep in the rear of the enemy. The Germans put up resistance only in isolated points along the line of our advance. There would be days when we saw no Germans at all, or they would try to stop our advance with hastily set-up defences, which we broke without any difficulties. They put up significant resistance in the fight for town of Gusyatin, on 22 and 23 March, 1944. Our 1st motor rifle battalion, and of course our company, took part in the town's liberation. During the night of 23 March, when the enemy was driven out of the city, Petr Shakulo and I stopped at the town's outskirts, where we settled in several huts to give some rest to the soldiers.

We could barely stand on our feet from exhaustion, as all day long we had walked on foot, eliminating separate pockets of resistance. Tanks did not always help us in those encounters, as they supported other battalions of our brigade. In darkness and in action we lost communication with company commander Titov and battalion commander Kozienko, as well as other companies of the battalion. Communication and co-ordination is the cornerstone in every action and one should never lose communication, but we were happy to have some rest after driving Germans out of the city. We decided that we would gain understanding of the situation at dawn, so we did not look for the company commander. Just in case, we put guards at the hut and arranged shifts. Night came, we managed to heat up the stove, took off our wet greatcoats and boots in order to dry our puttees and fell fast asleep. Late at night the guard, who went into the hut to warm up a bit, heard a knocking on the door. The guard opened the door, and heard German language, shouted 'Germans! Germans!' and opened submachine-gun fire.

Other soldiers woke up; many of them made it outside the hut and also opened fire. However, the Germans managed to disappear, shouting 'Ivanen! Ivanen!' – this is what they called us, the Red Army soldiers.

Lieutenant Shakulo gave a scolding to the guard for his negligence. We had some sleep until dawn, put our clothes and shoes on and in the morning found the company and battalion commanders. Other companies of the battalion arrived, we had a snack with what God sent us and marched forward on foot. It was quiet, the enemy was nowhere to be seen. Apparently, they had been straggling Germans, remains of destroyed units that ran into us during the night. Anything could happen in that war. For example, when our battalions left the town, all kinds of supply and support units of the battalion and brigade stopped there. They forgot about security, as they knew that the city was liberated from the Germans. German tanks rushed into town in the evening and held a St Bartholomew's Day massacre – breaking, burning, destroying and squashing everything that was in the streets, as there was no one who could put up resistance. The Germans burnt our battalion's field kitchen and several cooks were killed. A few eyewitnesses, who made it alive out of Gusyatin, including deputy battalion commander for logistics Zadiran, told us the sad story. On 24 March, 1944, other tank units of our Tank Army arrived at Gusyatin and after some heavy fighting the Germans were once more forced to leave it. So, Gusyatin was liberated twice, and all the merit for the liberation of the town went to the other units, which had liberated the city for the second time, not to our brigade.

I recall a march on foot in the spring of 1944. We would walk in the dirt, barely moving our feet, our greatcoats weighed a ton because of the rain, and I would think: 'It would be nice to get into a hut, have a hot soup or *schi* and have a nap for some twenty-five hours'.

All kinds of thoughts could be in one's head during marches, both good and bad ones.

We were happy when tanks from our Brigade's tank regiment caught up with our battalion and we moved on as tank riders. We had just one objective – to capture Kamenets-Podolsk. Running a bit ahead, I would say that it took the Brigade two or three days to arrive at the town. Both people and tanks were tired; the vehicles couldn't take such stress either. Tanks stopped more and more often because of small technical breakdowns, especially broken tracks. Of course we tank riders assisted in tank repairs, so as not to fall behind the battalion.

The battalion's march continued from Gusyatin, the enemy was not putting up serious resistance. Our tanks and the tank-riding infantry crushed separate pockets of resistance. In other cases the Germans did not put up a fight and abandoned villages, sometimes leaving an insignificant delaying force behind. We stopped in a village in order to refuel our tanks and load them with ammo, as well as to make some small repairs. I have already mentioned that the march was very hard and halts were necessary. Villagers gave us food and we lay down for a nap in their houses. As far as I remember, the day was sunny. We were afraid of an air raid, and camouflaged all vehicles well. Indeed, enemy bombers did arrive and bomb the village, but for some reason chose the part which had no tanks or soldiers stationed in it. Evidently, the German pilots did not notice us. After the planes left, we heard women weeping – there were casualties among the civilian population.

At the same halt the following incident took place. A tank driver, apparently after a liberal dose of moonshine, started his tank, but selected reverse gear instead of first gear. The tank broke through the wall of a hut, moving the table to the other wall of the hut while some officers and hosts of the house were having lunch at the table. The driver realized that he was going in the wrong direction and stopped the tank just in time. It was amazing that no one was hurt, but everyone was covered in clay and plaster and the wall of the house was destroyed. Those who were sitting at the table in the hut got off lightly. One of the officers jumped up from the table and with a gun in his hand ran to the driver's hatch. The driver was scared to death, closed all hatches and sat quietly in the tank, while the others calmed down the officer, who was threatening to shoot the driver. As the result the tank was driven away, and the tank regiment commanders decided to leave the 'horseless' tankers (those, who had lost their vehicles) to repair the house.

Later in the day we started to gather for a march and the commanders decided to continue the advance during the night because of the enemy's air force. In the twilight we started our night-march on tanks. We rushed through villages and towns with lights on the tanks. There were supply vehicles with us, and Studebaker trucks, and this all gave the impression of a huge tank column moving on the road.

At dawn, or rather, early in the morning, we ran into the Germans – infantry and two or three tanks (Tigers and Panthers). A battle commenced. Tanks opened fire from both sides. The 76-mm guns of our Brigade's artillery battalion also opened fire, some guns were set to fire with open sights. Lieutenant Shakulo and I led our platoons in assault. We both commanded our platoons: 'Get up, for the Motherland, forward, run!' We picked ourselves up for the Motherland and ran forward together with everyone. It was good that we did not have to run far – the enemy was less than 100 metres from us.

We rushed into the outskirts of the village, some of the German soldiers were killed, the rest fled. Artillery knocked out one German tank; the second one left the village together with the infantry, while the third one stayed where it was, abandoned by its crew. Its front armour plate had the marks of our shells and its armour was cracked on the side. Apparently it had run out of fuel. Such was the attack.

Every soldier's action in assault can be considered an heroic deed: it is heroism to attack under machine-gun and artillery and mortar fire from the enemy, not knowing whether you will survive or not. One had to have a lot of stoicism, bravery and courage to overcome all this and drive the Fritzes out of their positions. Kill or be killed – this is the only law of war. It is a scary thing to assault the enemy, you have to overcome your fear, overcome yourself, get up from the ground, get up and make at least the first step to get as close as possible, in short rushes or sneaking on the ground. It is very hard, and then you rush towards the enemy, who concentrates his fire on you. First you run, but sometimes you do not have enough breath to run all the way to the enemy's trenches, especially across a ploughed field. Then not only can't you run, but it is hard even to walk, especially in springtime, when your feet sink deep in wet soil. As a rule, though, attacking soldiers will always try to run and at the same time fire at the enemy from submachine-guns, even if they cannot see him. This has a psychological impact on the enemy, so I always ordered my soldiers to fire on the move.

After we had rushed into the village under enemy fire and halted for a short break, I learnt that my friend Lieutenant Petr Shakulo was wounded. Petr was not very lucky: in every operation he would get wounded. Our tanks arrived – they managed to knock out another tank, which was burning in the village, and we moved on with our mission. It was the morning of 24 March, 1944. Besides company commander Titov and I, the company had only one officer left – machine-gun platoon leader, Lieutenant Kolosov.

In the second half of that day, the German air force delivered a strong raid against our battalion and tanks. I rarely saw our fighter planes. The Germans bombed us very often, but the fighters never covered us. The anti-aircraft machine-guns of the brigade were a futile weapon against the German air force; they were simply afraid of opening fire on the Germans, as they feared they would be destroyed. Ground-attack aircraft would support us, bombers would do so more rarely, but I only saw our fighter planes during the Orel operation. A lot has been written and said about there being no fighters in 1941 and 1942, but they were not even there in 1944, when the Germans were strafing at 50 metres altitude, massacring people and tanks. They said that there were no airfields for our fighters. Maybe this was so, but the explanation did not make our life easier. At that time we did not think anything bad about our air force, we were proud of them, we were happy to see them 'working' on the enemy. Only at the end of my life did I start to ask questions: why hadn't our fighters protected us from the enemy's air force during our marches?

On that day, 24 March, 1944, the German air force almost completely destroyed the battalion. We suffered high casualties in personnel and the tank regiment lost many tanks. The rest were not spared either. The air raids started at noon and lasted till evening. One wave of aircraft, fifteen or twenty of them, would drop their bombs, and as soon as our battalion column gathered for further advance, the next wave would arrive. This lasted for several hours, until the twilight came. 'Luckily', the tank that I was riding on with my platoon threw a track and we had to halt to repair it. The Brigade advanced further, but we stayed behind for the repair. It was right after the first air raid, and I did not see the other air raids on the Brigade. Having completed the repair of the track, we moved on, and two more tanks joined us on the road. We arrived at the battalion when it was already dark. I found battalion commander Kozienko and tank regiment commander Stolyarov; they were both happy to see us, a significant reinforcement. The battalion commander asked me if I had seen company leader Titov. I reported that I had not. It turned out that our company commander Petr Ivanovich Titov had disappeared, and they had been looking for him before darkness fell, searching all the area around, but failed to find him.

Soldiers of the battalion, who had previously scattered in the fields and hidden in all possible ways till darkness, started to gather at the village, which was almost totally burnt down. The battalion suffered high casualties in personnel, while the tank regiment lost a lot of tanks. In my company, except for Kolosov and myself, we had some 30 or 35 soldiers left, the other companies had even less – ten or fifteen soldiers each. Kozienko and Stolyarov gave me an order: advance on three tanks with the remains of the company and machine-gun platoon of Lieutenant Kolosov towards Kamenets-Podolsk, capture its outskirts and then act depending on the situation, but try to hold on until the main forces of the brigade arrived. They stayed behind to gather personnel and tanks after the air raids.

THE BATTLES FOR
KAMENETS–PODOLSK

At dawn on 25 March, 1944, we reached Kamenets-Podolsk. Our company on three tanks bypassed the city from the west and approached the outskirts from the south. It was still dark. The Germans did not expect Soviet troops from the south, but when we approached the bridge across the Smotrich river they opened fire on us, although not very intensively. Trucks and other vehicles were parked on the bridge. It was some sort of a barricade, which even had a tank without tracks in it. The river had steep banks, up to 10 metres high, which did not allow tanks to cross the river. My attempt to enter the city over the bridge was stopped by enemy fire. The machine-gun fire did not cause any harm, but the snipers were deadly. I decided not to risk and suffer useless casualties, but rather to wait for the main forces of our Brigade to arrive. We occupied a small house not far from the bridge, and sent a scout party to the bridge. The men came back and reported that the it was impossible to bypass the barricade on the bridge, while sniper fire gave them no chance to lift their heads from the ground. While we were waiting for the main forces of the Brigade to arrive, soldiers of the company started to inspect the trucks that the Germans had abandoned as we arrived. The large trucks were filled with German uniforms, equipment, food and even wines of different kinds and countries of origin. The food and wines came from all over Europe. My men gathered German weapons and ammo, some wrapping themselves in MG-34 machine-gun ammo belts – just like the seamen in the times of the Russian Civil War. What could I say – they were mere boys. Many soldiers picked up new German jackboots, but the beautiful and shining German officer long boots did not fit me – they were too tight, although I tried many of them, and I really wanted to have them. We gathered food, wine, Cuban cigars in special boxes, cigarettes, chocolate, cookies, sweet breads, canned fish and meat. We had a nice meal with all that food and smoked cigars and cigarettes. The cigars were Cuban, just like the ones that Churchill had.

The main forces of the Brigade arrived at noon. Battalion commander Kozienko called me; tank regiment commander Stolyarov was also present. I reported the situation, and the tankers also reported that the bridge was impassable and guarded by the enemy, although not in strength. The commanders ordered me to go to the right of the bridge, to try to find a crossing or a ford across Smotrich river and advance to the centre of the city. They gave me the same three tanks and, of course, Kolosov's machine-gun platoon as a supporting unit. I was ordered to maintain communication over tank radio. I gathered the squad leaders, gave them an order to advance, and we left the area at the bridge, moving along the course of the river. Three tanks drove up to us, the company mounted them and we drove off to look for a ford or a convenient place for tanks to drive through river. We found a place that was kind of convenient, and crossed to the other bank of the river. Tankers reported to Stolyarov that we had found a ford and entered the city's outskirts on the opposite side. However, the top of the other bank was almost vertically faced with stone, one-and-a-half metres high. The tanks could not overcome the obstacle, no matter how hard they tried. This obstacle could be called an anti-tank wall, but in reality it was built to strengthen the riverbank in case of flooding. We had to dismantle this stone wall in order to make a convenient driveway for tanks. The tankers did not have so much as a crowbar, but we somehow managed to break down the stone wall; one tank negotiated the obstacle and drove off into the city with Kolosov's machine-gun platoon on it. The other two tanks could not get over the wall, however. We tried for a long time, but we could not do anything. Then the tank that drove into the city came back.

Lieutenant Kolosov told me that he was wounded, and I saw the fresh bandage myself. His tank had come under fire from a German machine-gun on a church bell-tower, with was almost in the centre of the city. Besides that, his tank could not move any further, as the streets were filled with trucks parked next to each other. It was not only hard to drive – it was hard to walk, so tightly were the abandoned German trucks parked. Later we learned that these trucks with all their commodities and food belonged to rear units of a large German formation that had retreated to the west. However, our Brigade cut their retreat routes and they had to stop in the city. There were very many trucks, at least 1,000 to 1,500 of them, and there were all kinds of things in them! I repeat that I never saw a larger amount of war booty anywhere else. It is interesting that there were no drivers in those trucks.

They transmitted an order over the radio for the tanks to stay put at the river, while the infantry was to advance to the railway station. It was a repetition of the earlier spoken order by the battalion commander. I advanced through the city with my company. The streets were packed with trucks, mostly heavy ones: Mahn, Opel and other types. We did not encounter the Germans — they ran away as we appeared in the city. Suddenly we heard artillery fire and shells exploding in the city. That was fire from our Brigade artillery. The company went out to the city's outskirts, to the higher bank of Smotrich river, and we saw an interesting picture. The entire Brigade, or rather, whatever remained of it after almost a month of fighting, assaulted the city. All types of weapons fired: tanks, artillery of the Brigade's artillery battalion, mortars and machine-guns. It was a beautiful battle scene, but it would have been nicer if they had hit the enemy, and not the friendly troops, especially my company. We shouted, waved our hats and hands (we did not have recognition colour flares), and ran around, trying to draw the attention of the assaulting troops, but it was all in vain. They continued their assault in an extended line, reached the river, waded in waist-deep in water (while my company crossed it on tanks, and we were all dry) and came up on our high bank and rushed into the city.

The company joined the battalion, and before I could report completion of the mission and Lieutenant Kolosov's wound, the battalion commander shocked me, saying: 'And where have you been? I have not seen you in the attacking line, and you are dry, huh?' At first I did not understand him. Then I felt offended. I had to remind Kozienko about the order that he gave to Kolosov and me three hours earlier. Tank crews had reported completion of the mission through radio. The battalion commander did not answer anything to that, but told the surrounding officers: 'Bessonov is cunning, crossed the river and did not get his feet wet.'

Soon we reached the eastern outskirts of the city. I am not mistaken – it was the eastern outskirts, as our 4th Tank Army and other mobile units of the front marched from north to south, thus practically cutting off retreat routes for a large group of German troops east of Kamenets-Podolsk. The Brigade and some other units took to the defensive in order to contain the retreating German troops to prevent their breakthrough on good roads with access to west and south to Dniester and direct their retreat on earth roads, full of dirt.

As it turned out later, the front failed to complete the encirclement. Because of significant losses in personnel and hardware, the mobile units of the first Ukrainian front just did not have sufficient strength to do it. It could be seen on the example of our 1st motor rifle battalion and other units of the 49th Motor Rifle Brigade – in that period we suffered irreplaceable losses in personnel. The weather failed us as well.

By the morning of 26 March, 1944, the town of Kamenets-Podolsk was fully liberated from the enemy. We were so happy that we spontaneously organized dinner with German snacks and wines. We sent the guards out, and all gathered in an abandoned house and celebrated victory all night long. I did not really like parties at the front line – I had my meal, had a bit of wine and left to check the outposts, where I found that one machine-gun crewman was dead. It was snowing heavily and I could clearly see footprints of the Germans who fled from the town. I gathered several resting soldiers and we ran along the footprints, but did not catch them and so we came back. Having reinforced the outposts, I gave the order to open fire on any shadow that appeared in the blizzard. The soldiers honestly followed my order and fired at any silhouette. By the morning it was all quiet, and the German exodus from the city was over.

By the morning everyone, except for the guards, slept like a rock. Exhaustion had accumulated during the unceasing day and night battles, when we barely slept for several hours or did not have any sleep at all, falling asleep literally while we walked

In the morning we organized the defence of the outside of the town, in the field in front of a ravine. To the left of us there were some village buildings – the mortar company of the battalion settled there. Further out there was the 3rd company, that had ten to fifteen soldiers

72

left under platoon leader Alexei Belyakov. The 2nd company also had no more than fifteen men, led by platoon leader Nikolai Chernyshov. Our company, which was temporarily under my command, had at least 30 soldiers, almost the same number as the two other companies combined.

Despite this, battalion commander Captain Kozienko, battalion's chief of staff Captain Belan and deputy battalion commander for political affairs Captain Gerstein decided to merge our 1st company with the 2nd company. The battalion commander called on me and declared this decision to me, as well as the appointment of Chernyshov, platoon leader from the 2nd company, to the post of company commander. I thought that I would stay the commander of my company, as it had more soldiers left than in the 2nd and the 3rd companies combined. Besides this, I had in fact been the company's commander in the course of all the previous days, receiving orders directly from the battalion commander. Having expressed my dissatisfaction, I asked them to keep me as the commander of our company, and not to merge it with the 2nd company, but merge the 2nd and the 3rd companies instead, appointing Chernyshov as the commander of the combined company. However, my arguments were ignored and the order remained the same. I had to obey the order – one cannot argue in the army, whether the order is wise or not, you have to follow it, especially at the front. What can you do, the commanders should know better, that is why they are commanders! That was the unsuccessful end of my first, but not my last, attempt to get promoted.

Our combined company dug in at the outskirts of Kamenets-Podolsk on a bad spot, in the open in front of a ravine, really more of a hollow. The opposite side of the hollow was higher, and our position could be clearly seen from there. At the same time, a bit behind us was a good natural defence – a mound. I proposed that we dig in there, but no one listened to me. Soldiers dug foxholes and put their weapons, which had no ammo, on breastworks; next to them they put German weapons with ammo and two or three German grenades. Each soldier had a bottle or two of wine to help them keep warm. There were no serious frosts, but living in the open under rain and snow at zero temperatures night and day is a really unpleasant thing. We shivered with the cold. Behind the mound we could at least light fires, but even in the foxholes soldiers found a way to keep themselves warm, covering the foxholes with German rain capes and blankets. I also had two blankets, and covered my foxhole with them during the night – it kept the trench amazingly warm. I would dig a foxhole myself or with my orderly. All soldiers and most junior officers had the small entrenching tool with them, including me. The soldiers had their entrenching tools in a case that they put on their belt, while I had a folding German tool that I carried in my hand. I carried it like this till the end of war.

We did not have gas masks – they only frustrated us in battle, especially the tank riders. I, like many of the soldiers, did not wear a helmet – they were heavy and slid down on to your face. Defending the city of Kamenets-Podolsk, we had to pick up German small arms: submachine-guns, rifles and machine-guns, as we had no ammo for our own weapons. Right up to the end of the operation some soldiers carried two types of weapons, their own and German weapons, before we received ammo for our weapons. The Germans tried to drop ammo and sometimes food to their encircled troops. Two containers with ammo fell in our hands, and company Sergeant Major Bratchenko took the parachute silk for industrial purposes. Silk could be traded for moonshine and lard in villages. Villagers made blouses and underwear from the parachute silk.

I would sleep little during the night, checking the guards, especially in the second half of the night – what if they fell asleep or missed the Germans, or did not pay attention to them? Anything could happen. Regular inspection of the positions became my obligatory habit, and my soldiers knew about my night checks and felt safer that their commanding officer was not asleep.

We stayed in defence for several days. Germans appeared on one of the days, but they did not attack the company, capturing several houses some 100 metres to the left of our defences. They opened fire, mostly from rifles, even on individual soldiers. Interesting indeed, that the Germans could approach secretly, and apparently were already there in the evening or in the night, but we only spotted them in the morning. This was exactly what I always feared – that we would fail to spot the enemy. However, most likely it was a small scout party that was searching the area trying to find retreat routes to the west and good roads that wheeled vehicles could use. We returned fire from all possible weapons, as we had plenty of ammo and we did not have to save it. Because of this need to save ammo we had not fired on the enemy freely for a long time. The Germans ceased fire, and so did we. At the same time we could hear heavy firing on the positions of the 3rd company (then it was the 2nd) and the battalion's mortar company.

The platoon leader of the mortar company, Lieutenant Novozhilov, was killed in that fight. The Germans were about to capture the mortars, and then Novozhilov ordered his soldiers to withdraw to another position, while he himself stayed and covered their retreat with a machine-gun — mortar crews had one just in case. The Germans set the house, from which he fired, on fire, but he continued to fire from that house until he himself burnt to death. This is how Lieutenant Sergei Vasilievich Novozhilov died on 28 March, 1944, a brave and cheerful officer. He sacrificed his life to save the lives of soldiers from his company. The Germans did not advance any further after Sergey's death, and, on the contrary, they abandoned a couple of huts next to the burnt-down house. We had to fold the left flank of the company towards the enemy, in order to keep them under our fire, and in that moment they almost got me — the bullet just scratched the skin on my side. Apparently, a German had fired an explosive bullet at me, and as a result for a long time I had a black stain on my right side.

On one of the days in late March 1944 a heavy snowfall set in, and it continued the whole night. I slept in my foxhole like a baby, covered by two German blankets. In the morning, when I woke up, it turned out that the foxhole was full of snow. There was so much snow that my soldiers literally had to dig me out. At the same time, Chernyshov was in the house, in the warmth — they had a stove there. He did not care to invite me to get warm, even though we were both platoon leaders. As soon as he was appointed company leader, his attitude toward me and to other officers of the platoon — Shakulo and Gavrilov — changed. I did not visit him in that hut, always stayed with the soldiers, had my meal with them, but I really wanted to have some hot soup or *schi*, or just some tea.

The Germans, under cover of the blizzard, abandoned their positions and disappeared. So, when we finally got out from the snow, the guys told me that there were no Germans opposing us. It was only then that we went into the huts to cook something hot. We were already tired of chocolate, cookies and canned food, as well as wine, too.

The enemy bypassed the town of Kamenets-Podolsk and moved to the west, abandoning cars and other vehicles on the roads in the blizzard. I have never seen so many burnt or abandoned vehicles. From the east, from Vinnitsa, the army units of the first Ukrainian front chased Germans towards us, but we did not have enough resources to stop the enemy at Kamenets-Podolsk and fully encircle him, as happened in Stalingrad. Disregarding their losses, abandoning vehicles that were stuck because of lack of fuel or mud, the Germans broke through to the west. The fighting was bloody and heavy. I remember that we used to find Soviet propaganda leaflets signed by Marshal G. K. Zhukov, calling for German soldiers to surrender, as they were surrounded and were to be destroyed if they did not lay down their weapons. It is indeed a pity that we could not repeat the Stalingrad scenario. At the same time, we threw the Germans far to the west.

As Lieutenant Petr Shakulo told me after his return, he was in a medical platoon in the small town of Orinin, near to Kamenets-Podolsk. The HQ of our 6th Guards Motorized Corps was also stationed there under General Akimov. Retreating westwards, the Germans tried to capture Orinin. Even wounded soldiers that could still hold weapons had to fight to repel the German attacks. The battle lasted for several hours and the outcome was uncertain until several JS-2 tanks arrived to assist the besieged troops. As a result, the German tanks were destroyed and the infantry scattered, some surrendered. This is how 100 wounded and the Corps HQ were rescued.

The battles for Kamenets-Podolsk were over. Some time in early April general army units arrived from the east.

THE BRIDGEHEAD
AT THE RIVER STRYPA

The Commander in Chief expressed his gratitude for the liberation of Kamenets-Podolsk to the soldiers of the Brigade in his Order of the Day of 27 March, 1944. Our Brigade and some other units of the 4th Tank Army received the honorary title of 'Kamenets-Podolsk', the full of name of the Brigade becoming '49th Mechanized Kamenets-Podolsk Brigade', while its commander, Petr Nikitich Turkin, was promoted to the rank of Colonel.

The Brigade again received an order to advance to the west, and drive out the enemy from our land. After a blizzard that lasted two days, there was deep snow on the roads and in the fields, sometimes with snowdrifts. The battalion again mounted tanks with the aim of chasing the enemy, to prevent the possibility of his consolidating positions on good defensible grounds. The weather improved, the sky cleared of clouds, the sun shone and snow melted away. It grew warmer. We encountered the enemy in some places, but the Brigade successfully defeated any German attempt to stop us. We did not have many tanks left, and even those that remained had already used up their engine lifetime and were constantly breaking down. The tank that I was on with my soldiers also broke down. After a day-long stop in a village (we were already in the Western Ukraine), our tank stopped and would not move on. The battalion commander ordered me to stay with the tank and wait for it to be repaired. A day passed by and in the morning the tank crew told us that the breakdown was serious and we were stuck for a long time. I decided not to wait for the completion of the repairs, but to catch up with the battalion on foot. I thought that I would fall under suspicion of deliberate avoidance of fighting. It took us a couple of days to catch up with the battalion. A huge mass of our troops from different units of the front marched westwards, and no one could tell me where our Brigade had gone. At a crossroads I saw a sign with an arrow saying 'Turkin's unit'. We followed the sign. Almost every unit used such signs in that period of time, in order to prevent soldiers from wandering around on the roads of the war looking for their units. One afternoon, I think, on 12 April, I found my battalion: it had been reduced almost to nothing. We had a mission to complete, and before my arrival the battalion only had the 2nd company with ten to fifteen men, or maybe fewer. Only battalion HQ remained more or less intact, but it also had some losses. Battalion commander Kozienko, and *zampolit* Gerstein and chief of battalion's staff Belan were happy to see me – I had at least 20 or 25 soldiers with me, all that remained of 1st and 2nd companies. Company leader Chernyshov and his staff were not in the battalion and no one knew where he was. Having fallen behind with a broken tank, the company commander only showed up some three days later.

Once with the battalion we got a hot meal, which we had not had for a long time – we received both the first and the second course; I remember this quite well. Only two officers were present in the battalion at that time – Junior Lieutenant Alexei Belyakov with the 2nd company and me. The battalion had a total strength of 32 to 35 men, or as they would put it, bayonets. The battalion's artillery battery and mortar company were missing, the submachine-gun platoon, machine-gun company, anti-tank rifle company, all were missing. All these units were lost in battle and destroyed by enemy air force. Officers of the artillery battery showed up a bit later – Senior Lieutenant Kashintsev, Lieutenants Harmakulov and Isaev, Lieutenant Zaitsev from the mortar company, Lieutenants Volkov and Karpenko from the machine-gun company. I think they all arrived without their equipment (45 mm guns, 82 mm mortars, heavy machine-guns) and with just a few soldiers. The 2nd and the 3rd battalions of our Brigade also suffered significant losses, also mainly from air raids.

The battalion was stationed in a village and stayed there for several days. Reinforcements arrived; these were soldiers drafted from liberated areas of Ukraine. The company received men well in their forties, who had only received basic training, and they were slow and timid. Besides that, they had never served in the army. Our company received twelve or fifteen such 'warriors'. The 3rd company, at that time it was the 2nd company, received men of different ages, including former partisans, who could handle weapons, all in civilian clothes. The same company got a new commander to replace Gulik, who had been killed – Senior Lieutenant Shtokolov. Lieutenant Mochalov arrived as the machine-gun platoon leader to replace the wounded Kolosov. At that time the machine-gun company as such did not exist, it did not have machine-guns either. It was Mochalov's first time at the front, he was not used to army service and commanding other people, so he had a hard time on active service. Sometimes he merely wept, as he could not control his men.

After a brief rest the battalion received an order to advance and set up defences on the bank of Strypa river in the village of Dobropolie. Further to the west was the town of Bulach, where German reinforcements were starting to arrive. The Brigade was not capable of executing offensive operations. Its personnel was almost gone, almost all equipment was out of action. Out of 450 to 500 tanks of the 4th Tank Army at the beginning of the operation, the entire army only had around 60 vehicles, all with some kind of breakdown. However, we could still hold defences against the enemy that was also weakened, and we had to hold out until the infantry units of the Front arrived. The Tank Armies lost contact with them and were at a significant distance from the front units (50 or 60 kilometres).

My company and I were transferred to the other, western, bank of the Strypa river; we dug in to the west of Dobropolie village. The village was small – no more than thirty houses, I believe. The terrain on this bank of the river was less defensible than on the eastern side, but that was the order. I sent an outpost to the nearest hill in order to get early warning in case the Germans appeared. When in a defensive position, I always appointed observers both during the day and during the night – that was necessary at the front. The bad thing was that I did not have binoculars: although I did not like having them with me as they were very uncomfortable, especially during assaults.

The company lived on food provided by villagers, as the battalion kitchen was not there. Many villagers abandoned their houses – the old people remembered the fighting of 1914–1916 – the Russian Army under General Brusilov had defended the area, so they said. Villagers took their cattle with them, leaving chicken and other poultry behind. This is why we mostly ate poultry – soldiers could cook very well and even baked doughnuts with sugar, as there was plenty of sugar in the village. We dug trenches on the edge of the village and had several days of quiet rest and sleep in the huts. The sun was already hot, by 12 or 14 April, 1944, it was already nice and warm weather, while we were still in our winter uniforms.

Somewhere is a small ravine where we would take off our shirts and fight 'German submachine-gunners', as soldiers at the front called body lice. We squashed the damned bugs with our fingernails, shook our shirts out above a fire, but it rarely helped – lice lived very well in the warmth. I had a sweater and in almost every stitch lived a parasite bug. I burned the sweater; lice snapped loudly in the fire. It is shameful to write about it with such sincerity, but what can you do – it was war and as a mobile unit, we did not have a chance to wash in the field bathhouse or change our underwear from January 1944. We slept and rested in warm clothes for at least four months, in wintertime anywhere at all: in foxholes, on tanks, in huts – all the time without taking our clothes off. This is why we could not maintain a good level of personal hygiene. I do not think that I should blame anyone for this, as we were all the time deep behind enemy lines. It was only after we disengaged, that we received new summer uniforms. It wasn't a problem in any of our other operations.

On one of those days Captain Belan (after the war and graduation from a military academy, he served as chief of traffic police in Moscow), chief of staff of our battalion, arrived along with our company commander Lieutenant Chernyshov, who had been missing for over a week. Lieutenant Chernyshov right away started to give orders, saying that this and that was wrong. I answered him with 'F★★k off'. Captain Belan stopped our quarrel, but I said that Chernyshov was picking on me. I said that if he had not been missing for a week and had arrived on time, he could have given all kinds of orders. I said that I had marched 30 kilometres in one-and-a-half days just to catch up with our battalion, and hadn't been living with a young village girl. Belan did not reply, but gave me an order – to take a squad of strong guys and reconnoitre the village that was some 3 or 4 kilometres from us (I think this place was Bulach). I was to find out the enemy's strength and report back.

Going on a scout mission in daytime in the open field, sinking in a muddy ploughed field, where bushes did not have leaves and wheat was not high, was a hard task. It was practically a suicide mission – Germans could merely shoot us down in the field or try to take us prisoners. Even without a reconnaissance we knew that the Germans occupied the village in front of us the day before – day and night we heard noise of the tank and truck engines from the village. But I had my orders and I had to fulfil them, as I did not receive any counterorders. I took two or three physically strong soldiers, and my binoculars, and off we went. It was fortunate that there was a ravine and we advanced 1or 1.5 kilometres in it. It was a hard walk in the ravine, we could barely pull our feet out from the mud; we reached a hill, lay down on a dry spot and started to examine the surrounding area. Inspecting the terrain through the binoculars, I noticed a column of trucks and APCs advancing on the road to the right of us towards our defences, a little bit to the right of the battalion. To the left of us, less than a kilometre distant on the neighbouring hill, we spotted an armoured personnel carrier and several trucks, apparently carrying infantry. The Germans slowly advanced towards our village. It did not make any sense to stay there any longer and we went back secretly to our lines. At one place we had to abandon the ravine and we were in the sight of the Germans that marched to the left of us on the top of the hill. However, they did not open fire, although they could easily have cut us all down from the APC, even more so when a Tiger tank joined them later. We could not run – we did not have any energy left. Even now I do not understand, why they did not kill us, when we barely dragged our feet across the ploughed field in some 250 to 300 metres from them.

Upon my return I reported to Belan what I had seen and pointed at the German unit that was some 300 metres from our line of defence. The Germans quietly stood there, without opening fire. Captain Belan did not say anything, but it seemed to me that he was upset about something. But what? With me coming back alive with all soldiers? But we did make it back, and Captain Belan reported to the Brigade HQ about the large column of German troops that moved to the right from our battalion and a small group of Germans to the left of us. Captain Belan went off to the battalion HQ to the other side of the river, taking Chernyshov with him, ordering me to stay in the trenches with the untrained soldiers on the western bank of the river.

On the same day, late in the afternoon, Katyushas fired a salvo. It was good that we were in our foxholes, because when the Katyusha missiles started to explode to the right of the company and then closer to us, we were all able hide in them. Several missiles exploded on the company's positions, but no one was hurt. When this nightmare was over and I peeped out from my foxhole, and saw a large piece of a missile that had not exploded lying just outside. The entire salvo had hit an empty spot and us, but they should have been firing on the neighbouring hill, where Germans were digging in – the Germans that I had fled from.

How can one explain this mistake in firing the salvo? Only by the fact that someone, apparently Belan, gave the wrong co-ordinates, confused two hills, or maybe just did not know how to read the map. The salvo could easily have knocked out the whole company, as at Skalat, when the 2nd and 3rd battalions suffered significant losses from Katyusha fire. The battalion HQ requested the results of the Katyusha salvo over the 'phone. I informed them that the salvo had hit an empty spot and the company, but no losses were inflicted and they should have shifted fire to the left. However, the Katyushas did not fire any more. Some time after the fire mission my soldiers reported to me that engineers wanted to blow up the only bridge across the river. The engineers confirmed that they had had such an order, while the battalion informed me over the 'phone that I was not to prevent them from blowing up the bridge. They also informed me that all communication with me was discontinued and that the 'phone operators were to leave me together with their 'phone and cable.

I was outraged, but they told me: 'It is necessary'. I thought 'Well, to hell with you all', but was more precise in my description of the commanders, using some obscene words. In general, our company officers only used such obscenities in extreme cases, if ever. We did not curse in vain and did not use such words to get the soldiers up to attack. I walked up to the engineers and asked their senior to blow up only the part that touched the western bank, approximately half the bridge, leaving the eastern part intact just in case. The engineers took heed of my request and did everything as I asked them.

I was left there as a condemned man, with a company of 25 or 30 soldiers, of whom half had not seen battle and were untrained – they had not even been sworn in. We had neither heavy nor light machine-guns. The bridge did not have a strategic significance, as its capacity was low. Dobropolie village also did not have any military significance, as it was located in a depression between the high banks of Strypa river. Even now I do not understand what the battalion leadership had on their mind when they left the company on the western bank of the river, holding literally a patch of soil. The battalion and the Brigade had no reinforcing units left after the heavy fighting before we reached Strypa, but we all knew that the enemy brought up fresh reserves, which were superior to our Brigade.

The engineers said that they hoped we would survive as they withdrew, expressed their sympathy and said that they were not guilty. They looked as if they were saying their last good-bye to us – apparently, they thought that we were already dead. I had to follow the order, what else could I do – an order is always an order.

I do not want to praise myself, but by that time I was already an old hand and was not planning to give up my life or the lives of my soldiers yet; I did not hope for luck either. I thought that it was impossible for me to hold the bridgehead anyway, and ordered my soldiers to join our bank with the remains of the bridge on the other bank using wooden beams, thus creating some kind of bridge across the river. Besides this, I transferred soldiers from the southern part of the village to the northern side, where the earth road to the bridge was located. I thought that the Germans would not attack across the ploughed field, where we initially had our defences, but would advance on some sort of a solid road. In each foxhole on both sides of the road I placed two soldiers, to make each other braver through mutual support.

A dark night fell. I was at the right side of the road with several soldiers. Everything was quiet so far. I checked the positions of the soldiers. The men couldn't sleep, but some were sleepy and I warned them to be at full alert, as we could overlook the moment of German assault. Personally I, fearing a German assault, was also awake. The Fritzes rarely attacked at night, but anything could happen, the possibility of a night assault could not be excluded, and I did not have much faith in my new soldiers. It all happened just as I thought it would. Just as dawn broke and the sky started to grow lighter, the

Germans assaulted the company. It was a surprise attack, but some soldiers opened fire. Some, especially the rookies, left their foxholes and ran to the bridge. Some of them were wounded; we bandaged them and sent them into the rear. The veterans were not hurt, as they fired on the enemy and did not run without a backward glance. We had to retreat.

I gathered all the soldiers at the bridge, and we opened fire from submachine-guns at the Germans, stopping them at the line of our foxholes. It was hard to see either the Fritzes or our own men in the gloom. I wanted to regain the positions, but assistant platoon leader Savkin talked me out of it, pointing at the green soldiers, who, putting it mildly, did not feel well, shivering with fear. They received several boxes on the ears from the more experienced soldiers for their behaviour. Such a 'teaching method' was rarely used, but in that case I did not object and did not stop the men. Wooden beams were carefully placed on the bridge, and we safely crossed to the other bank, digging in at the bridge. Day came and I informed the battalion commander that we had had to abandon the western bank of the river. As an answer I received an order: 'Come back to the other bank the same way that you ran away from there, immediately recapture the positions.' Why on earth did they need that bridgehead?

I had to fulfil the order, and for the successful completion of it I studied the enemy's positions, noting his weapon emplacements. I got some understanding of where the enemy was, how many Germans were there and what they were doing. It was quiet and calm, except sometimes the Fritzes fired single shots at us; we did not return fire. Preparing for assault on the lost positions, some soldiers cooked food – one still had to eat. I talked personally to every green soldier, de-briefing his behaviour in battle. I told them that fear was natural for everyone, but one should never lose control over fear and let it grow into horror of the enemy. I gathered the squad leaders separately and shared the object of the assault among them.

We sneaked across the bridge and suddenly stormed their positions. The Fritzes were about to have their lunch and did not notice our rush, as we approached quietly without any shouting. I did not really think that the Germans would be so scared and shocked by our assault that they would flee from their foxholes without a single shot, leaving weapons and unfinished lunch behind. Sergeant Poddubny scared the German machine-gunner so much by popping up some 10 to 15 metres in front of them that the guy ran away, leaving a battle-ready MG34 and his lunch in the canteen. His first course was in the canteen and the second course – pasta with a piece of meat – was in the canteen lid. Many of my soldiers did not even fire a shot, so rapidly did the Germans make their escape. Then the 2nd company commander, Shtokolov, with a dozen former partisans arrived on the scene. All those men were quite drunk and all of them, except for recently appointed 2nd company commander Senior Lieutenant Grigori Andreevich Shtokolov and Lieutenant Alexei Belyakov, were dressed in civilian clothes. Shouting 'Hurrah!' they threw themselves behind the fleeing Germans, but were stopped by fire from a nearby forest. If they had appeared a bit earlier, they would have spoiled our quiet surprise assault. When they reached our foxholes, Shtokolov asked for the MG34 from Poddubny, the guy who captured it. I permitted him to give it away – we did not need it anyway, it was quite hard to operate – in fact, I did not know how to use it myself.

Shtokolov, in turn, went to the battalion commander and exclaimed: 'This is how you should fight the war! I just went there and captured the German trenches, the Germans fled and as a proof here is the machine-gun that I personally captured in battle. This is how partisans fight!'

When I reported to the battalion commander about the completion of his order, he rebuked me for cowardice as a reply!

The day was quiet; the Germans did not show up or open fire at us.

As darkness descended, I inspected the foxholes, cheering the soldiers up, especially the green ones, and warned them that they should not leave their positions without orders, otherwise the Germans would slaughter us all. As soon as I walked away from the left flank of the company, the Germans sent a strong artillery and mortar barrage against us, making use of six-barrelled mortars. The Germans rarely used them; they did not have many. It was a strong weapon, but could not be compared with the Katyusha. We called that mortar '*Vanyusha*', in other places they called it something different, a donkey, for example. Sergeant Savkin, my orderly, and I had nowhere to hide, there was firing all around us, and we lay down under the steep riverbank. Shells and mines from the six-barrelled mortar exploded, red-hot splinters were flying in the air – it was all shining against the background of a night sky. It was sheer hell. It is incomprehensible how we survived. The horrible crash and noise of the guns that must have been stationed close to us filled the air. I had not experienced such heavy bombardment for a long time, not since fighting at Kursk in 1943. All this fire descended on a single company, 25 or 30 soldiers. Apparently, the Germans were very angry and upset because we drove them away from the village with losses in soldiers and weapons in the daytime, when they did not expect the attack and while they were having their nice lunch. Losing a weapon is infamy for a soldier.

The barrage lasted 20 or 25 minutes, although how could I check my watch at that time? Not only the green soldiers, but also the old hands, were very scared as well. I can't lie, I was scared too, especially given the fact that there was no shelter to hide in. After the barrage was over, the Fritzes attacked with superior forces. The soldiers of the company could not take the fire, and fled again. The experienced soldiers put up some resistance, but then they also withdrew to the bridge with the fleeing green soldiers. I could not stop the retreat from the trenches, even less now that some soldiers were wounded and we had to carry them on rain capes. I decided to leave the western bank, reported this decision to the battalion commander and received the order to leave the bridgehead and take position to the left of Shtokolov's 2nd company.

It is interesting that several days later Shtokolov with his company (without our participation) wanted to drive the Germans out of their positions on the western bank of the river, but got almost completely wiped out. Only a small group of partisans, including Shtokolov himself, survived. The Germans were finishing them off as they ran in the open to their foxholes on our (eastern) bank of the river.

The battalion commander saw the hurricane of fire that descended on the company and apparently realized that it was impossible to hold the other bank, and there was no point in that. Half of the newcomers were out of action, mostly wounded, and again I had almost no soldiers left.

The Bridgehead at the River Strypa

From my point of view, one cannot send untrained soldiers, who are not used to army and front line discipline, straight into battle. As our company's Sergeant Nikolai Chulkin told me after the war, many of those recruits hid in their trenches, put their guns on breastworks and fired without aiming. I never saw anything like that. Two or three soldiers were picked off by the Germans at point-blank range, but still managed to jump out of the trenches and dropped unconscious only after they reached the bridge. The battalion's medic told me that one of those recruits had fourteen bullet wounds, but survived. In the very first German attack two soldiers, Chaschin and Khalilov, went missing in action, as they got scared and ran off in the wrong direction. One of them, Chaschin, came back after almost a month, while the second guy joined another unit.

That was the end of my adventures on the bridgehead at the Strypa river in April 1944. The company dug in at the high bank of the river. Days quietly passed by, the Germans did not bother us, and we did not fire on them much. Sometimes our Brigade artillery fired on the targets that they spotted, but that was quite rare. We did not see our company commander, Lieutenant Chernyshov, I think he was sent to receive additional personnel in the rear or somewhere else. To the right of us were defences of the 2nd company, where I had a friend – platoon leader Alexei Belyakov, while Senior Lieutenant Shtokolov was appointed the 2nd company's commander. He had arrived shortly before from the reserve and had already caused a stir. Lieutenant V. K. Mochalov arrived in late March or early April to fill the position of the machine-gun platoon leader of a machine-gun company. He stayed in our company, as there were no machine-guns or machine-gun crews. We continued to feed on the poultry of the villagers from the village that the Germans had driven us out of, Dobropolie. In the mornings two or three soldiers would go to that village, bring chicken or something else and we would boil this in canteens over the fire. By that time the Germans had abandoned the village and dug in on the hill behind the village.

On 27 April, 1944, an infantry unit replaced the Brigade, and we went into reserve. The battalion was transferred into rear area, and we stationed ourselves at a forest edge in vicinity of Kopychintsy town.

During the two months of action in the Kamenets-Podolsk operation of March and April of 1944 we suffered significant losses in personnel and military hardware, especially tanks. We had travelled over 350 kilometres in action during this period. Our Brigade liberated the towns of Manachin, Podvolochisk, Volochisk, Skalat, Gusyatin and Kamenets-Podolsk. Writing about losses in the battalion is the hard part, but I am obliged to show to our descendants how hard it was to achieve victory, and how much blood we shed to achieve it.

The three motor rifle companies of our 1st motor rifle battalion had at least 300 soldiers at the beginning of Kamenets-Podolsk operation (3 March, 1944), 100 soldiers in a company. When we disengaged, the 1st and the 2nd company that was combined with the 1st had no more than 20 or 25 men including me. The 2nd company (former 3rd company) had even less, 10 or 12 men, together with Junior Lieutenant Belyakov, which put the total strength of the battalion at just 30 or 35 men. I cite the numbers excluding the new soldiers that were recruited in early and mid-April, but they also suffered losses in action at Dobropolie village. Losses in the three companies were almost 90%.

The machine-gun company of the battalion also suffered significant losses – all the Maxim machine-guns, the main support weapon of our motor rifle companies, were knocked out together with their crews. Before the operation the company had 40 or 50 soldiers. The anti-tank rifle company, which also had some 40 or 50 men, merely ceased to exist. The mortar company lost its mortars and most of its men – before the battle it had 30 or 35 soldiers, out of whom only platoon commander Lieutenant M. P. Zaitsev was left. The artillery battery (45 mm guns) lost all its guns, and the majority of the battery men were killed or wounded. Before the operation the battery had 25 or 30 men.

The rest of the matériel, as well as most of the transport vehicles of the battalion was destroyed. The 4th Tank Army had no more than 60 tanks left out of 450, the tank regiment of the Brigade had just few tanks left of the initial 33 tanks. Out of those that remained, all were damaged.

No more than 50 or 55 men remained out of 550 soldiers and NCOs of our battalion. Losses among officers were also high. Out of 45 officers no more than 50% remained, the rest were killed or wounded and sent to hospitals. Just six out of 22 platoon leaders were left. Young soldiers, 18 or 19 years old, the cream of our country, died for the liberation of their Motherland from the German Nazi invaders. Officers, platoon leaders and company commanders, also died, often being just little older than their soldiers – they were 20 to 22 years old. One can always replace losses in military hardware, tanks and equipment, but one can never replace losses in personnel...

IN RESERVE AT KOPYCHINTSY

We marched on foot from the front line to the rear area, while the battalion command went there by car, 'pilots', as we called them. We walked without any haste for several days, before we finally arrived at our destination. We built shelters and settled there. For some reason only I was present in the battalion out of all the junior officers, the others fell behind somewhere. The battalion commander called on me and appointed me officer of the day in the battalion. A heavy rain started during the night; I was tired and my sentries were also tired. We lay under the tarpaulin that made do for the tent that we had not set and fell asleep. In the morning the battalion commander found me and woke me up; but he was not angry with me even though I had slept and not organized breakfast for the men of the battalion. I quickly corrected my mistake and told the cooks to start making food.

Replacements started to arrive, many officers, as well as soldiers and NCOs, came back from hospitals. Senior Lieutenants Fomin and Grigoriev (he was appointed the battalion's chief of staff), platoon leaders Lieutenants Shakulo, Gavrilov, Guschenkov, Drogovoz, Kravtsov (he had to spend over two months recuperating after the burns he received) came back. As we were receiving personnel, we started training and putting the units together. We taught them what they would need in battle, tried to strengthen discipline, eradicating laxity that had appeared in behaviour at the front. No one saluted at the front line. Some liberties that could not be tolerated in an army in peacetime appeared in relations between soldiers and commanders at the front. We did combat training at company and platoon level with live ammo. We had to teach green soldiers everything: taking care of weapons, assembling and disassembling the PPSh submachine-gun (we did not have rifles), applying camouflage on terrain, advancing in rushes, digging foxholes, sneaking on the ground, mounting a tank and skilfully dismounting it, even on the move. We even taught them how to shout 'Hurrah!' Soldiers fight the way you teach them. We taught them to attack in squads, platoons, to sense comradeship. In short, we knitted the platoon and the company together in one fist, so that we would be superior to the enemy in battle, so that it would be his *Kaputt*, not ours.

We lived in shelters that we built out of pine-tree branches, some people covered the shelters with tree bark. The battalion commander, his deputies and other staff officers lived in staff vehicles or in tarpaulin tents, which the company did not have, and when it rained we covered our shelters with rain capes. The weather in the Ukraine was warm. Studying was studying, but we were young and tried to entertain ourselves as best we could. Some of us went to the nearest village Maidan, and exchanged some war trophies for moonshine, lard, wheat bread and even milk. We even arranged parties in the village – we sang and danced, while some stayed with the girls till the morning. We were young and healthy and strong, we were happy to live without thinking what lay ahead of us.

Shakulo, some other officers and I were awarded with the Order of the Red Star. That was my first decoration of the War. Many soldiers from the company were awarded as well. Lieutenant Zaitsev was appointed deputy battalion commander for logistics, Lieutenant Volkov was appointed commander of battalion's machine-gun company, Lieutenant Chernyshov was appointed the 1st company commander. Newly arrived officers were appointed commanders of the 2nd and 3rd companies, although, from my point of view, I and Belyakov and Shakulo deserved to become commanders of our companies. We had all had secondary school education, graduated the six-month course in a military academy, had been in the battalion for a long time and had a two-year record of service as officers, but we remained just platoon leaders. I just do not know why it happened that way. Later I was also not lucky in my career and decorations, but we somehow did not pay attention to that – you survive and that's enough, what else can you desire? Commanders in higher offices, however, reacted quite sensitively about the unfair distribution of decorations. There was a rumour that battalion commander Kozienko beat up *politruk* Gerstein, as in his opinion, Gerstein had been awarded with a higher order than Kozienko himself for the Kamenets-Podolsk operation – Kozienko was awarded with the Order of Bogdan Khmelnitski, while Gerstein received the Order of Great Patriotic War 1st degree. Kozienko was temporarily suspended from the office of battalion commander for that fight, but before the next Lvov operation he was re-appointed. As it turned out later, a Lieutenant Colonel, a teacher from the Military Academy of Armoured Troops, entered the battalion for an internship during the period of Kozienko's dismissal. He started to require us to learn and know the field manual of the armoured troops instead of the infantry field manual. Although we were not tankers and never led tanks, we even had to pass some exams, but he quickly left and returned to the Academy.

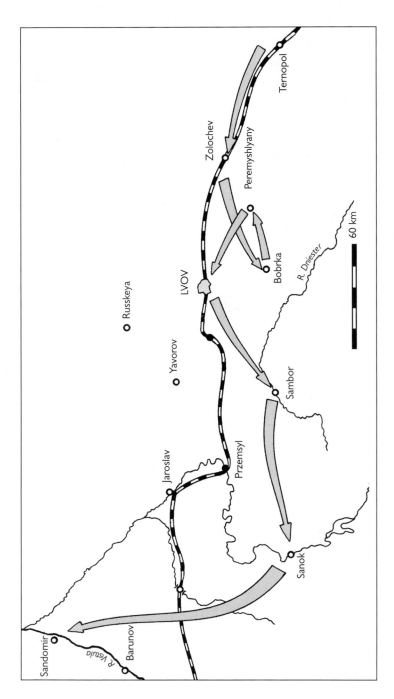

Map to show the Lvov-Sandomir operation, July to August 1944.

THE LVOV–SANDOMIR
OPERATION

Our 'vacation' and training for the battles to come was about to end. In early July 1944 our battalion along with the other battalions of the 49th Kamenets-Podolsk Mechanized Brigade, marched on foot towards the front line, to the concentration area, from which we were supposed to go over to the offensive. Intensive fighting was ahead of us.

We only marched in darkness and till dawn; in daytime we stayed in forests and groves, taking camouflage measures. By night the road to the front turned into a mighty stream of troops of all branches of service: infantry, artillery of all calibres, armoured personnel carriers. Tanks drove on other roads in order to confuse the enemy. Camouflage and concealment requirements were strictly followed, all soldiers understood its necessity – otherwise we would have been bombed. Regardless of how hard it was to find a good place for daytime rest, battalion commander Kozienko tried to position the battalion near some water, by a small river for example. It was of great significance in the hot summer days in Ukraine – one could wash or cool down tired feet, or wash their foot wrappings after exhausting night march in huge clouds of dust. All movement died out in daytime – we feared air raids.

We arrived at the concentration area after several days. We stayed for some five days in a copse, waiting for further orders. After this, on one summer evening, Studebakers drove up to us, all personnel of the battalion climbed aboard those trucks and we moved closer to the front by a forced march. The problem was that the drivers did not have sufficient driving experience, and sometimes made mistakes when advancing in columns, but all worked out well. In the morning we dismounted from the trucks and dispersed in the forest in case of artillery strike.

At dawn on 14 July, 1944, after an extensive artillery barrage and numerous air strikes, the infantry's offensive operation began; the goal was to break through the strongly fortified German defences. On 17 July, after breaking through the German positions, our 4th Tank Army entered the gap with the mission to penetrate deep into the enemy's rear in the direction of Lvov. Only our 1st motor rifle battalion was thrown into the breakthrough, we rode on tanks of the 56th Tank Regiment. The second and the third battalions along with the Brigade's tank regiment in the meantime attacked the Germans, who tried to close the gap in their defences, counter-attacking from north and south. The battalions suffered significant losses in personnel and tanks in a heated battle; the tank regiment of the Brigade was almost completely wiped out. However, the enemy also suffered losses and had to give up its intention to close the gap in defences. As a result of that battle, our battalion, our Brigade and the 6th Mechanized Corps in general had all the conditions necessary for a raid into the enemy's rear. Thus, the burden of fighting during the raid fell on our battalion, the only one that had not suffered losses in the first days of the operation.

We were hit hard during the march to Lvov, especially by the German air force, which never stopped strafing our column, trying to slow down our advance. We tried to advance at night, but summer nights were short and we had to advance in daytime as well. The enemy tried to stop us with all the means at his disposal, setting ambushes and covering forces, but it did not help him much, and we continued our march forward. We also suffered from heat, especially when we dismounted tanks and had to march on foot because of the air raids. What was an air raid? Normally 20 or 25 Junkers bomber planes, escorted by Messerschmitt 109 or 110 fighters, flew in. The bombers were in battle formation even before they reached us and strafed along our column, or attacked from the side, normally out of the sun. First they all dropped their bombs, aiming for the tanks and simultaneously fired the large-calibre machine-guns, trying to set them on fire. The planes attacked twice or three times. During an air raid the tank riders would immediately jump from the tanks like lemmings, trying to run away from the road, diving into some natural shelter, or just lie down and wait for the raid to be over. The tanks also

Above: Moscow youth. This photo, taken in 1932 in Moscow, shows children from Evgeni Bessonov's neighbourhood. The author stands second from the right.

Left: A photograph of Bessonov taken while at the Kamyshlov military infantry academy in 1942.

A junior officer, holding a submachine-gun, watches as his troops fight their way into a wood. The submachine-gun was the weapon of choice for many tank riders and it meant they could combine firepower with mobility.

A junior officer leading Soviet infantrymen forward through wooded terrain. Junior officers such as Bessonov were expected to lead from the front and suffered enormous casualties as a result. In four years of war the Red Army alone lost 90,210 company commanders and 296,744 platoon commanders killed in action.

An action shot of Red Army soldiers changing position during an attack. The lead soldier is armed with a Degtyarev light machine-gun.

A T-34-76 tank, heading to the front, fires at a distant enemy position.

A Maxim machine-gun crew opens fire on a village occupied by Germans. The Maxim was a morale-boosting addition to any attack as well as a crucial way to 'soften up' any enemy position.

A Soviet divisional ZIS-3 76mm gun being towed by a Studebaker US6 truck drives through the streets of a liberated European town.

A T-34-76 ploughs its way through a forest.

The wreckage of a German Mittlerer Zugkraftwagen 8t Sd.Kfz.7 destroyed during a Soviet assault.

A KV–1 heavy tank mounts a slight incline. Its complement of tank riders follow in its wake, ready to offer infantry support.

Tank Riders on a column of T-34-85 tanks move through the streets of a European town. Riding a tank was a hazardous affair. Near Lodz a tank carrying Bessonov's men was hit by a shell from a German Tiger: 'The explosion killed almost everyone, some soldiers were simply blown to pieces and nothing remained of them'.

Another photo of T-34-85 tanks with tank riders. Despite the hazards, riding tanks meant that infantry could at least travel at speed.

These remarkable photographs show Soviet infantry taking cover as they come under German fire during a battle for possession of a forest. Fighting in such terrain was extremely hazardous. Bessonov and several of his men were wounded by splinters when a German shell struck a tree in August 1944.

A sparsely camouflaged Soviet artillery column moves forward. Dodge 3/4s pull ZIS-3 76 mm divisional guns while Willis jeeps tow 45 mm antitank guns.

This photograph was taken in Poland in November 1944.
Left to right: Bessonov, Petr Shakulo and another soldier.

A photograph taken in November 1944, somewhere in Poland.
Left to right: Lieutenant Alexander Fedorovich Guschenkov, commander of the machine-gun platoon of 1st company; Lieutenant Oplesnin, commander of SMG platoon of the 1st battalion; an unknown soldier; Senior Lieutenant Nikolai Konstantinovich Chernyshov; commander of the 1st company; another anonymous soldier; and Lieutenant Grigori Andreevich Shtokolov, commander of the 2nd company.

A certificate awarded to members of Bessonov's brigade to mark the liberation of Prague. Signed by Colonel Pushkarev on 10 May, 1945, the award notes that the brigade received the thanks of the Commander in Chief for their efforts in freeing the city.

The 1st battalion of the 49th Mechanized Brigade photographed on 9 May 1945 taking a rest while on their way to Prague.

left the road. On a hot sunny day, just beyond the town of Zolochev, the German air force bombed the battalion's column all day long, 'with no lunch break', as we said: one group would leave, and the next one would arrive right away. That was why the tanks stopped and the Brigade's command, with the consent of the battalion commander, ordered the tank riders to march on foot with all possible camouflage and concealment. In daytime the heat exhausted the soldiers, there were problems with water, men lost their energy and our feet seemed to be made of lead. Some soldiers chafed their feet sore to bleeding. I also got sore feet, for the first and last time in my life. Tanks stood in shelters till darkness and then caught up with us; during the night the battalion again marched ahead on tanks. This measure helped us to avoid losses in personnel and tanks, and we reached the necessary point after the night march. The enemy temporarily lost us; the German air force searched forest edges and ravines, but it was in vain. We marched to Lvov in this manner for several days more.

I liked to sit on the front armour of the tank, on the machine-gun mounting (on the right side of the tank), holding on to the main gun barrel with my left hand. However, one could really only do this when the nights were quite light, with good weather and a good road; normally the tank riders would stay behind the tank turret. Just one time I was inside the tank – I had an hour's nap there. It was not too comfortable – bumpy, hot and strange. I mostly travelled on the first tank – there was no dust and there was a good view. However, the danger was that the very first enemy's shell was for you – after all, that was the first vehicle. This is exactly what happened once.

We had travelled on tanks almost the whole night, with lights on. Before dawn, as the sky grew grey, the column stopped in front of a small hill for a short break. That was in front of small town Bobrka, south of Lvov. I decided to leave the first tank and stay behind the turret of the third tank – a more usual place for me and my soldiers. I just wanted to take a nap, if that was possible. Apparently, my intuition helped me, not for the first time. As soon as the column moved forward and the first tank reached the top of the hill, the Fritzes opened fire, the first tank was knocked out and caught fire and then exploded. Two or three soldiers who were on that tank died, the rest, some eight of them, survived. The men were lucky, they jumped off the tank in time, ran away from it and took cover in a roadside ditch. The company also dismounted the tanks and dispersed in a line. We lay down and started to dig in just in case. We could not lift our heads, so heavy was the German machine-gun fire, artillery also fired on us (later we learned that this was in fact German tanks – Panthers).

The order 'Forward!' came from the company commander. I got my platoon up to attack, other platoons of the company also stood up. We reached the top of the hill, where our knocked-out tank was, and could not advance any further because of the storm of fire coming from the Fritzes. The platoon suffered casualties – both dead and wounded. The soldiers went to ground, as they could not stand the machine-gun and artillery fire of the enemy, as well as the sniper fire. With the assistance of the squad leaders I managed to spot a couple of German machine-gun nests that were dug-in some 150 to 200 metres from our line. I pointed them out to a runner and sent him to an artillery observer and to the battalion's mortar company; by that time they themselves had already seen the targets. Brigade artillery and our 82 mm mortars opened fire but failed to suppress the German gun emplacements. As soon as we got up from the ground, the Fritzes pinned us down again; the Brigade's command did not send tanks to support us, apparently sparing them for further battles. We, tank riders, also could not attack without tank support, and we lay down and tried to wait for the tanks to arrive.

Another 'Forward!' order came, that time with the addition of 'or you will be executed.' I think that it was the company commander himself, Nikolai Chernyshov, who thought up this addition. I very much doubt that the battalion or brigade commander would have come up with such an order; I never heard anything like that from them either in this and or in the following battles. No one ever scared me with threats of execution, there were no reasons to do so, I always followed my orders without question. We would have to attack the Fritzes and die for the sake of others' lives. However, it took us a long time to organize the attack, almost the entire day. Yes, we were afraid to charge against tanks, we were simply afraid. The company did not have anti-tank weapons (anti-tank grenades, petrol bombs, were already becoming obsolete). It was not only me who was afraid, other company commanders and platoon leaders were also afraid. The enemy's fire was heavy and deadly, no one wanted to die, regardless of how brave or dashing you were. The worst thing is to become a cripple, it is better to die right away. When you attack and feel that your comrades are falling next to you, you are horrified – 'It must be me next.' But on the other hand, one had such a huge anger against the Germans: 'just wait for me to get there', that one was ready to crush everything around and no longer thought of death.

So, I got infuriated after the execution warning. I ordered the squad leaders to get the soldiers up to attack – I was also in the line. The soldiers did not get up – they lay on the ground, no one wanted to die. I also did not want to die, I was just 21 years old, but I had received an order, I could not just wait for the enemy to leave the village. I jumped up from the ground under heavy fire from the enemy and shouted the command: 'Get up! For the Motherland, for Stalin! Follow me, attack, forward!' Just a few men got up, it was mostly squad leaders, the rest remained on the ground; fear chained them to the ground. I ran a few metres forward and noticed that it was just several men in the attacking line. I had to come back, run along the line of soldiers and get them up from the ground by force, literally pulling them up from the ground by their waist belts. This was all under the enemy's machine-gun fire. My orderly ran behind me and shouted to me: 'Comrade Lieutenant, get down! Get down, comrade Lieutenant, or they'll kill you!' I just ran forward, getting the soldiers up. All of a sudden I noticed that wheat ears in front of me were falling off their stems, as if they were cut down by scissors. They were cut by machine-gun fire that the Germans were aiming at me. I had not seen such concentrated fire before. I got in a terrible rage, forgot that I could be killed and started to kick the lying soldiers with my feet and the handle of my entrenching tool, getting them to move. Eventually, everything ended well for my soldiers and me – I was not even wounded, I got the soldiers up and the platoon ran down from the hill into a depression at the outskirts of Bobrka. At the same time Petr Shakulo's and Gavrilov's platoons assaulted the enemy. The Germans fled, leaving a Panther tank behind – apparently, it was out of fuel. When we ran up to the tank, it was still warm from the working engine. It took me a long time to come to my senses after that assault, I sat on the ground behind a house and thought of nothing. They called for me, but I did not answer. It was a miracle that the Germans did not kill my orderly and me as we ran along the line of soldiers, getting the soldiers up.

When everyone calmed down and we came to our senses, I heard laughter, jokes, we started to recall the recent engagement. In order to relax we all took a shot of vodka. There were a lot of jokers in the war, we called them *hohmach (a Russian slang word for comedian – translator's comment)*. They started to joke about me: 'Bessonov, why did you run along the front, not forward, during the attack?' Another *hohmach* answered: 'Lads, he was so scared that he forgot the direction of the attack.' The third one: 'No, he drew German fire on himself, to make it easier for the Slavs (this is what we called soldiers on the front) to attack the Fritzes.' This was all accompanied by the roar of comrades. 'He is a real *hohmach*, he knows how to deceive the Fritzes!' Those big lads thought it was funny, they laughed like horses, and did not have the slightest idea why I had run along the front, not forward. I still get scared when I recall that incident, but that time I was really lucky that I remained safe and sound. I never forgot that town of Bobrka.

The soldiers did not hold it against me that I got them to attack by force. On the contrary, they turned everything into a joke, and they were happy that they survived. It seems that this episode stayed in my memory because of its uniqueness. I never again had to go through anything like that in the rest of my battle experience. On the whole the soldiers were brave and followed orders without questioning no matter how hard it was for them. I had faith in their ability and I knew that I could fulfil orders with them. They saw me in the attacking line and participating in the deadly battle. They saw that I did not hide behind their backs and this is why they trusted me. I never doubted their stoicism, did not humiliate their self-esteem and treated everyone equally. Some soldiers showed extreme courage, for example, Poddubny, Savkin, Chulkin and others. These brave men were my support. I took heed of their useful advice in battle, and as a rule I tried to fulfil their requests and shared everything that I had with them, mostly food. So did they. I never left wounded on the battlefield and I knew that if I were wounded, they would not leave me. Our problem was that with our fast advance on tanks we did not always have time to bury the dead, and when we buried them, we did not always mark that place. It was only after the end of an operation, when we were in reserve that we defined more precisely who was killed and where, but even then it was only approximate. That was the misfortune of the tank riders and tank crews when fighting far behind enemy lines. We sometimes carried the lightly wounded with us on tanks, they were taken care of by medics or sanitary officers; heavily wounded were left in villages for the villagers to take care of them. In general, it was the battalion and company clerks' job to keep a tally of the dead and wounded.

We did not enjoy the rest for long; a 'Forward!' order came, as our tanks caught up with us. That horrible day, 18 July, 1944, the day that I would remember for my whole life, was drawing to an end. One must acknowledge that the Germans set up a good covering force on that spot, skilfully used the terrain and acted very competently in that battle. The road, as I have already written, first went up to the top of the hill, and then went sharply downwards with a right turn. To the right and to the left of the road were steep hillsides, we had to jump down from them when attacking. At the same time, from my point of view, the German covering force was small – two or three Panthers and Tigers, and up to one company of infantry. To compensate for that, they had a lot of MG34 machine-guns, snipers as well as an 81 mm mortar battery. The Germans were well prepared for defence, skilfully placed their weapons and set their tanks in ambush. We, a column of tanks, advanced at full throttle, without advanced point, without any reconnaissance. An encounter battle is a very complicated type of combat, and one must know how to command it. We were lucky to have such minor casualties both in our company and in platoon. We failed to find one soldier – Babaev, a native of Baku. We searched the entire hillside, checked the houses, but he was nowhere to be found. It was a pity – he was a good soldier.

All night long we continued our advance towards Lvov. We encountered small groups of the enemy, but none of them could compare with the covering force the Fritzes had at Bobrka. At dawn of 19 July we stopped for a rest – we really needed it, especially the tank drivers, as after the hard night they would fall asleep right in their tanks, on their seats. We, the tank riders, could have a nap on the tank's armour during the march, although the tank was not a car and it did not have real shock absorbers. Any suspension consisted of special kernels (cylinders) that slightly softened the tank's movement on uneven roads.

We lay in wheat fields, our tanks were camouflaged in ravines. We had a snack with what God had in store for us, washed ourselves and started to put ourselves in order. Officers, who were older than me, started shaving. It was quiet and calm, the sun was shining, the sky was blue, not a single cloud in the sky. How much beauty is around and what a great happiness it is to be alive!

An incident took place during that break that I remember very well. Lieutenant Alexander Guschenkov, machine-gun platoon leader from our company, was shaving. Lieutenant Petr Malyutin came up to him to shave after Guschenkov was done. Guschenkov had a German Parabellum pistol. It was quite a rare piece in our army, the officers did not like it as it was quite complicated, but it did fit comfortably in one's hand.

So, Lieutenant Malyutin came up and took the pistol, which he had apparently never seen before, and started to study it. Without thinking he put the bullet in the cartridge chamber, pulled the trigger and a shot sounded. The bullet hit Guschenkov in the left shoulder and went right through the muscles. At first Petr did not even understand what had happened, until Alexander told him: 'Pete, you wounded me.' Malyutin was scared to death, but all worked out more or less well – he did not kill him, just wounded Alex in the left shoulder. Guschenkov was quickly bandaged and sent to hospital, but his misadventures did not end with that and he had to avoid a deadly danger once more: as he told us later, the Germans, some retreating unit, rushed into the village where the hospital was stationed. They suddenly burst into the house where the wounded were, rushed into the rooms and slaughtered everyone who was there. Alexander Guschenkov jumped from the window of the second floor and ran away into the wheat fields, firing back at the Germans with his Parabellum. He was lucky that it grew dark quickly after the attack. He got into the army hospital several days later. Unfortunately, this was not the only case when the Germans executed wounded and medical personnel. I think that there is no justification for such atrocities.

I also had a case when I wounded a fellow officer, a machine-gun platoon leader. It happened like this: our battalion attacked the Fritzes and almost threw them back from the road, when my soldiers reported: 'Comrade Lieutenant, the Germans are attacking from the left!' I did not have binoculars – they only frustrated me in battle, but after looking attentively, I indeed saw Fritzes with their give-away helmets with 'little horns' running to the left flank of my company. One of them was especially annoying – he kept hiding and popping up again from the wheat. For some reason I had a rifle, in fact, a German carbine. I did not think long, aimed, and as soon as he showed up, I fired. All of a sudden I heard horrible obscene curses from his direction. It turned out that this was a Russian, and he had found a German helmet in action and put it on for safety. I did not kill him, but had shot his nose through. He immediately threw away the German helmet, they bandaged him and sent into the rear, as someone wounded by a German bullet. What else could I do? Well, the bullet was indeed German. How can one put on German equipment during an offensive! One can use them in defence, but with certain caution.

On the day Guschenkov was wounded our column marched forward unharmed for half a day, not encountering the enemy. The air force was not there either. However, this did not last long – in the afternoon the enemy threw their air force against us again. Given the lack of fighter escort (we did not always have anti-aircraft guns in the column either) the Germans merely taunted us without any disturbance. They strafed low over the column, and we suffered losses both in tanks and personnel. Why were our fighters not in the air? I think the only reason was that our Brigade was far away from the fighter bases, and fighters had limited range capacity. With the mission to liberate Lvov, our Tank Army, including our 49th Mechanized Brigade were deep in the enemy's rear, almost 100 kilometres ahead of the general army units, that mostly advanced on foot and were engaged in constant fighting with the Germans.

THE BATTLE FOR LVOV

On 19 July we spotted German defences in front of a village. The battalion dispersed and formed a line; our company deployed and advanced towards the village, to the left of the road, while the 3rd company under Senior Lieutenant Kostenko advanced to the right of the road. We had learnt lessons in the battles at Bobrka and the 2nd company remained in battalion commander's reserve. In a ravine we encountered two men in Soviet uniform. They said that they were Il-2 pilots, shot down by German fighters during a ground attack mission at the outskirts of Lvov and were trying to get back to the Russian lines. They asked for food, we gave them bread and canned food and advanced in attacking line. The pilots told us that there were no Germans in the trenches, and they were right. However, there was a barbed wire fence in front of the trench – Bruno's coil, as it was called. This was a roll of barbed wire one metre high and one metre wide. We tried to jump it over, but it did not work out. I ordered several rain capes to be put over it, and we crawled over them to the other side of the obstacle. It was nice that the enemy was absent, otherwise we would have been stuck in front of that obstacle.

We entered the village and the villagers emerged one by one out of their shelters. Some soldiers went into the houses and were given milk and white bread. They brought me some, but I did not drink the milk, just had a piece of bread. For some reason the kitchen had again fallen behind and we did not have any food from the evening of the previous day. When we left the village, none of us were hungry any more. After that village we marched both on foot and on tanks. The German air force did not leave us alone and thus we moved westwards in stages.

Twilight set in, the German air force finally departed and we could continue our march in a normal manner. Later in the evening I and my platoon reached some village, unfortunately, I no longer remember its name. Ahead of us, about one or two kilometres away, lay the city of Lvov. When I reported to the battalion commander, he permitted the soldiers to rest. He gave an order to me to advance on Lvov early in the morning of the next day. It must have been 20 July, 1944, my birthday – I was 21 years old.

Because of platoon leader Petr Shakulo's light wound, I was put in charge of his platoon as well. Petr's assistant platoon leader was Sergeant Savkin – a brave man, I knew him well from battles in Kamenets-Podolsk and had a great respect for him. Savkin was a reliable man, soldiers obeyed him and respected him. It was just us two officers that remained in the company.

I should say that only our 1st motor rifle battalion approached Lvov, or, rather, a company and the battalion HQ – Battalion Commander Kozienko, Political Officer Gerstein and Head of Staff Grigoriev, my platoon and Shakulo's platoon (without Shakulo himself). The 3rd platoon with the company commander Chernyshov was left behind at some road crossing (platoon leader Gavrilov was wounded) in case the Fritzes appeared. Guschenkov was also wounded. The 2nd company (company commander Shtokolov) was also left as a guard at some hill. The 3rd company (under Kostenko) was left to assist the 16th Guards Mechanized Brigade, which was stuck in street fighting in the town of Peremyshlyany, south-east from Lvov. The 2nd and 3rd battalions of our Brigade were somewhere else, while the 56th Tank Regiment left our battalion, fulfilling other missions. Thus, the battalion commander ordered me to capture Lvov with two platoons, which had 30 to 35 men. A huge city and a handful of soldiers.

We approached Lvov from the south, not from the east; the enemy did not expect us there and there were almost no German troops in the area. To be honest, I was afraid to enter the city without armour support. I did not like to assault or advance without tanks. Tanks always meant additional courage for us and additional fear for the enemy. We supported each other in battle, especially in built-up areas and forests. It is hard to fight without tanks, as it is hard for them to fight without us, the tank riders. Both the tank crews and ourselves were used to this co-operation. Without tanks we felt like a naked person in the winter, I cannot find any better comparison. It is bad without armour.

In short, on 20 or 21 July, 1944, I summoned the squad leaders and explained the mission, that had been given to me by Captain Kozienko, battalion commander (one month later he became a Major). At dawn I and two platoons of our company, as well as the machine-gun platoon of the 3rd company of our battalion under Lieutenant Tsikanovski, attacked Lvov. The city was built in the western manner, alongside large apartment houses there were individual mansions, surrounded by iron fences or mesh. There were a lot of small crooked, sometimes steep, streets in the city in addition to the wide boulevards.

Trenches could be seen at the outskirts of the city. It was these that we attacked in a line. Just in case I sent one squad (seven or eight soldiers) ahead as a scout party. The scout party reached the trenches and reported that there were no Germans there. I ordered the squad to come out on to the asphalt highway and advance into the city on that highway. I turned the company to the road as well, and we followed our advanced point on the roadsides. This is how we entered the city – ahead of us, some 150-200 metres away, there was the vanguard, and the rest of the company proceeded as two columns of one on the roadsides. Two local men welcomed us. One of them held a tray with glasses, while the other held two bottles of vodka, pouring it into the glasses. Each one of us came up to them had his shot of vodka and marched on. I also did this with thankfulness, I even had two shots. We entered the city from the southern outskirts, along Kultparkovaya Street. To the left of the road there were small houses, one and two storeys high, while to the right there was a wooden fence. We did not encounter enemy, it was quiet as if there were no war, and the sun was at its hottest. But we could in no case be off-guard, as we were not waging war against amateurs. On the contrary, we faced well-trained, strong and resourceful soldiers, one could expect anything from them. I warned my soldiers that we had no right to relax because of the small size of our force, which was only armed with two Maxim machine-guns. One of the Maxim crews was under Sergeant Ivan Zakharievich Chechin – a young, brave and self-confident fighter, with whom I fought side by side till Victory Day.

We did not advance deep into the city but consolidated our position in the empty houses at the city's outskirts, as the battalion commander ordered it. In any case, we advanced one block into the city. The battalion commander and his staff were stationed in front of the city, but established telephone communication with me. Our kitchen was again absent – it was burnt in an air raid, so I sent soldiers to look for food in surrounding houses. We managed to get hold of some food from the locals – in any case, we did not go hungry. Senior Lieutenant Kashintsev, the commander of the artillery battery of our battalion arrived together with Israel Solomonovich Tsikanovski (we called him Semyon). Kashintsev brought along one 45 mm gun, which was towed by the crew, but it only had a few rounds. The rest of the battery, supply trucks and prime movers were destroyed by the German air force during the march to Lvov.

I liked Kashintsev, sometimes stuttering, but ever cheerful with a sharp mind and a good sense of humour. At that time he was 27 years old. He was an interesting person and a veteran of many previous battles. I was glad that he came. Then Tsikanovski and I had someone to consult with about how to capture a huge city with a company of soldiers. We did not advance deep into the city, I was afraid of entering the maze of narrow streets, which had no shelter and where it was impossible to dig in. We could not advance through the gardens because of high metal fences of private houses. Somehow, there had been more space in Skalat and Kamenets-Podolsk – we had not encountered any fences of that type. We did not have any tanks with us; we would have felt safer with them. Of what use was the 45 mm gun with five rounds? Just a joke. We did not have any information about the enemy, its positions and presence of enemy armour. The battalion commander did not give a detailed mission to us – such as where to advance in the city. He did not bother us, we did not bother him, and that was a mistake.

It was quiet and calm, no one fired at us, the German air force was nowhere to be seen, and we had food. They were warm sunny days. After days of intensive march and battles on the way to Lvov this was bliss to us. We prepared to face the enemy: placed our machine-guns, even put the 45 mm gun into position. We dug trenches by the houses to defend against air raids. We had a schedule for observers and a squad on duty. Tolya Kashintsev and I decided to inspect the nearest houses. I sent two squads ahead to check what was happening in front and to the sides of our street and, without going too deep into the city, interrogate the locals, if any could be found anywhere. So far the city looked dead – locals were nowhere to be seen, some houses were abandoned.

Searching the area, Kashintsev and I found a German hospital, which was stationed in three or four four-storey buildings. As far as we could understand, it was a hospital for mentally ill soldiers. We found some German personnel of the hospital. In broken German I ordered them to feed the patients and take care of them. They understood me and we did not come close to that psychiatric clinic. We had enough things to worry about, while Germans could take care of their mentally ill countrymen without our help.

We inspected several other houses, in a brick one we found the locals, who had gathered in that house from other buildings, more vulnerable to shelling. Our scout party came back, reporting the absence of Germans in the nearest houses. Other soldiers, who volunteered to examine the surrounding area, also came back. They spotted a German airfield close to us, but the enemy had abandoned it. The soldiers brought some food staples – mostly all kinds of canned food.

Night passed well; on the next day we did not receive any instructions from the battalion commander, and we were happy. Of course, we should have entered the city instead of having a rest, but we were exhausted and did not know anything about the enemy. We were all tired from our march to Lvov and especially tired of the enemy's air force. German pilots strafed low, almost at ground level, firing their machine-guns and raining their bombs on us. They did all they could to prevent our advance, while we could only repel the aircraft with small arms fire. The effectiveness of this fire was the same as the effectiveness of medicine given to the dead. And all of a sudden we were in a quiet place: no shooting, no bombing, no hunger either. It was nice and warm, summer time. It seemed like a resort to us, at least a nice holiday house for us.

The next day a sniper opened fire on us. As soon as someone appeared in an open place, a shot sounded. We could not spot his firing position for a long time. Finally, through binoculars we found out that a sniper had fired from the attic of a five-storey building. Late one afternoon volunteers secretly approached the building and went up to the attic, but the sniper was off and away, while neither I nor my soldiers were quick-witted enough to leave an ambush there. Most likely, he was not even a German, but a Ukrainian or Polish independence fighter on his own. He never reappeared.

Two or three days passed like this, and we were still hanging around in the city's outskirts. Tsikanovski, Kashintsev and I were not brave enough to assault a huge city with half a company of soldiers – 30 or 35 people. The battalion commander did not bother us and we did not bother him, but all of a sudden company commander Senior Lieutenant Chernyshov arrived. It would have been better if he had never shown up. All he did was cause confusion and mess; later he again disappeared. Chernyshov made a decision to advance to the city centre; we advanced along one of the streets. At that instant a person in civilian dress appeared, who showed a Soviet passport and started to convince Chernyshov to advance faster to the city centre. Despite my admonitions not to trust the guy, he did not agree with me and ordered us to advance. An order is always an order, we had to comply, and we cautiously continued our advance along the street.

Before we could cross many streets, German infantry with two armoured personnel carriers showed up in our rear. It was as if they were waiting for us to go deeper into the city and then cut us off from the battalion staff. There was not much infantry, but the Germans were armed with machine-guns, the worst being the APCs with machine-guns; we did not have a weapon to combat them. The civilian disappeared, soldiers later told me that he ran to the Germans. The Germans opened a storm of fire from all types of weapons, mainly from machine-guns. We were not ready to strike back, but many soldiers kept their heads and returned fire. I do not remember how I ended up with a submachine-gun in my hands, but I also opened fire on a machine-gun crew from behind the fence.

However, we could not deliver a single attack, as we were separated by the street. Some soldiers fired individually, others ran away behind the houses, almost to our previous positions. Chernyshov ran back to the platoon, which was in defence in the rear of the battalion HQ. He told me: 'You manage things here yourself, while I go to see the battalion commander,' and then disappeared. Somehow I organized the defence and calmed the soldiers down, suppressing the confusion.

It was amazing that we did not have losses, because there was no shelter except for the houses, and the doors were locked as a rule.

Sergeant Savkin showed stoicism and courage in that fight. This man was never at a loss and was always acting as platoon leader for Lieutenant Shakulo, when the latter was wounded, and he was trusted as an officer. In that fight Savkin with several soldiers had to keep the Germans at bay all day long. It was good that they hid behind a high metal mesh fence and the Germans could not overcome it under fire of our soldiers. The German APCs were also helpless.

Nikolai Savkin was angry at me because I did not support him with another group of soldiers in that fight. Only after it grew dark did I reach him with my soldiers; the Germans had already abandoned the battlefield. Apparently, the Germans wanted to delay us for some time, depriving us of the possibility of advancing to the centre. A soldier went missing in that fight, he was around 40 years old, and our search for him did not produce any results. Savkin's soldiers told us that that soldier was Polish and was from either Lvov or its suburbs. Probably that soldier just went home, deserted – it is hard to say. Anything can happen in the war; that's why war is war.

I should mention that during the battles in Lvov a Lieutenant (I do not remember his name) arrived with a battery of 120 mm mortars. He failed to find his unit and decided to stay and fight the battle together with us. Of course, we warmly welcomed him. His battery had four mortars with a full *boyekomplekt* [complement] of mines, each mine weighing around 16 kg. The Lieutenant was dashing. Many times we climbed into the attics of a tall building and he adjusted the fire on the enemy from there. In any case, it was of assistance to us. In order to be on the safe side and not be convicted of desertion, the Lieutenant asked for a letter that would state that he took part in battles for Lvov. I wrote such a letter, signed it and got it stamped with the battalion's stamp.

One day in late July (24 or 25) a T-34 tank showed up some 500 to 700 metres from us. Apparently, it did not notice us and we could not establish communication with it. The tank disappeared in the labyrinth of the city streets and we never saw it again. It was only many years later that I learnt the story of that tank and its crew. The tank was knocked out, the whole crew died except for the driver. They were all awarded with the status of Heroes of the Soviet Union. The crew of that tank is considered to be the first one to enter the city, although it was Tsikanovski and me with our soldiers who entered the city first. Apparently, battalion commander Kozienko did not report on time to the brigade commander that we had entered Lvov. The only thing that consoles me is that we did not fight for history, and we did our soldier's duty without paying attention to who was first and who was second.

In the course of those battles Lieutenant Oplesnin, submachine-gun platoon leader from our battalion, went to the city centre dressed in civilian clothes with a local Polish guy, who could speak German. Several times they ran into German patrols, but everything went well, and knowledge of the language helped them.

Also in late July (25 or 26), our tanks from the 10th Guards Tank Corps arrived, but they entered the city at some distance from us. Their actions made us bolder, and we also advanced into the city in order to cut the road that fleeing Germans used for retreat and capture the railway station and crossing. We completed the mission, consolidating our positions in two smaller abandoned buildings, there was not even any furniture in the rooms. The city was not damaged, neither our nor the German air force bombed it, and it seems that it was only our half company that was involved in street fighting in the city. As soon as our tanks entered the city, The Germans evacuated the city almost without a fight. The Lieutenant that joined us with his 120 mm mortars was with me throughout the battle. He rained down his mines on the highway that the Germans used for retreat from Lvov, we cut another highway, and the Germans only had one road for withdrawal. However, quite soon the Germans ceased movement on that road as well, having chosen a less comfortable but safer route of retreat.

I decided to send several soldiers to find out what was in front of us, whether the Germans had stayed in their positions or abandoned them. They returned and said that there were no Germans. They brought along several piglets from a huge refrigerator that they found – the Germans had not managed to evacuate food supplies from there. There was a lot of canned food and other stuff, but mostly the refrigerator was filled with piglets. I had to send other soldiers to the refrigerator; we managed to keep some food for the future and cooked a fantastic dinner. It had been a long time since we had had such an abundance of food. In general, I did not forbid the soldiers to get their own food, especially given the fact that we had not seen the battalion kitchen for a long time. However, I strictly warned the soldiers and they never looted the locals, as they knew my strictness and harshness in this respect.

On 27 July, 1944, Lvov was fully liberated from the enemy. The battles for the city ceased. I should mention that the city had been under German occupation for three years (1941–1944), but we met five or six Jews, who had been hidden from the Germans in a shelter by their acquaintances. One evening, some time after Lvov was fully in our hands, Semyon Tsikanovski told me that we had been invited by several Jews for a dinner on occasion of the city's liberation. For three years these people had been suffering, but survived and were happy. They welcomed us in the warmest possible way. The table was served just like before the war: Moskovskaya vodka, sausage, ham, canned meat and fish. How on earth did they manage to get all that food? Everything was very tasty, and we had a nice evening, just like being back home.

We stayed for several days in Lvov. The 2nd and 3rd companies arrived in those days – they had separate missions. After the arrival of the rear and support units the Brigade has finally gathered all its units.

On 29 July the battalion received a new order – to attack towards the Polish town of Peremyshl. However, several kilometres before the town our Tank Army commander, Lelyushenko, directed the battalion to the south, towards the town of Sambor and further towards the Carpathian foothills, towards the oil fields. There was no major action, the enemy retreated and did not try to delay our advance. Only in one place, at a large village, did the battalion encounter resistance. We dismounted our tanks and rushed into the village. The terrain was swampy behind the village, pitted with large trenches, apparently for drainage. Tanks could not offer any significant support to us in this terrain. We had to attack right from the village without tanks or artillery support.

My platoon attacked some sort of a factory, as it turned out later, a distillery. The enemy stopped us with heavy small arms fire, and we had to lie down in the swamp. We did not suffer losses, but the enemy's fire prevented us from advancing further, especially because in front we could see the stone wall of the factory. We could not see the enemy, while we ourselves lay exposed. As soon as the Fritzes spotted any movement in our lines, they fired, forcing me and my soldiers to lie completely still. It took me a lot of effort to make it to a dry spot, seven or eight soldiers made it out of the swamp with me. We ran behind a house and started to look around, trying to find a way to drive Fritzes out of the factory's brick buildings.

I ran forward on dry land, trying to find a better way to attack the enemy, and show the soldiers, who were stuck in the swamp, a route of retreat to a dry place. The Fritzes noticed me and opened fire on me, not from small arms, as it was usually, but from a small-calibre mortar, apparently a company mortar. We encountered such mortars sometimes, although they quickly disappeared. Shells exploded not far from me. I ran, paying no attention to the fire on me. I ran as fast as my feet could carry me, while mines exploded behind me, all falling short. I ran at least 50 metres like this, before I ran behind a house. I was not even wounded, but by hunting me, the Fritzes had been distracted from the soldiers in the swamp, and they managed to run and sneak to a dry spot and hide from the enemy's fire. If the Germans had aimed longer, I would have been in serious trouble from mortar fire. I would run and a mine would explode behind me, then I would accelerate and it would fall short again. Owing to my talent as a sprinter I got off unharmed. I rarely ran that fast.

When twilight fell, we left that swampy area, joining Lieutenant Shakulo's platoon. Shakulo arrived from the hospital while we were at Lvov. He was lightly wounded at the beginning of that operation. Company commander Chernyshov was not there, and no one knew where he was. As early as during the day Shakulo and I received an order to gain possession of the village behind the swamp. We decided to attack the village along a good road, as soon as it grew totally dark. At first fortune was on our side, but as soon as we almost reached the edge of that village, the Germans opened a withering machine-gun fire on us. We lay down, and I consulted with Petr Shakulo what to do next. Eventually, we decided to wait for the Germans to make a pause in their fire, rush to the nearest houses of the village and act from there. So we did, although the Germans fired on us with great accuracy – tracer bullets flew low and close to the ground. We hid behind the folds of the ground and managed to avoid losses.

When we reached the first hut, we realized that it was an APC that had fired on us. We did not dare go further – it was dark and nothing could be seen. We did not know where the enemy was, what his forces were, where the village streets were. We quietly withdrew and established a defensive position some 150 to 200 metres from the village on the banks of those large drainage channels. As dawn came, we looked around and decided to dry our uniform at that spot. As it turned out later, we were right to retreat from that village – at dawn we spotted the arrival of German tanks in the village, and Tigers were a formidable opponent

Exhaustion was overwhelming, and in the daytime, in the sunlight, we fell fast asleep. Apparently, the men at the combat outpost also fell asleep, and the Germans took advantage of this. They secretly approached us through the ditches, captured a sleeping soldier from Shakulo's platoon and dragged him to their side as a 'tongue', a prisoner for interrogation. That soldier yelled like an animal, as the Germans wanted to take him prisoner in broad daylight. Such a thing had never happened even at night, and this was during a warm and sunny day, with the sun was at its peak. The soldiers woke up at this animal cry and opened fire, and some ran to rescue the man. One or two Germans fell dead, the rest dropped our soldier and ran away. No matter how hard we tried to get them, they disappeared. The soldier that the Germans had captured was barefoot, as he was drying his foot rags and boots in the sun. Many soldiers got wet in that swamp, and had to dry their clothes.

In general, the soldier got off lightly, he was even laughed at. We could not calm down for a long time after that incident, and Petr Shakulo gave a scolding to the soldiers who fell asleep on duty. This was the result of our carelessness, the guys forgot that they were in the war. One had to sleep in a special way during the war. Of course, we were always short of sleep – not always hungry, but always short of sleep. During even the slightest breaks in the fighting we would fall asleep. I was always sleepy and slept in every possible place and at every opportunity. Exhaustion was relentless – we were tired all the time in battles, both in day and night time. Breaks were short, as a rule.

We informed the battalion commander that enemy tanks and APCs had entered the village, but we had not captured it and thus failed the mission. The battalion staff also saw the Fritzes' armour in the village, and ordered me to stay where I was, dug in with my platoon, while Petr Shakulo with his platoon was transferred somewhere to plug a hole in our defences that had to be filled.

During the day of 30 July a soldier came and reported that I was invited as 'a guest' by the third battalion's company commander Senior Lieutenant Varennik. Escorted by this soldier and my orderly (I would never go anywhere alone at the front), I went for 'a visit'. Varennik welcomed me warmly. The snacks were excellent and there were also some drinks. We had a nice time together with him. I was glad to talk to my brother-officer, as at the front, in battles one could rarely meet a comrade, especially from the neighbouring battalion. Also, I did not think that the officers from the other battalions knew me, although personally I knew Varennik. Later he became deputy battalion commander of the 3rd battalion. In that period his company was to the right from my platoon. There were no other units, the leadership forgot about us, neither he nor I had a 'phone line to the battalion HQ. This is why we had such a nice resting session with him at the table, no one bothered us, even not the Germans – such a thing was quite rare at the front. The next day, 31 July, we disengaged and left this 'water battlefield'. For some reason I was again the only commanding officer left in the company. Company commander Chernyshov did not appear, while the platoon leaders – Gavrilov, Guschenkov and Shakulo were wounded, Shakulo for the second time.

After these couple of days of rest, we received an order to advance again towards Sambor, a town some 80 or 90 kilometres south-west of Lvov, on the Dniester river. Captain Kozienko, battalion commander, again did not appoint me company commander to replace Chernyshov, appointing machine-gun company platoon leader Lieutenant Karpenko for the office. Karpenko was a battalion veteran, he had fought with the battalion as early as in the summer 1943 at Kursk. I do not remember where Chernyshov was, probably lightly wounded. Several days later, on 2 August, Karpenko was killed in the vicinity of Sambor at his command post in a trench by a single splinter that went right into his heart. Telephone operators, orderlies and platoon runners were in the trenches next to him, but they were not hit, although the mine exploded closer to the telephone operators' trench...

Near Sambor we dismounted the tanks at a forest edge. We received an order and the direction of advance; our companies deployed in a line and quickly walked forward. The enemy was not seen, no one fired on us – apparently, the Germans did not expect our assault in this area. We reached a village. Behind the village was a wheat field, on the river Dniester, and on the other bank of the river we saw a city. From my point of view, the offensive was poorly organized. Even now, recalling those fights, I cannot understand why it was so. No one knew where the enemy was, there was no reconnaissance done by the Brigade or its battalions. 'Forward!' – and that was it, we were supposed to hope for the best after that. Oh, this hoping for the best! The entire battalion, or to be more precise, what remained of it, almost got slaughtered.

The company reached the village, which only had one street, and we had to check the houses just in case. A threatening silence hung in the air. I was used to relying on intuition, and I did not believe that there weren't any Fritzes in the houses. Machine-gun platoon leader Lieutenant Petr Malyutin from our MG company, however, did not agree with me, saying: 'There are no Fritzes in the village, because it is quiet.' It was this very quietness that scared me. I was about to send a squad of soldiers to check what was going on in the village, when Malyutin went out to the middle of the road and started to inspect the village through binoculars. A shot sounded – the bullet hit him right between the eyes and the binoculars fell apart into two pieces. Lieutenant Petr Nikolaevich Malyutin was killed on the spot. He was older than we were – he was around 36 years old; we dubbed him either 'grandfather' or 'old man'.

There were no more shots; soldiers hid behind the huts, not daring to go out in the street. We did not attack the village at all. The battalion commander sent an order to advance towards the river in order to capture the bridge across the Dniester and further towards the city, leaving the village alone. We said, to hell with those Germans in the village, they would have had to retreat anyway when we captured the bridge. An order is an order, so I left the village with my soldiers and we quickly advanced across a field to the river. As soon as we got 100 to 150 metres away from that ill-fated village, we saw a line of Germans attacking us from the rear. The Germans walked openly and fired submachine-guns at our line. To be honest, we were lost when we saw the German attacking line behind us. Despite of all soldiers being experienced and having been in all kinds of troubles, we were taken aback.

I did not lose self-control and shouted to my soldiers: 'Fire on the Fritzes, fire!' I also shouted to the Maxim machine-gun crew: 'Turn the machine-gun and fire on the Fritzes!' I was not even shouting, I was yelling at the top of my lungs. Many soldiers opened fire, while the others ran from the enemy's line, retreated and thus frustrated Tsikanovski's machine-guns – they could not fire on our soldiers, of course.

Neither I nor the other officers managed to bring order and organize resistance, no matter how hard we tried – soldiers dispersed, at least it was good that many fired on the Fritzes. When no more soldiers were left in front of me, I also ran along the hillside to the road and lay in a ditch. I saw a light DP machine-gun, some soldier dropped it in panic, so that he could run faster – I grabbed it and opened fire on the line of German soldiers, as there was ammo in the drum.

As I fired, my garrison cap fell from my head, I put it back on and continued to fire, before I ran out of ammo. I did not have my own submachine-gun with me, although it would have been nice to have it in that moment. When I ran out of ammo, I withdrew, sometimes sneaking and sometimes in short rushes to the rear, where the fighters ran, or rather, frightened soldiers, one could not call them fighters – they had got scared by a bunch of 40 or 50 Germans! Later they said that there was also an APC, but they must have lied – the eyes of fear see danger everywhere.

Our group was not larger than the German one, though, but we had Maxim heavy machine-guns, although they ceased fire quite soon. It was either due to my fire or that of some stoic soldiers, but the Germans did not pursue us and quickly left towards the bridge, carrying their dead and wounded – apparently, our fire on them had been successful.

The Germans left, while we gathered together and started to debrief the clash with the other officers (including 3rd company commander Kostenko) and gathered the scattered soldiers. Our subordinates assembled too. I noticed that machine-gunner Ishmuhammetov sat there without a weapon, and realized that it was he who had dropped the machine-gun; I sent him to pick it up. It is infamy for a fighter to drop a weapon. Soldiers came back with a feeling of guilt, they were ashamed of their fear and cowardice in battle. The proud ones suffered twice as hard in their feelings, we also did not spare ourselves.

We distributed the returning soldiers between the companies and ordered them to dig in just in case. If memory serves me well, by some miracle we had no losses. The machine-gun platoon of the 3rd company under Lieutenant Tsikanovski had disappeared during the fight, but as it turned out later, they had had to hide in thick vegetation on the Dniester shores for some time. Several days later they caught up with the battalion on the march.

We were all hungry after the skirmish and arranged some snacks. During the meal one of the officers asked me: 'Where did you tear your garrison cap?' I took it off and saw two torn holes in it – in the front and in the back. It was only then that I recalled that the garrison cap had fallen from my head as I fired the machine-gun and told the story. The guys told me: 'You were really lucky, Bessonov, if that sniper had aimed several millimetres lower, you would have been dead.' They were right, I was lucky, really lucky. How many times have I been lucky? Quite a few. Luck at the front is quite an important thing. However, such luck does not happen very often.

By the evening our company, as well as the other companies of the battalion dug in on a dominant hill with a steep slope towards the river, some 150 metres from the river. Some units to the left us also tried to attack Sambor. The cannonade lasted some thirty minutes, Katyushas also took part, as well as heavier missiles, launched from the ground, not from trucks. Sometimes their missiles (M-31) were launched together with the launch frame, in order not to waste time for preparation. However, those units also attacked in vain, their assault was repelled and the Germans still held the bridge across the river and Sambor proper.

On the night of 2 August a heavy rain fell from the sky, water fell like a shower. The deluge continued all night and the whole day after. We had to ladle water out from the trenches with mess kits, and we were all soaking wet. The soil was so saturated with water that it turned into a total quagmire. In the evening the Germans decided to drive us out from that hill. Eight to ten T-VI Tiger tanks emerged from the bushes by the river. Probably, there were more Tigers, but I could not see all of them. At the time I did not understand how Tigers had appeared against us, and even now I cannot explain how they appeared. Regardless of how they made it there, the main thing was their assault on our defences. The Tiger is a serious thing. Our 76 mm gun could penetrate its armour only at a range of 50 metres.

The Tigers advanced slowly, with frequent stops, sometimes opening fire. We all hid in trenches, afraid to make a move. A tank could fire even on a single soldier, but they fired over our heads on some targets in the undergrowth behind us. It was good that infantry were not escorting the tanks. Apparently, they wanted to squash us with tanks without infantry support. At that very moment the rain shower and wet soil, as well as the steep slope played their positive role. The tanks were some 50 metres from us, when all of a sudden a miracle happened – the Tigers skidded on the wet soil and stopped. The tanks were stuck on one spot, their tracks were spinning, but the tanks could not move. We were lucky that because of the Tiger's weight its tracks did not have good cohesion in the mud. The tanks could not approach our defences and they retreated to the line of attack, and then disappeared from our sight. Had it not been for the rain, they would have squashed us in our trenches. It was hot before the rain fell, and the soil was dry. Nevertheless, we suffered casualties – it was in that fight that Lieutenant Karpenko was killed and I again had to take over the company, though not for long.

FIGHTING ON THE SANDOMIR BRIDGEHEAD

T he next day we left that position and quickly moved on tanks to the west, towards the Vistula, where Soviet troops had captured a bridgehead on the western side of the river. We entered Poland.

The march was quiet, we did not participate in any action on the way from Sambor to Sandomir bridgehead. Even the Luftwaffe did not disturb us. We completed our 200 kilometres' march, reached the Vistula by 15 August and safely crossed the river on a bridge of boats. The German air force constantly bombed the bridge, but at the time when we were crossing, the Luftwaffe was not there. We were lucky.

Our Brigade's task, as well as task of the entire Tank Army, was to assist the units holding the Sandomir bridgehead. However, the heavy fighting companies of all battalions of the Brigade had suffered significant losses in personnel, and the tank regiment had lost many tanks and other equipment. Our company had fifteen or twenty men left, and other companies did not fare better, some even had less. After crossing the Vistula we advanced into the bridgehead and stopped in a young forest, setting up tents. We did not have anything to go into action with – neither tanks nor soldiers.

Several days later we received insignificant replacement personnel from hospitals and rear units. The men that joined the company were of different ages, most of them were older, the bulk of them had never seen battle, and some of them did not know how to handle a submachine-gun. It was not a nice gift, as the saying goes. But we had to go into battle with them, so we trained them a lot. Chernyshov appeared, on 20 August he took over the company, while I returned to my second platoon. Two companies were formed in the battalion. There were not enough men to form the 3rd company. All in all, we were given no more than a week to form the units.

For the first time at the front they screened a film for us – *Two soldiers*. However, we did not have a chance to finish watching it - a *kukuruznik*, or corn plane (this is what we called a U-2 plane) *(the name probably comes from the joke that those planes could not fly higher than corn – translator's comment)*, flew by, the pilot turned off the engine and shouted to us through loudspeaker: 'Slavs, turn off the film! The Germans are about to deliver an artillery strike!' Everyone dispersed very quickly. The pilot was right, after some time the Germans hit the place with artillery fire. We finished watching that film after the war, in the autumn of 1945 in Vesprem, Hungary. They did not show any more movies to us at the front. I rarely saw artists or war correspondents or mobile shops during my time at the front. Just once, in June 1944 when we were at Kopychintsy, an army ensemble came to visit us, that was about it for cultural activities in our 49th Mechanized Brigade. All of a sudden a military shop appeared on Sandomir bridgehead. Once squad leaders, led by Sergeant Pavel Poddubny, walked up to me and asked me if I had money. I gave them some money, but I do not remember how much. I could not have had a lot of money, as my salary was 900 roubles, out of which 700 I sent to my parents through bank transfer, and I had to pay party membership fees and do some other payments, leaving around 100 roubles for myself. So, when the military shop arrived, it turned out that those guys bought a couple of *Troinoi (brand name – translator's note)* eau-de-colognes and some other small things. They invited me to their tent and proposed drinking the eau-de-cologne. It would have been nice to have a drink, but my stomach would not take eau-de-cologne, and the men drank it themselves.

In late August, about the 26th, the Brigade was transferred to the front sector where the Germans were pressurizing the infantry units of the army. We had to stop the enemy and throw him back to the initial positions. Our battalion, as well as the Brigade in general, was seriously weakened; other units of our army also suffered significant losses, but a tank army is a tank army, it is not a needle in a stack of needles, so our arrival was not left unnoticed by the Germans. The very fact of our arrival deterred the enemy. We were happy that the German air force was almost not present – they either were exhausted or transferred from Sandomir bridgehead to another front sector. However, German artillery was very active instead, and the worst part was that they opened more or less accurate fire with large-calibre shells. However, we successfully camouflaged our positions, made to dig in and did not have losses from that barrage.

On an evening in late August 1944 the company received an order to move to the attack position, closer to the German lines and wait for the order to assault the nearest hill. As far as I remember, another platoon leader in the company was Lieutenant Gavrilov. I led the first platoon, Sergeant Savkin led the second and Gavrilov led the third one. The company that was supposed to have 100 men had not more than 40 soldiers.

I moved the platoon and company forward, ordered them to dig in, appointed observers and we had a chance to 'listen to the grass growing' for a couple of hours, that is, to have a nap. At dawn an orderly ran to me from company commander Chernyshov with an order 'to attack the hill'. We had neither tanks nor artillery support. The Brigade had suffered heavy casualties in tanks, the artillery battalion must have also been hit hard. As often happened at the front, we did not have the slightest idea about the enemy – how strong he was, where the positions were and whether he had tanks.

The sun started to warm us; it was quiet, one could hear only birds singing from the nearest forest, which was not yet occupied by our troops. I replied to the runner that I was about to start the attack; he left, and I again fell asleep. The runner from the company commander ran up again, with the same order and with threats from the company commander. I again replied that we would commence the attack any time soon and fell asleep again – such things had never happened to me before. The runner woke me up and again reminded me of the attack – this time, the company commander ordered him not to leave me before I started the attack. I slept under a bush on soft grass (I did not dig a trench), I had been dreaming about something peaceful and I really did not feel like dying in that quiet hour… I tried to think of death as little as possible, but at that moment I was merely over-whelmed by exhaustion and quietness and I really wanted to sleep.

I feared a German attack from the left, from the forest – we were on the leftmost flank of the battalion, but I had to fulfil the order. I got the company up and we advanced in short rushes. The enemy did not open fire and we advanced some 100 or 150 metres ahead. So far everything was all right and I already had hopes that we would quietly capture the hill without shooting and soldiers dying, but my dreams did not come true.

The enemy opened a storm of rifle and machine-gun fire. A German self-propelled gun, the so-called 'assault gun' (*Sturmgeschütz*) with 75 mm barrel, appeared on the hill and opened fire. Soldiers lay down, using all folds of the earth, every little hillock, to hide from the bullets. As I could not find a better place, I also lay down in the shade of a bush, a small creek with steep shores behind me. My soldiers also opened fire on the enemy, but we did not even have heavy machine-guns – the machine-gun platoon had ceased to exist a long time before that battle; we only had submachine-guns and light machine-guns. The German assault gun opened fire with its main gun even on individual soldiers, and very soon all fire from our side ceased. It did not matter how hard I shouted, soldiers did not shoot – no one wanted to die hit by a 75 mm shell. Apparently, the Germans saw me waving my hands, demanding soldiers to open fire and generally making a show. Next to me, not far away, a soldier was lying and the assault gun went right after us. The shell exploded next to the soldier, he was thrown into the air and dropped dead on the ground. I quickly jumped into the creek, and hid under its bank, bending down. The creek was not deep at all, so I did not even get any water in my long boots. The second shell exploded next to the bank, but it did not get me again, and I quickly ran away and threw myself down behind a tree. I was fine, just with some strong ringing in my head. The assault gun ceased fire and stood peacefully on the hill.

While I was thinking what to do, our ground attack planes flew in, Il-2 Shturmoviks, approximately twelve or fifteen planes. They first dropped their bombs and then started to plough up the enemy's defences with missiles and fire from their guns and machine-guns. The assault gun disappeared from our sight, the enemy ceased fire, and under cover of the air attack I got the company up. We rushed forward as fast as we could, while we still had energy and while the enemy was depressed, and we tried to reach the top of the hill as quickly as possible. After we reached to top of the hill, the Shturmoviks ceased their attacks, assumed formation, waved their wings to us and flew away. I was very happy, it was for the first time that I saw such a successful cooperation of infantry and air force. I wish we had had it all the time! We also waved our hands to the pilots, shouting 'Hurrah!', thanking them for assistance. Apparently, it was the Brigade staff that organized the air support, as the hill was of great significance.

We found trenches, a well, several houses and barns on the hill. On the rear slope of the hill there was a steep descent into a deep hollow with a village; one could see a dozen huts and barns there. The Fritzes fled to the left of us, into a wood, evading the hollow. As we passed the German trenches I was starting to decide in which direction the attack should be continued – into the hollow or towards the grove, where the Germans fled – when a mass of large-calibre shells dropped on us.

Debris from barns, huts, the well, the shells, all flew into the air. The fire was heavy, explosions were going off all around us, and for a moment I was lost, thinking that that was the end for me and my soldiers. Some of my soldiers ducked by the destroyed huts and the well, others threw themselves towards the wood, as there were no explosions there, some ran down the slope. I ran away, stopped at a place where shells were not exploding and started to stop and gather soldiers around me; squad leaders assisted me in that. We ran along the ridge of that hill, stopped at the grove edge, lay down and started to dig in. The Germans were out of sight. The artillery strike that caught us by surprise suddenly stopped, apparently the Fritzes were saving ammo or thought that the job was done. They would often do that – deliver a short artillery strike on a concentration of infantry and then have a break. It was interesting that we did not suffer heavy losses from that artillery strike, just a few soldiers were wounded, but I found out that two soldiers were missing, they were greens, apparently, and they had run away when we were attacking the hill. I had noticed before that they always stayed by themselves, did not contact the old pals, only talked to each other. I had told the squad leader and the assistant platoon leader to keep an eye on those two, but they had other things to do in the attack, and the two soldiers ran away. To hell with them, they could not run far – and the river bridgehead was not that big. If those two had deserted, they would have been caught.

Company commander Senior Lieutenant Chernyshov arrived and gave us another order – to advance right through the wood, where the Fritzes had fled from the hill. When we deployed in a line and started our advance through the wood, the 2nd company of our battalion arrived; it had orders to advance on the right of our company. It cheered us up, as we were to advance with reinforcements, not alone. In general, attacking in a wood is different from other types of combat, say in open terrain or in built-up areas. You can't see the enemy – there are trees, bushes and high grass all around; you don't know what is going on with your neighbour. I rarely fought in such terrain. The Germans rarely set up defences in forests, and as a rule did not launch attacks in forests.

We walked for some time among the trees without any shooting. Company commander Nikolai Chernyshov was next to me, this was quite rare – apparently, the battalion commander had scolded him and he decided to lead the company himself. We all knew that Germans were dug in somewhere in the area, but still, the heavy machine-gun fire that they opened on us was sudden. As the enemy was close, the bullets did not whistle but flew as a dense swarm. When they hit a tree they made a sound, as if someone hit a tree with an axe, the sound was loud and juicy, one could hear that it was a strong impact. We had to lie down. We somehow dug in and started to look around, but because the young forest was dense we could see nothing, although we knew that the Fritzes were somewhere next to us. Company commander Chernyshov was shouting: 'Bessonov, forward! Get the soldiers up and attack!'

I had to fulfil the order and shouted (because of the exchange of fire we could barely hear each other) to my assistant platoon leader and Sergeant Savkin: 'Get the men up and attack!' They were lying on the ground and looking back at me, as if they were saying, 'Why don't you get up yourself? Get them up yourself!' And they were right – that was my job.

Ah, whatever! During a pause between two machine-gun bursts I drew myself up to my full height and shouted at the top of my lungs: 'Get up, get up, you this and that! Follow me, charge, forward!' A short and clear message – the situation called for it. Savkin and my deputy platoon commander (I forgot his name) jumped up from the ground at the same time as me and the whole company followed. We ran the distance to the German trenches, but they did not like hand-to-hand fighting and fled. We did not pursue them – they fled and to hell with them. We stopped in their trenches to have a break and decide what to do next. In principle, we had completed the mission, but German tank engines could be heard in front of us. The German tank engines had a special sound – a mournful one, different from our tank engines. It was hard to say how many tanks there were just from the sound.

Chernyshov walked up to me, sat down under a tree and we discussed the situation and further action. Chernyshov reported the situation to the battalion commander over the field 'phone and received an order to wait for the tanks to arrive. At that moment the Fritzes opened artillery fire, most likely from tank guns, and shells exploded, both short and over us. They did not know the company's position and fired at random.

A shell hit the tree, beneath which Chernyshov and I were sitting; splinters wounded several men, including me. Chernyshov was not hit. All this happened in a twinkle of an eye – I did not even manage to realize that I was wounded and did not lie down on the ground – but something just bent me. I quickly ran away from the spot, shouted to Chernyshov that I was wounded and quickly – running and walking – went to the battalion's aid post. They bandaged me in haste, and I went to the Brigade's medical and sanitary platoon. It turned out that I was wounded in the right side of my chest, both shoulders and the left foot. They disinfected my wounds in the medical platoon and bandaged them. I was hoping that I would be sent to a hospital, but my dreams did not materialize. I did not want to stay in the medical platoon and went back to the battalion. I reported to the battalion commander and received permission to stay at the aid post. A couple of times I had to go to the medical platoon to change the bandages, the wounds healed, but the movements of my right hand were still limited, the wound was sore, the pain echoed in my chest (these splinters are still both in my shoulders and in my chest).

For about a week I hung around the kitchen (it had finally arrived and started to provide food to battalion's men), until the battalion was transferred to another sector, where the situation became difficult. In my absence the platoon was led by my assistant platoon leader, a Jewish Senior Sergeant, whose last name I totally forget. He arrived in my platoon in June 1944 from an army unit. A brave and steady NCO, he was a good assistant to me. He proved himself a good soldier in action in Lvov. Soldiers of my platoon and even the company, especially the old hands, took to him straight away for his calm character, bravery and smartness in battle. He deserved to be reckoned with. It was a pity that soon after I was wounded he was killed, mortally wounded by a shell splinter in his chest. He was just 22 years old.

After I was wounded, tanks arrived to assist the companies. Just three T-34-85 tanks arrived, but they increased the morale of the soldiers. Already then, in mid-1944, the tank crews were afraid of *Panzerfausts* and we tank riders would sit at the front of the tanks when in forests. In such cases tanks were ordered to fire just armour-piercing shells at enemy tanks, not high-explosive shells. Everything seemed to be clear and tank crews were supposed to know that order and stick to it, but as the saying goes, every family has its black sheep. One of the tanks fired only one shell, it hit a tree and cut down all who stood next to it. Senior Sergeant Safronov, medic of our company, veteran of the battalion, was killed. He was 43 or 45 years old, we all respected him, he was a cheerful and brave 'uncle', he always provided first medical aid to wounded soldiers and was highly respected in the company. I enjoyed good friendly relations with him; when there were no soldiers around, he rarely addressed me with full military rank, but called me by name. Why did he have to be in the attacking line? Apparently, he wanted to provide medical aid directly on the battlefield.

As they told me later, both companies went through the forest and dug in in the field in front of the forest, among abandoned village houses. It was a good place to set a defence. The Fritzes – both infantry and tanks – disappeared out of sight and did not disturb the company, and our tanks also left.

A heavy thunderstorm started in the afternoon of the next day, and rain poured down. The company posted observers and soldiers hid in their shallow trenches, covered with rain capes. The night was pitch dark, nothing could be seen even at short distances. It was on that night that the Germans quietly attacked the battalion. It was quite untypical of the Germans, they rarely attacked at night, especially in such bad weather. Apparently, the battalion position was also important for the Fritzes. In flashes of lightning our observers spotted the Germans and opened fire, but it was too late, the Germans were already among the trenches and they rushed into the battalion defences. The soldiers could not put up proper resistance – they jumped out of the trenches and ran back towards the rear, but the Germans ran together with them. All the soldiers were mixed up, you could only see who was who in the lightning. The battalion's soldiers (two companies, 20 to 30 men each), reached the initial lines in their 'cross country race' and stopped there. The Germans did not advance further, digging in almost at the forest edge. With the end of the thunderstorm and dawn, our company put itself in order and counted losses. We did have losses, but they were amazingly low.

An order to recapture the positions that we fled from came from the Brigade's commander. A Katyusha battery (four vehicles) arrived to support the battalion. Soldiers had a chance to dry themselves after a horrible rain shower and prepare for an offensive during the day. The battalion commander ordered everyone from the battalion's support units into the attacking line. As he said: 'Send everyone, except for Bessonov.' Junior Lieutenant Burkov, deputy battalion commander arrived to see that the order was fulfilled. Those support unit men that did not have weapons received them and some 25 or 30 of them were sent to the battalion companies.

I had a chance to see the Katyusha rocket launchers, their equipment for launching and aiming. As I have written before, they did not aim very accurately, twice I saw them hitting friendly troops, not the enemy. One time, at Dobropolie village, they hit positions of my platoon. It was a horrible weapon. If I am not mistaken, each vehicle (rocket launcher) carried 16 rockets (1.8 metres long), that made 64 rockets per battery, and they were all fired in one instance. The sound of their launch was quite loud.

In the afternoon Katyushas fired on the Germans; after the completion of the salvo the battalion launched the attack and quickly captured the trenches that it had had to abandon in the evening, during the thunderstorm. As some participants of the assault told me, the Katyusha salvo destroyed almost all the Germans. There was no resistance from the German side – there was simply no one left to fight. The positions were regained. That was it.

After several days the Germans calmed down, stopped their attacks and went on the defensive. In mid-September (15 to 17) we handed over our sector to a general army unit. We were transferred to the second echelon of the first Ukrainian front for replenishments in personnel, military hardware and equipment. During the operation that had lasted around two months, we had travelled 600 kilometres, in many cases we had to fight our way through. We liberated many settlements, including the cities of Lvov, Bobrka, Zolochev, Peremyshlyany and others. Our 6th Guards Mechanized Corps was awarded for the Lvov-Sandomir operation, mostly for liberation of Lvov – the Corps received an honorary title of 'Lvov', while our 49th Mechanized Brigade was awarded with the Order of Bogdan Khmelnitski. The Lvov-Sandomir operation was over for us.

PREPARATIONS FOR
THE PUSH WEST

The battalion, or rather what little remained of it, was lodged in huts in Vengertse Panenske village, which had been abandoned by locals. We buried platoon leader Lieutenant Savin and a private, who had been killed at the Sandomir bridgehead, at the edge of the village. The craftsmen of the battalion made monuments for their graves. We took full advantage of the lull and got our hair cut by the company's handy-men, washed in the field *banya* (which in summer, and in winter, was nothing more than a tarpaulin tent), changed our underwear, 'fried' our uniforms in barrels and wrote letters home. While we were settling down, Lieutenants Petr Shakulo and Alexander Guschenkov came back from hospital, while Senior Lieutenant Grigori Vyunov arrived to replace wounded Gavrilov, who was still in hospital. As far as I remember, he was a political officer and had never led a combat unit before. We were not too curious, and he also tried to avoid the question as to why they sent him to us. The main thing was that he was a good comrade, a calm and cheerful person with a gentle character. He was around 30, and he was a bit too stout for a platoon leader, though of course he grew thinner later on. A new medic, a Sergeant, also arrived in the company. I do not remember his last name, and I probably never knew it, as everyone called him 'Brotherly Heart' – because of the way he began conversations with many men. He was around 40, or maybe a bit older. A cheerful and cordial person, he quickly became part of our team.

The company's personnel lived in huts, most of us slept on plank beds, on hay covered with rain capes. Most importantly, we had a roof over our heads and a stove; although it was a bit crowded, it was not a problem. Company commander Chernyshov lived separately from us, while we all lived together; the company's Sergeant Major Bratchenko also stayed with us. We slept on beds, two people on one bed, but sometimes just on hay. It was warm in the house, and as a rule we could take off our uniforms for the night. During the day we trained the personnel, and entertained ourselves in the evenings in different ways. We had a lamp made of an empty 45 mm shell – we burnt petrol with salt in it. Sometimes we would play cards, write letters, or go for a visit to the neighbouring company. We would often have conversations with the soldiers of the platoon. We would normally talk about ourselves, our relatives, sometimes soldiers had some requests or recommendations. If the company's Sergeant Major could do something (he was the main administrator in the company), we informed him about the soldiers' requests. Bratchenko really did not like to hear comments about his work, but he corrected his failures quickly. The soldiers liked these discussions, they felt that they were taken care of and knew that I was on their side.

Tsikanovski and I were awarded with Orders of the Red Star for the Lvov-Sandomir Operation. If Kozienko had taken the initiative and reported the action of the battalion or even our half-company in Lvov on time, then it might not have been impossible for us to have all received higher decorations, but I could not change things. I am also somewhat at fault in that I did not act decisively and did not go into the city centre.

On 7 November, 1944 the battalion commander organized a dinner for all the officers of the battalion to commemorate the 27th anniversary of the Great October Revolution.

The soldiers also received a special holiday meal, but it was all served without alcohol. For some reason we never received the daily *Narkom's* (named after the Defence Minister who introduced the ration – translator's note) 100 gram ration of vodka, but we found a solution – we started to make our own moonshine. Brotherly Heart, our medic, was responsible for making it in our company. The command persecuted underground moonshine manufacturing, but it was still widespread and flourishing. Moonshine made from sugar beet was strong (it could even burn), but it stank like hell so it seemed that our moonshine-making technology was far from perfect.

Battalion commander Kozienko would regularly inspect the companies and destroy the distilling equipment, but we would assemble it again and continue brewing alcohol. We would come from our training, have a half-glass of moonshine, and it would feel great, millet porridge seemed tastier. For some reason they only gave us millet meal – millet soup and millet porridge… There were heaps of potatoes of Polish owners lying in the fields, but we were forbidden to take them – the local population was sent away from the front area, but some managed to stay, while others visited every week or even every day. We secretly ate these potatoes though, but not every day. We were afraid of being punished for looting if caught, but everything worked out well.

We did not abuse the moonshine; we drank it but controlled ourselves and didn't drink too much. I could hardly stomach this drink, and my comrades even laughed at me because of this. Alexander Guschenkov, however, was a big fan of alcohol; there was nothing he liked more than drinking. The battalion commander sometimes rebuked him for this.

Kozienko had an old bastard serving as his orderly, who was always snooping around and then reporting to the battalion commander. We would normally kick him out of our house, but somehow he still knew everything. He himself also brewed moonshine – it was for the battalion commander and his deputies. Some smart guy found out where he was brewing it and when the orderly was away, he stole the whole supply of alcohol – quite a big disappointment for him and the battalion's top brass! Deputy battalion commander Burkov decided that it could only be officers from our company and right away came to our house. But we did not have the moonshine in our house – although we got to taste it a couple of days later. It is still not known who stole it. I should also mention that in October Burkov was promoted to the rank of Captain and awarded with the Order of the Red Banner. He visited all companies and celebrated the new rank and the decoration with the officers. He was very happy, as he had been Senior Lieutenant for a long time. That was one of the negative features of the Brigade's staff – not only did we not receive a lot of decorations, but it was also hard to get promoted.

Meanwhile we trained the soldiers in the field – we knitted the platoon together, training on company level was more rare, while shooting was very rare. We were afraid of the Germans spotting our positions – the front line was just next to us. This is how we lived.

Alexander Guschenkov travelled to Sandomir a couple of times in order to exchange some of our trophies for lard, vodka, sausages and white bread, but we quickly ran out of trophies and had to switch back to millet and moonshine. As cold weather set in, we received our winter clothes. The Motherland took good care of us and we were well dressed for winter – winter hats, mittens, padded trousers, warm cotton or woollen underwear, while officers received woollen uniforms and fur vests. We did not receive sheepskin coats or felt boots.

During the autumn of 1944 a second woman, a cook, appeared in the battalion. The first one was our battalion's doctor Praskovia Pankova. At first I did not notice her, but then they told me that we had a new cook. She was a redheaded girl, no older than 25 years, quite chubby and short. Cooks were normally men, but we had a woman. One time I went to see her. I walked up to the kitchen and asked: 'Do you have anything to chew?' She rudely answered: 'No, get out, don't disturb my cooking.' I answered: 'Well, I just came here to see you and get to know you, my last name is Bessonov' 'So it is you, Bessonov? I know most of the men, but I see you for the first time,' she said. 'Your friends say that you are always somewhere far ahead, while Petro Shakulo, Guschenkov and Mikheev told so many stories about you that I must give you something from my reserve stock.' She gave me a can of American ham, some sausage and bread. I could only thank her and left to the company with the food. This is how I got to know Lelka. Everyone called her that and I have no idea what her last name was.

The Germans would often fire on the village from large-calibre guns, but there were no casualties. There was just one air raid, but that time our fighters repelled the German aircraft and even shot down one or two planes. Nevertheless, we stuck to blackout rules – although light from our lamps was weak, we covered windows with blankets and only stoked ovens at night so that the Germans would not see our smoke.

The Brigade's staff organized training for platoon leaders and the company sent me there. The deputy brigade commander Lieutenant Colonel Grigori Starovoit conducted our training session. He ordered me to prepare a lecture on 'Company procedure during marches.' I do not remember what I spoke about and what were the comments, but in January, 1945, on the recommendation of Lieutenant Colonel

Preparations for the Push West

Starovoit I was appointed to lead the forward security detachment of the Brigade and travelled around 600 kilometres on three tanks in front of the Brigade with my platoon from the Vistula to the Oder.

To the west of the village where we were there was a dominant hill. At regular intervals, according to the schedule, I had to occupy it together with my platoon in order to warn the unit if the Germans attacked, although it was significantly far behind our defences (some 5 or 7 kilometres). The Brigade would also send a couple of T-34 tanks and sometimes guns from the artillery battalion, normally a section of 76 mm guns (two guns). We did not like going there, as we had to live in poorly built dugouts and we only received food in flasks from the battalion kitchen. The Germans sometimes delivered artillery strikes on the hill, but my platoon did not suffer any losses.

In November we had a chance to get a photograph taken at a Pole's shop. In one picture I stand with Petr Shakulo and a soldier from the machine-gun company, the second one was given to me as a gift by Alex Guschenkov. Besides Guschenkov, there are submachine-gun platoon leader Oplesnin, Chernyshov's orderly, 1st company commander Nikolai Chernyshov, the 2nd company commander Shtokolov and his orderly in the picture. Alexander Guschenkov, machine-gun platoon leader of our 1st company, wrote on the reverse of the picture: 'For good and long memory to Evgeni from Alex. Remember how we fought together, how we drank and partied together in Poland – 28 November, 1944.'

The war left such a tragic trace
And put so many men in graves
That after twenty, thirty years
Survivors don't believe they live

K. SIMONOV

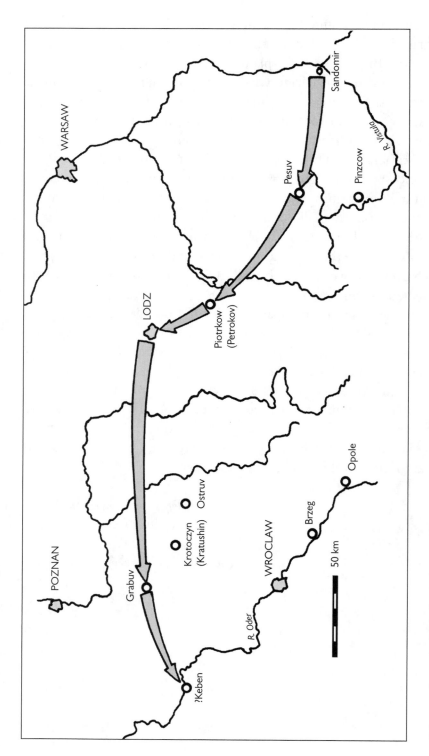

Map to show the Vistula–Oder operation, 12 January 1945 to 26 January 1945.

THE VISTULA–ODER OPERATION

Our preparation for the upcoming battles on the Sandomir bridgehead was over. In late December, 1944, we marched on foot from the village where we had been staying, not far from the front line. Our battalion concentrated in a forest, and for several days we slept at campfires using branches of pine trees to sleep on. After that we built dugouts and installed stoves that we made from empty fuel barrels. Rain capes or pieces of tarpaulin served as doors for dugouts. Frost was not that heavy – 10 to 12 degrees – but we were freezing to our bones. Of course it was warmer in dugouts. We did not have any training during that period; we were given all our time for rest. We slept as much as we wanted, checked our weapons and did all kinds of small things – mostly we played cards and wrote letters home.

They took us officers to the front line several times. We went to the trenches to work out the routes of advance for tanks with tank riders. We also got to know the tank crews. We did not know when the grand offensive was to start – such things were kept secret. However, one could feel that the moment was coming, and this is why we were somewhat excited, even nervous. The two worst things are waiting for something and catching up with someone.

Finally, the big day, 12 January, 1945, came. After a long artillery preparation and air force strikes, infantry units of the front went over to the offensive and in a dashing assault captured the first and the second defence lines of the enemy. Artillery preparation and air force strikes lasted at least one-and-a-half hours, if I am not mistaken. Guns, including 76 mm to 152 mm, 82 mm, 120 mm and 160 mm mortars, as well as Katyushas firing on the enemy defences. Bombers and Il-2 Shturmoviks raided the defences as well. It was a permanent rumble; we even had to shout, as we could not hear each other. The enemy's positions were covered with a thick cloud of smoke, some debris was flying in the air, and something was burning and exploding there. The enemy could only return sporadic fire, as almost all artillery and mortars were suppressed.

After the Field Army's infantry units broke through the defences, our turn came. The task of our Brigade as well as the whole Tank Army was to enter the gap, develop the advance towards the Oder and then capture a bridgehead on its left, western bank.

Our company, just like the other companies of the battalion, moved forward in a column on tanks of the tank regiment. It was a total mess on the road, other combat units and all kinds of supply units were also on the move; some trucks and lorries moved against the main stream of vehicles, slowing down our offensive. It was dangerous to drive off the road – mines were all around, and engineers had not yet had time to clear them. M-1 *emochka (loosely translates as 'small M' car – translator's comment)* car of the Brigade commander hit a mine and Colonel Turkin survived by pure luck (he got off with light shell-shock), although his driver and the orderly were killed and the car was blown to pieces. Platoon leader Lieutenant Shakulo from our company was wounded on 12 January, he was hit by something that broke his leg. When he left for hospital, I was ordered to lead his platoon as well, although the acting platoon leader in his platoon was Sergeant Savkin – a wonderful guy, a brave and skilful soldier.

During the entire day of 12 January, 1945, we were advancing forward successfully, though slowly. Clouds were hanging low in the sky, and the enemy's air force was not present. It grew dark early in January, and already at twilight we ran into the enemy's stronghold in front of a village. The enemy opened fire from machine-guns and tank guns at point-blank range.

We quickly got off our tanks, deployed in a line and lay down on open terrain. We tried to dig in, but the battalion commander and tank regiment commander ordered us to attack. It was almost dark already, which suited us well – this meant fewer losses. As often happens in night action, the company split – Vyunov's platoon attacked to the left, while I attacked on the right flank with my two platoons. Despite enemy fire, we rushed into the village and the enemy fled. Our tanks supported us by fire, but did not enter the village, staying where they were. Apparently, they were afraid of the Tigers positioned behind the village and firing intensively on our tanks. They did not fire at us, infantry, though, as they were afraid of hitting their own infantry that was fleeing through the village.

I went to the opposite side of the village with two platoons and occupied the German trenches. The Germans could no longer be seen. The night battle that followed stayed in my memory very well, as we had to repel German counterattacks till very dawn. I did not have communication with either the company commander or the platoon of Senior Lieutenant Vyunov; I did not even know where they were. Machine-gun platoon leader Alexander Guschenkov noticed the direction of my attack and, without losing his head in this hell, came to assist me with his two Maxim machine-guns and his men. He took up a position on the right flank of my two platoons, as my right flank was exposed. The other companies of the battalion covered the left flank, which were also in action. The third platoon of the company with its leader was also somewhere over there. Guschenkov's machine-gun crews were a great help to us.

Fire ceased for some time and I decided to walk along the newly captured German trenches in order to support my men and show them that I was with them. This is important for soldiers, especially in a hard situation. Sergeant Savkin drew my attention to German hand grenades, mess tins, helmets and clips that were hidden in niches of trenches. I ordered my men not to touch them, but one soldier either forgot my order or just started jumping in order to get warm, and touched something. An explosion sounded in the air, the soldier was thrown 2 metres up in the air and he fell dead into the trench like an empty sack. That was the only casualty we had from boobytrap mines.

The Germans counter-attacked after some time, but only with infantry – their tanks stayed where they were. At that time our T-34s had already driven up to us, and together with them we repelled the attack. The German infantry fell back, while the German tanks opened fire on the village, setting some houses on fire. Combat at night is generally very hard, and this engagement lasted the whole night. You cannot see a thing; you only fire at flashes or barely visible shadows. In darkness you cannot see the results of your own fire and of course it is less effective than in daytime.

As far as I remember, there were at least thirteen to fifteen Tiger tanks, but I cannot say how many infantry they had – it was too dark. Just three T-34-85 tanks supported me. The tank crews were green and it was their first battle. They rarely fired on the German tanks, being afraid that the enemy would spot their muzzle flashes, and when the houses caught fire, they tried to retreat as far as possible into the dark shadow. Although they did not retreat far, their retreat had a bad effect on the morale of my soldiers, most of whom were also green, but even the old hands were scared. They held on with their last bit of strength, but kept on firing at the enemy. However, they were all looking back at our tanks – they were afraid that the tanks would just leave us and drive to the rear. So I had to run back and forth – first to the tanks in order to stop them, if they had retreated too far, bring them back or even ask them to fire, then run to see how Guschenkov was doing, and then back to my men. The whole village was on fire, shells were exploding all around, and bullets and shell splinters flew shrieking through the air. Our DP machine-guns and submachine-guns were firing. The Germans tried to attack our flank, but Guschenkov's machine-guns cut them down almost at point-blank range and they ceased their attacks.

Nevertheless, two or three soldiers abandoned their foxholes and hid behind a hut, which was still on fire. I brought them back to their initial place – back to the trenches. If you do not nip panic in the bud, then your unit becomes uncontrollable. This is why I strictly warned the squad leaders of those two soldiers who ran away from the trenches without order. So, almost all night long I had to run back and forth from trenches to tanks and then back to trenches, all the time under enemy fire. I was steaming, I was constantly thirsty; it was good that there was a well nearby, my orderly scooped water from the well with a canteen and I gulped it down. The whole village was on fire, it was as bright as day. I had to lead almost a company in action in these conditions – two platoons and a machine-gun platoon, plus I had to force our tanks to fire, while the tanks were always trying to retreat to a safe place. This running around almost cost me my life. I could be seen for miles in the burning village, so as soon as I jumped into a foxhole, a shell exploded on its breastwork. The breastwork was smashed, while private Ivanov and me were deafened by the explosion. The worst thing was that the trench was just few metres from a burning house and it was too hot in that foxhole. The foxhole was clearly visible against the glare of the burning house, but the second shot never came, apparently Germans thought we were dead. I quickly moved to another foxhole, permitting Ivanov to go to the first-aid station, as he was slightly shell-shocked.

Before dawn the Germans ceased fire and then altogether disappeared from our sight. Apparently, their mission was not to destroy our battalion and the Brigade, but rather to delay our offensive for as long as possible in order to rescue their units from destruction and encirclement in another sector of the front. Despite the intensity and length of the battle, our losses were insignificant. At dawn Guschenkov and I found company commander Chernyshov and 3rd platoon leader Vyunov. I reported the losses to the company commander and we exchanged our opinions about the engagement. The battalion's field kitchen had managed to cook breakfast by that time and we sent two or three men from each squad with mess tins to bring the food, just like we always did. My orderly and I had breakfast from the same mess. If we could, we washed our messes after meals or wiped them with grass. If someone was still hungry, it was always possible to get extra food, as they cooked food for the whole battalion and the battalion had losses...

We started to march after breakfast, first on foot and then we clambered aboard the tanks. The battalion was moving as the Brigade's forward task force, and the Germans did not try to set up serious defences, but by the end of the day a strong German delaying force stopped us. Our companies attacked several times, but were thrown back with losses in personnel. German artillery, especially anti-tank guns, were especially active. We had to stop and dig in. During daytime the enemy did not let us move – as soon as they spotted movement they opened fire. Only with the arrival of darkness could we move – we put ourselves in order and counted our losses. Just as I was lying down to have a nap, an orderly found me and passed on the order of the battalion commander to go to battalion staff. When I came to Kozienko, I saw deputy brigade commander Starovoit and tank regiment commander Stolyarov at his CP. They were all in a tent that was set up in a hollow. They had a portable electric lamp in the tent. It was not battalion commander Kozienko, but tank regiment commander Stolyarov who addressed me: 'You, Bessonov, have got an important mission,' he said. 'With three tanks

Tank Rider

you and your platoon must cut the road that the Germans are using, you must stop them, advance forward and capture the German artillery, thus securing the Brigade's further advance.' I really did not want to go there to die, I really wanted to sleep. That was my second night and second day without sleep. Yes, it was an order, but I lost my self-control: 'Don't you have any other officers except Bessonov in the battalion? I always have to go first, I've been 48 hours without sleep already!' Lieutenant Colonel Starovoit answered to me: 'We did not choose you at random, we believe that you will complete the mission and we are more doubtful about the other officers.' Major Kozienko repeated the order: 'Go and fulfil the order.' What could I do, it was an order and I had to obey it! The tank platoon leader also came up to us. We knew each other from previous battles and quickly developed a co-ordination plan. I had a comment to make here as well, saying that the tanks should assist the tank riders, not hide, as it was in the night action for the village the night before. Major Stolyarov was not offended with my comment; on the contrary, he drew the tanker's attention to it: 'A tank is designed for a battle, it is not just a coach for tank riders.'

At night from 14 to 15 January we moved forwards to complete our mission. I put a squad (seven or eight men) on each of the three tanks that I had. The tanks deployed in a line some 20 or 25 metres apart. The tanks drove forward at low speed on my command. There was intensive German traffic on the road, and so the Germans could not hear the noise of our tank engines. It was a dark and cloudy night, one could not see stars. We advanced towards the road and stopped some 30 metres from it. As we had previously arranged, each tank fired one round from its main gun, a long machine-gun burst and then ceased fire. At the same moment the tank riders jumped off the tanks and rushed to the road, firing their submachine-guns on the move at the German vehicles. When we ran up to the road, the German column stopped. Cars stood there filled with luggage and sacks full of German food and wine. The Germans ran like a hare before hounds – I was always amazed by how quickly they could run. Apparently, this was a retreat or relocation of a large unit's staff. The enemy was thrown from the road and the way for Brigade lay open. We threw the bags on the tanks and rushed forward, capturing an artillery battery with prime movers, one of which still had the engine

158

running. We did not see the Germans, but in the darkness we could hear that they were running away, breaking bushes and tree branches. Yes, Germans were fast runners, great runners – especially when death was looking them in the eye.

We advanced a bit further on tanks, some 2 or 3 kilometres from the road. The tank crews reported to Stolyarov that the mission had been completed, German traffic had been stopped and the Germans were nowhere to be seen; we also reported our co-ordinates. I did not have a radio and had to maintain communications with the command through tank radio. We received an order to wait for the main body of the Brigade. We had to wait for it for a long time; it was growing light. Visibility was good. A cold day came, we waited in a forest and there was no wind. We had a snack using the German food – of course, we shared the food with the tank crews. Tanks with tank riders of our battalion appeared. Battalion commander Major Kozienko arrived, but I did not see the company commander Chernyshov. During the whole operation I was receiving orders from battalion commander or even Major Stolyarov, the tank regiment commander, and in fact never saw the company commander. At that point the battalion commander gave a new order – to inspect several houses located far from the road.

I deployed my platoon in a line, and the enemy fired several rounds at us, but they all missed. We rushed into the houses, and in close combat, even in hand-to-hand fight we destroyed the Fritzes. Some of them fled, and we did not pursue them. My platoon did not have any losses. The mission was thus completed and we came back to the battalion.

Brigade commander Colonel Turkin arrived and again sent me forward as a vanguard on three tanks, gave me a route of advance and pointed out a place where I should stop for a halt. The depleted platoon of Shakulo, who was wounded, was also with me. The vanguard moved forward some 5 to 7 kilometres from the main body of the Brigade, maintaining communication over tank radio in order to warn the main body about enemy forces. The vanguard is always the first unit to receive a blow from the enemy, in some cases a deadly blow from an ambush, so one always had to be careful.

That was the beginning of a long journey on Polish soil, up to the Oder and then to the Neisse river. In general, one has to know how to ride on a tank, how to jump off it and how to mount it. We had a special training session for that during our time in reserve. It is harder to do in wintertime than in summertime; besides that, armour is cold and there is no protection from the wind, and one has to hold on to something in order not to fall from the tank during a cross-country march. There were railings on the tank's turret, but they were not enough. There was an incident when during a cross-country march one soldier was knocked off the tank by a tree branch, which hooked round neck and threw him on the ground. No one noticed his disappearing – apparently, everyone was asleep, and the soldier had to travel on alone on foot, following the tank tracks. It was good that the column stopped soon after the incident and the soldier, who was from Petr Shakulo's platoon, was able to catch up with the battalion. For a long time the man was the butt of friendly jokes from the 'Slavs'.

In wintertime soldiers tried to sit behind the turret, on the tank's warm radiator. I would sometimes stay behind the turret, where I sat and dozed off at night and stood during the day and looked forward, in order to see the terrain and be able to control the situation. I would normally be on the second or third tank, as the radio worked better there. Continuous communication is a cornerstone of combat, especially when you are to the enemy's rear and when we were detached from the main body of the Brigade. Our mission was to attack along the route of Keltse [Pesuv], Lodz, Petrokov (or Petrokuv) [Piotrkow], Ostruv [Ostrow], Kratoshki [Krotszyn] and on to the Oder, to Keben on the other side of the river. It was generally dangerous to be in front of the Brigade. If you missed the enemy, all its forces would crush on you and soldiers of your platoon. On the other hand, I felt quite free – no command around, and I was my own boss. Besides that, we had lots of food we had captured from Germans and we never stayed hungry, and we had some alcohol to wet our whistles. The grey hilly fields of Poland were lying before our eyes – fields covered by snow, fields of poor peasants. To the right or to the left of the road there were small villages, some ten buildings each. Shots sounded from them sometimes, but our order was – just forward. We would report the name of a village, from which we were fired upon, but we never engaged the enemy. Sometimes we saw huge fields without a single border-strip. Normally in the centre of those fields stood large brick houses, surrounded by barns – these were the houses of richer Poles. However, we had no time to enjoy the view. The first tank reported: 'A supply column in sight, what should we do with it?' The tank commander and I sent a message back: 'Crush them!' We fell upon them, firing on the move without even dismounting from the tanks; the supply column was blown to pieces and we moved on.

At the end of the day on 15 January, 1945, we reached the village of Bobzha. As always, I parked the tanks, appointing one squad to guard the tanks and observe the road. Just when I was about to report the completion of the mission to the battalion commander, all of a sudden a strong explosion rent the air. I rushed there. A tragic incident had taken place. The head of engineers of the battalion, an experienced battle engineer and a veteran from Kursk, had decided to defuse an anti-tank mine. He unscrewed the top fuse, but the mine was frozen to the soil and he could not move it. Then he took a bar and hit the mine. The following explosion blew the engineer into pieces. He apparently forgot that German anti-tank mines also had a bottom fuse. It would have been easier to tie a rope or a cable to the mine, hide in a shelter and pull it – everything would have been all right then. The mine had at least 8 or 10 kilograms of explosives… This is how our battalion's engineer died, a modest and good comrade, who made such a tragic mistake. We were all very sorry about his death.

We did not rest for long, as I received a new mission. I was given two tanks and two 76 mm guns; a machine-gun platoon under Lieutenant Vasily Mochalov attached to us. It is strange that it was not the machine-gun platoon from our company, but anything could happen at the front.

It was a responsible and dangerous mission. We were to move 5 to 7 kilometres to the right of the main road to a road crossing and delay the retreating enemy forces at least till dawn or force the enemy to retreat on other routes, in worse conditions: on earth roads, not on the highway. But we only had a platoon – 20 or 25 men with two Maxim machine-guns. The guns that we had were too weak against Tigers, and the tanks, as it later turned out, were not the ones that we had during the day and were significantly damaged. They could not even fire, so it would have been better if we hadn't had them at all.

We reached the road crossing safely. Gun crews and tanks took up a position at the only house by the crossing, while the infantry lay down in front of the house. However, no matter how hard we tried to dig in, we could not do it – the soil was frozen solid. It was frozen to a significant depth and was hard as a rock. Soil rescues a soldier in combat from mines and shell explosions, while here soldiers had to lie in the open like sitting ducks. We did not see the enemy. It was a cold winter night. Silence was deceptive, as always in the front, and we did not have to wait for long.

Deputy battalion commander Captain Maxim Tarasovich Burkov came over on a motorcycle, apparently to offer me support and control, or maybe just because they had little hope for my task force. After bringing Burkov, the motorcycle returned to Bobzha village. Burkov was a wonderful person and enjoyed great respect among the officers. He informed me that there would be no reinforcements (although earlier they had been speaking about it). He told me that we had to hold the crossing till dawn at all costs with our task force and see it from there. We walked into a house, where some of my soldiers were resting – it was warm inside. There were no owners of the house; they had abandoned it even before we arrived. We had a snack, given the fact that we had something to eat. Burkov laughed and said: 'Where do you get all that food, Bessonov?' However, we did not drink alcohol, even the German wine. I had a bit before I was sent to the crossing, and it was enough for me, while Burkov also did not want to drink it – it was not the right moment. We walked outdoors and heard a motorcycle coming over from Bobzha. We thought that it was our motorcycle again and Burkov even walked up to roadside and raised his hand, but the motorcycle rushed by us at high speed. Soldiers opened fire on the motorcycle in the gloom, but they were way too late and it disappeared.

A truck drove to our crossing from the forest after some time. My men opened fire on the vehicle and it stopped some 10 metres from the tank, behind which I was standing. I shouted to my orderly 'Fire!' but he paused. Germans started to jump out from the back of the truck, shouting '*Ivanen! Ivanen!*' I pulled an F-1 hand grenade from my greatcoat pocket, loosened the pin, pulled it out and threw the grenade into the back of the truck, continuing to shout to my soldiers: 'Fire! Fire!' Then I threw the second hand grenade into the truck, but none of my grenades exploded, although I distinctly remember that I had pulled out the pins.

The Germans, at least fifteen of them, all ran away in the direction that the truck emerged from. I am sure that some of them got hurt by the fire of my platoon, but there were no bodies. We did not pursue them – how could we find them in darkness of the night? Maybe we did wound someone, but we did not look for the escaping Germans. I forbade my soldiers to search the body of the truck, where my unexploded grenades were lying – I feared that they could go off. I climbed up the truck and inspected it myself, but did not find the grenades in the dark. I have been puzzled for a long time as to why the grenades did not explode and have not been able to come to any conclusion, but in subsequent battles I started to change grenades for the new ones more frequently and thoroughly inspected them, especially the fuses.

At midnight of 16 January, the artillery section leader reported that at least ten Tiger tanks had appeared at the forest edge in front of our defences. I ordered them to open fire on the tanks. The two guns of the battery opened fire on them, but in the darkness you could see the armour-piercing shells hitting the front armour, ricocheting and flying off into the sky with a loud ring. Our tanks also fired a few rounds and ceased fire. The tankers reported to Burkov that the tanks were not working properly and could not fire on the enemy: the first tank could not rotate its turret, while the second one also had some defects. Besides that, the second crew only had the driver and tank commander. When Burkov learnt about this, he just spat on the ground, cursed and said that the tank regiment was supposed to know what kind of tanks they were sending on such a responsible mission.

Nevertheless, our fire stopped the enemy's tanks, but they opened intensive fire with armour-piercing and high-explosive shells on our defences. We spent an awful night at that road crossing. The enemy's shells were exploding next to tanks and guns, but we did not have losses and even the house that we had abandoned did not catch fire. Soldiers had only been able to dig skirmisher's trenches, which secured them from bullets, but not from artillery fire and splinters, while Burkov and I did not even have those shelters – we sat behind a tank.

Captain Burkov asked me: 'What do you think, will we make it alive from here or Germans will crush us here?' What could I, a 21-year-old Lieutenant, answer to this? As far as I remember, in order to calm both of us down, I said: 'Let's sit under the tank till dawn, it is not much time left, and we will see then! We will complete the mission. We will retreat to the hill which is behind us.' After that we had a smoke. Officers at the front received *Kazbek (Russian brand name – translator's note)* cigarettes or light tobacco in packs. I rarely smoked, but in hard situations I normally smoked *mahorka (tobacco for hand-rolling issued to enlisted men – translator's note)*, giving my good tobacco away to those who preferred good tobacco and cigarettes.

We were just a handful of soldiers at the crossing, while the enemy concentrated both tanks and infantry against us. Of course, we could not put up stubborn resistance. But the tanks did not attack us, and we with Mochalov's machine-guns were able to throw attacking German infantry back all night long. Germans, as a rule, would not attack during the night, they only attacked at dawn or in daytime, so I thought (and I shared this with Burkov), that the Germans would attack *en masse* at dawn. Apparently, the enemy simply did not yet know what forces he was facing, it was impossible to see at night-time, but with the coming of dawn the Germans would attack with all their strength. They had to capture the road crossing in order to retreat to the west and avoid destruction by other Red Army units. Our infantry was not a problem for German tanks, 76 mm guns were also too weak, while our two broken-down tanks could not fire and would be knocked out right away by the Tigers.

Before morning Captain Burkov made a decision to withdraw to the hill which was behind us, behind the road. 'Let's say good bye to each other: apparently the Germans will not let us leave this road crossing alive. The dawn will come and Fritzes' tanks will crush us.' This he said to me. Before it grew lighter we withdrew our artillery and then ourselves went to the hill, following our guns. Having completed this manoeuvre, we wanted to dig in at the hill, but the soil there was also too hard, and we just lay down on the ground. It was growing light, and we had to watch out. Our two tanks also arrived – they safely hid behind the hill, as the reverse slope of the hill was steeper than the one facing the Germans.

At dawn the Germans started their attacks on the hill. At least ten German tanks impudently attacked our positions. Yes, things looked bad for us. A line of attacking German infantry was walking across the field on our left flank, on our right flank there was also a battle – we could hear machine-gun bursts and gunfire. It was hard to understand what was going on over there. The Germans destroyed one of our tanks, the one that could not rotate the turret, on that hill. The second tank was firing on the Tigers and even made them stop half way up the slope. The battle intensified. We thought that reinforcements had arrived, but everything was mixed up and we could not tell where the enemy and where the friendly troops were. Then Burkov ordered us to withdraw the artillery into the forest, while we stayed on the hill, which did not have any place to hide in. Then he gave us an order to retreat as well. It was only later that I understood that Burkov ordered us to retreat to the forest in order to save soldiers' lives, to save them for future battles… Before we reached the forest edge, Burkov was heavily wounded – he was standing on the step of a truck, and was hurt when the driver accidentally passed too close to a tree. We laid him on a rain cape and carried him along forest edge toward Bobzha village, from which Kozienko sent me to the road crossing and ordered to hold it till dawn. I fulfilled the order – it was already morning.

Of course we could stay at the road crossing, but we could no longer contain the enemy – the Germans needed ways of retreat, and they would have merely squashed us with tanks, as we could not dig proper trenches. Nevertheless, we fulfilled the order of the battalion commander and held the positions almost till noon withdrawing only on Burkov's order. It was hard to carry Maxim Tarasovich: the soldiers had to take turns very often. Soldiers drew my attention to footprints of Germans jackboots on the snow – the soles of their jackboots were covered with large nails. The footprints went deep into the forest. We sent out a squad to find a further road to Bobzha and followed the squad at some distance, but did not encounter any Germans. Then we reached the well-rolled road that went to that village and curved to the right along forest edge. We were planning to check who was in the village, when a truck appeared on the road. The driver of the truck was an officer whom I knew. He told us that the village was occupied by our forces – the 2nd and the 3rd battalions of the Brigade, while behind a hill, in another village he had seen 1st battalion commander Kozienko.

I asked him to drive Burkov to the medical platoon, as the driver knew Burkov as well. We put Burkov into the back of the truck, and I sent some soldiers as escort, and the truck left, while Lieutenant Mochalov, the machine-gun platoon leader and I went on to the battalion with our men. The soldiers, as well as Vasily Mochalov and I, were happy to have survived that hellish merry-go-round. We were walking on the road in a crowd, laughing and making jokes with each other. I lost my feeling of alertness, which happened to me quite rarely; if there had been an ambush, they would have slaughtered us all in no time. Several soldiers even drove on abandoned German motorcycles without fuel – they rolled down the hill very well even without the engine working.

The battalion met us fully armed, it turned out they mistook us for Germans. As they told me, they were about to open fire on us, but saw two tall guys – me and especially Mochalov – we called him a 'beanpole' because of his height. They were happy to see us, as they thought we had been killed at the road crossing.

I started my report about the battle at that road crossing and the entire situation to the battalion commander. I also reported that I had fulfilled his order to hold the road crossing till dawn. First of all I reported Captain Burkov's wound and where they had sent him on a vehicle. The battalion's political officer, Gerstein, and the battalion's doctor, Senior Lieutenant Pankova, who was Burkov's wife, immediately went to the medical platoon. They came back after some time and informed us that Captain Maxim Tarasovich Burkov had passed away. He was 25 years old. It was a big loss for the battalion. A warrior, an officer, who had been in the war from its very first day, a decent person, a brave and good comrade and commander, was dead. In my memory he will remain as a tall, physically strong and cheerful person that never lost heart. His wife, Praskovia Pankova was expecting a baby at that time, and Maxim Burkov's son was only born after his death…

The 2nd company commander Senior Lieutenant Shtokolov, being drunk, was heavily wounded in that village. He liked to drink and he drank a lot. He was wounded because of his own stupidity. As Alexander Guschenkov told me, the drunken Shtokolov grabbed a submachine-gun and started to fire on an abandoned German APC, and the APC just exploded. Shtokolov was seriously wounded along with several others. This is how it was at the front – bravery was sometimes next to stupidity. Besides that, eyewitnesses told that in Bobzha village the 'Slavs' overslept the arrival of retreating German units that broke into the village at night. The battle lasted all night till dawn. The 3rd battalion of our Brigade under command of Major Alexander Grigorievich Chuyah as well as the tanks of our Brigade's tank regiment saved the situation. The enemy forces were thrown back with heavy casualties and the situation was restored, but our losses were also high. The only conclusion is that you can sleep, but one eye has to stay open and one ear should still hear. It was war. Our battalion had been sent to another village from Bobzha and did not have losses.

We were in defence the whole day of 16 January, our task was to prevent the breakthrough of retreating German forces to the west. Everything worked out fine, however, the Germans did not appear, apparently having taken other retreat routes. On the next day, 17 January, tanks of our tank regiment caught up with us and the battalion moved forward on tanks. We continued our advance to the Oder at high speed, through Petrokov, Ostruv and Kratoshin. Along our route there were some other smaller villages and towns, which I do not remember – it's been more than half a century since that time, during which I did not keep a diary. As usual, I was sent forward as the advanced point with my platoon on three tanks. Marching behind enemy lines is no mere parade, one had to be careful all the time. We had orders not to engage small enemy groups, not to linger – just move forward! Nevertheless, we had casualties both in men and in matériel. One gets used to heroism and self-sacrifice of men in battles, and takes it for granted, but it is impossible to get used to the death of people around you.

THE ADVANCE TO THE ODER

We advanced quickly across Poland, the enemy put up resistance only sometimes, but I did not engage the enemy – this was the job of other units, the main body of the battalion or the Brigade. It was good that the enemy's air force was not active owing to bad weather – clouds were hanging low, it was foggy and snowed sometimes. Breaks were short, mostly to give rest to the tank drivers and for small repairs, snacks, stretching our legs and urinating. We encountered rivers sometimes. As a rule, we were able to capture bridges intact and cross the rivers. If a bridge was destroyed and the ice was strong, tanks crossed the river on it. Sometimes the ice broke under the weight of the tanks and they had to ford. There were only one or two crossings like that, not more. Some tank riders did not dismount tanks in those cases and got really wet, and there was no time to dry clothes later on. Normally the tank riders would dismount the tank and cross a river on ice not far from the tank crossing.

On the night of 18 January, 1945, having overcome enemy resistance, we rushed into Petrokov. The Brigade did not stop in the city and quickly drove through it, shooting at the houses right from tanks. Having travelled through the city, we continued our lightning march to Lodz, and at dawn on 19 January we captured the city's southern suburb.

We dismounted and got behind some houses, in an open field, and started to dig in just in case of a German air force attack or artillery or fire strike. The enemy was silent. Some soldiers did not follow my order and only dug skirmisher's trenches, so I had to make them dig deeper. The soldiers did not like digging in – it took a lot of energy, and sometimes it was in vain – either the enemy did not open fire or

169

we had to leave the area right after the trenches were ready. I ordered my soldiers to dig in for many reasons: first, we would have lower losses from enemy fire, but the main thing was that soldiers could panic under strong artillery or air strike, abandon their trenches and flee in the rear, and panic always meant higher losses. Front line experience had taught me this, and I enforced it strictly. Probably this is why we had lower losses compared with other companies. I was unrelenting on these matters, as I knew it could save the lives of the soldiers and NCOs who were my subordinates. They complained and were angry with me, but I always strictly followed my rules.

In front of us we could see a nice panoramic view of Lodz and the German defences with dug-in tanks. The enemy did not open fire, nor did we fire either. The whole of 19 January was quiet. However, there was a small exchange of fire between Russian tanks. A tank column appeared to the right of us at noon. Several tanks of our tank regiment opened fire on the column. Tanks from the column returned fire. The exchange of fire lasted for a short while and suddenly stopped. It turned out that those were the tanks of the 1st Tank Army of the Belorussian front approaching the city, while we, the 4th Tank Army, were part of the first Ukrainian front. Such things tended to happen at the front, but fortunately we soon realized that these were Russian tanks and I think no one had losses.

In the suburbs of Lodz, where we dug in, I was checking how well the soldiers had dug in and walked at my full height in front of foxholes in sight of German tanks, displaying my bravado. A Partorg, a Communist party secretary of our battalion, told me that I should not walk so openly, I could be killed – he was amazed by my bravery. I remember that I answered him that a tank would not bother to fire at me, while submachine-gun fire would not reach me. After that the party secretary started to respect me, and paid attention to me for the second time after the following incident.

We were supposed to leave – as it turned out, we were not intended to capture Lodz. The tanks formed a column on the road, and the 'mount the tanks' order came. Our tank stood between two houses. I walked up to the tank commander and told him to move the tank a bit further forward and park behind a house, so that the enemy would not see us mounting the tank. Why should we take risks? As a response some officers from the tank regiment and our battalion criticized me. No one understood the logic of my request; all kinds of shouting, obscene curses and insults about my person were flying through the air. The tanks did not hide behind the houses, as I requested, but remained where they were. While they were cursing me, two shots sounded in the air and both shells hit the tanks that stood between the houses. After this the tanks immediately moved forward and hid behind the houses. The great officers that had cursed me walked up to those tanks and saw a horrible picture. A high-explosive shell from German Tiger tank had hit the back part of the tank, when soldiers of our company had already mounted it. The explosion killed almost everyone, some soldiers were simply blown to pieces and nothing remained of them. Some seven or eight soldiers were killed. The other tank did not have soldiers on it. The Germans did not fire any more. Colonel Turkin, the Brigade's commander, walked up to the scene, and when he realized what had happened, he told Stolyarov and Kozienko: 'You know, Bessonov was right.'

We left the suburbs of Lodz, and again my platoon on three tanks was ahead of the Brigade. I had already mentioned that the Army's, Corps' and Brigade's task was to advance to the Oder as quickly as possible and establish a bridgehead on its western bank, in area next to Keben (northwards from Wroclaw). Having travelled some 50 kilometres from Lodz, we stopped for a rest, in order to refuel tanks, replenish ammo and have a nap, if the situation allowed it. After all, in seven days, from 12 to 18 January, we had travelled over 200 kilometres in heavy fighting. In 24 hours we would travel up to 50 kilometres almost without any sleep. We were quite exhausted. Penetrating deep into the enemy's rear, we were supposed to capture good river crossings and destroy enemy reserves, if we could not bypass them. Our rest was short and on the night of 21 January we moved on. The Poles did not meet our warriors with the same attitude everywhere. Some met us with joy, others with distrust. Sometimes villages did not have a single living soul – all the villagers would escape as soon as they heard the news of approaching Russian tanks.

Once, when the battalions stopped for a break after a day-long march, I was ordered to move forward with five tanks in the night and capture an important road junction. The commander of the tank regiment Stolyarov personally led the task force, and I was on his tank. Suddenly we spotted Fritzes, and Stolyarov asked me: 'What should we do?' 'Crush them!' I answered. He dispatched this order to all the tanks over radio. It was actually clear that we did not have any other choice. The Germans were superior to us in numbers, but owing to the element of surprise, we smashed the well-armed unit into pieces. My soldiers displayed miracles of bravery, decisiveness and fearlessness in the running battle. Some stayed on tanks, while others dismounted. Trucks and APCs were burning, their crews abandoned some of them, dead bodies of German soldiers were all around. We even managed to burn two Tiger tanks, while all the surviving German infantry fled. For some reason we did not manage to take any prisoners, all the surviving Germans ran off. The remains of the column managed to disappear in the darkness, and we did not pursue them. The way forward for the Brigade was open.

My soldiers were coming up to me, excited and happy with their victory. We captured some war booty, but it was not the main thing, the main thing was our success. This shows the importance of the element of surprise in a night attack. The Germans did not expect such boldness from us, and did not organize the security of the column as they usually did. They paid dearly for this. For some reason I remember that battle very well, probably because of our success and the absence of losses on our side.

In our joy we even had a bit of a drink and drank a symbolic toast to Stolyarov and his tank crews. We slaughtered so many Germans in that battle, that even Stolyarov, an experienced front line commander, got sick, but alcohol got him back into shape. Until dawn we moved forward, fulfilling the order given to us. We stopped in a village to get ourselves warm and stayed there till evening, waiting for the main body of the Brigade.

During the night of 22 January the Brigade moved on. From that time on our company was riding on JS-2 tanks instead of T-34 in front of the Brigade. The Brigade was reinforced with three such vehicles.

We moved at high speed, overtaking the German units that were retreating on other roads; we were also travelling at a significant distance from our infantry units. The situation called for a lightning speed advance, in order to deprive the Germans of the chance to man the defendable and sometimes already fortified areas, especially the ones along the Oder. On the night of 23 January we rushed into

Ostruv and after a short but stubborn battle we captured the town. It was in that town that the Germans used *Panzerfausts* for the first time against our tanks, but they missed. We did not stay in that city for long, although the city had warehouses stuffed full of food, while we were already out of it and we should have picked it up from there – our field kitchen fell behind, as usual. Having quickly left the city, we moved on. I made myself very comfortable behind the turret of a JS tank, as the space over the tank's engine was much larger than that of a T-34, and fell asleep. I slept so well that I did not even notice that our column had stopped.

As it happened, the Brigade commander with his staff had travelled with our battalion that night. They woke me up, and I jumped off the tank and walked forward. There I saw a JS-2 tank lying on its side on the ice of the frozen river. One could hear groaning and desperate pleas from under the tank. For some reason no one was brave enough to assist the suffering men. I did not think long, and crawled under the tank and pulled four soldiers one by one from under the tank. It turned out that they were safe and sound, but a bit squashed and really scared. There were three or four soldiers more under the tank, but they had been crushed by the tank. As it turned out, the first JS-2 tank safely drove across the bridge, but the bridge could not stand the weight of the second tank and it fell on its right side, pressing against the ice those who sat on the right side, as well as the tank commander. Those soldiers who sat on the left side of the tank, were thrown to the sides and they got off with some bruises. I was on the third tank. One of the soldiers that I pulled out later became my orderly – it was Andrey Ulianovich Drozd. I went through the rest of the war with him.

My soldiers wandered off to the huts in order to warm themselves and have a snack. An orderly found me at the capsized tank and informed me that Brigade commander Turkin had called me. I ran up to the Colonel and reported with all due ceremony. Majors Skryago, Kozienko, Stolyarov and someone else was there. Turkin told me: 'Bessonov, order your soldiers not to execute any of the Germans who are in the village houses.' I said, 'Yes' and ran to fulfil the order.

There were indeed Germans in the village. My guys were kicking them out of the houses, taking away their weapons. If a German resisted, they would finish him off, but in other cases they did not harm them at all. However, they confiscated all the Germans' watches. I ordered them to draw all the German soldiers up in column of two, but not to harm them. 'We were not going to execute them,' squad leaders told me, 'we just took their weapons.' I came back to the Brigade commander and reported that his order had been fulfilled: all prisoners had been gathered from the huts and formed up. No one was planning to execute them. I noticed that in front of Turkin there was a tall guy standing at 'attention' in German uniform. The guy was holding a garrison cap on the bend of his arm and was reporting to Turkin clearly in Russian. It turned out that the man was an Uzbek. According to him, in 1941 he had graduated from Tashkent infantry academy as a Lieutenant and was taken prisoner by the Germans in 1942. Then he was a commander of a construction or security company with a rank of Ober-Leutenant (A Senior Lieutenant in our rank system). His company included almost every nationality of Europe: Russians, Ukrainians, Poles, Belorussians, Frenchmen, Czech and others, some 60 to 80 men. According to him, there was a German battalion staff and two companies of German soldiers in the nearby village. That village was not on the main route of our advance and we did not go there.

Colonel Turkin ordered the Ober-Leutenant to lead all his soldiers eastwards, into captivity, but did not order any security to escort them. I have no idea where they went. In my opinion they most likely just scattered.

No matter how hard the tank crews tried, they could not put the tank back on its tracks, and we had to leave it there. The Brigade in the meantime moved on, sometimes engaging the enemy in short clashes. We were held up with the capsized tank anyway.

Anything could happen at the front. One day those of us on the three tanks travelled too far during the night and they ordered us by radio to stop and wait for the main body of the Brigade. Some soldiers went to look for food in the village and they found some. I had excellent men, they could find anything anywhere! They brought two or three containers of milk and white bread that was still warm. We had not seen white bread and milk for a long time, and had an enjoyable meal. We were sitting in the house, enjoying the warmth. All of a sudden the door opened and a Senior Lieutenant walked in. I looked at him and saw something familiar in his face. The guy was smiling with a broad smile and asked us: 'You have something to eat, Slavs? I said: 'Sit down, Muscovite, but we have nothing except bread and milk.' He replied: 'How do you know that I am from Moscow?' I did not want to tease him and answered that he was a teacher of craftsmanship in the 1st Soviet School, which was later renamed in the 341st school, and used to be the school's *Komsorg*. I studied in that school from 1931. He said that everything was right and we even recalled common acquaintances. Everyone was amazed. Could it really happen that, so far from Moscow, two men who knew each other met in the fourth year of the war. Such things also happen generally in life, not just in war. And again we could not stay there for long – we had to move forward, only forward.

In the night of 24 January we attacked the town of Kratoshin straight off from the march. We travelled through the town quickly, and there was no serious opposition from the Germans; they just fired on us at several places. They were afraid to face our tanks with tank riders. In Poland we would often travel through small settlements quickly, without dismounting tanks, firing from the tanks and throwing the enemy out of our way. On 25 January we captured the town of Gernstadt in a battle.

It was good that the enemy's air force was not there, and we could march both during day and night. As a rule, during the night we would stop once for two or three hours. We tried to get into houses, into a warm place. There were almost no stops during the day, and even if we had them, breaks were short, no more than one hour. It was rare that we stopped for a long time to warm the soldiers. We only had food twice a day – morning and evening; if the kitchen was there, the food was hot. Thus, in order not to be hungry during the day, we made do with trophies – mostly German tinned meat and hard tack. Sometimes we saw small loaves of black bread in plastic; the bread was not too hard, but it was tasteless. We did not really like it, but we ate it anyway. Our Russian bread would also freeze in our back-packs in the frost, if you did not eat it on time.

We stayed in a large village almost the whole night. Our company was housed in the former village school. According to practice, we appointed guards and dropped to the floor. I was not even hungry, like most other soldiers – we were almost dead from exhaustion. In the morning, after breakfast (our field kitchen was still with us) we walked up to the tanks to mount them, and I saw a carcass of a pig on our tank. I asked Savkin: 'What is this, are you looting the civilians?' He swore by God that it was not our pig, but the tankers'. To hell with that pig, I thought, if the tankers took it. There were no owners anyway.

Almost all day long we moved on without a battle. Although we were in the German rear, there were no German troops, and we did not hear a single shot during the day. Such days were rare and we were happy, especially given the fact that the enemy's air force was not there either. We had suffered losses in previous battles from the German air force, and although the losses were insignificant, the air force had delayed our advance. Finally we stopped, and parked our tanks by the walls of houses so that they would look like parts of huts and would not be so visible from the air. A tank crew officer walked up to me and said: 'Bessonov, the spirit is mine, the pig is yours!' And he pointed at the water tank that was filled with spirit. I answered: 'Isn't it your pig, as Savkin told me?' The tanker replied: 'Don't be angry with the men. They know you and they know that you would not allow this, so they said that the pig belonged to us.'

What could I do? I could not carry the pig 70 kilometres back! I called Savkin and shook my fist at him. He just said: 'I'm sorry!' Anyway, we were all hungry. 'Well,' I said, 'Fry the pig, and do it fast, the order to move on can come any time.' To be short, we fried a lot of pork on a stove in a house (the owners were not there). We ate all we could eat and fed the battalion commander with his staff, as well as the tank crews. We finished the pig and fed everyone that walked up to us. My soldier Shamrai cooked the food – he was a partisan from the Lvov area and a cook in civilian life. It is a pity that he was killed in Potsdam. At that moment a 'mount the tanks' order came, and we again moved ahead at high speed.

There were cases when I slept so well during the night that I did not even wake up during the small night clashes with the Germans that occurred in some villages. The soldiers sympathized with me and did not wake me up; the squad leaders could manage by themselves – if necessary, they fired on the move. During the day we sometimes ran into horse-drawn supply columns. All the personnel and their escorts were dressed in German uniforms. Among them there were all nationalities except for the Russians – Kalmyks, Uzbeks, Tatars,

Kazakhs, people from the Caucasus and Poles. Apparently, the Germans did not trust the Russians and did not allow them to serve in supply units. We had different attitudes towards those men, but we did not show cruelty, did not abuse them and did not execute them. I think once we fought a supply column of Kalmyks and soldiers of other nationalities, as they tried to resist – they lost their heads and opened fire on us, and my soldiers did not like it. War is war. I never saw Russians or Ukrainians in supply columns, but met Vlasov's men in battle many times. They always put up stubborn resistance and besides that shouted all kinds of offensive curses at us. They knew that there would be no mercy, and we did not give it – we never took them prisoners. Besides, they never surrendered, unlike the Germans.

Sometimes tanks broke down and had to stop for small repairs. In such cases the tank riders would as a rule stay with the tank. But if a tank needed more serious repair, the tank riders would travel along on another tank. One of our tanks broke down, and Sergeant Nikolai Savkin with his squad stayed in that village. Retreating Fritzes entered the village after we left and burnt the tank in battle. Savkin himself was killed, along with his men, among them Bespalyuk, Polischuk and others…That's how it was, there were no major engagements, but platoons had fewer and fewer soldiers left…

We went through the whole of Poland fighting constantly. Sometimes the enemy put up stubborn resistance, while sometimes our arrival in a city or a village was totally unexpected for the Germans. One village still had electric lights and even a policeman on a street crossing when we drove in. At first he did not understand which tanks these were, but as soon as we drove closer, he realized who we were and ran away from his post, he was off like a flash. I have already mentioned that Germans run very fast.

I also remember the following incident. We stopped after a march at a detached house, and the soldiers decided to go into one of them to get warm. It was dark and quiet in the house. As soon as some five men walked into the house, several shots sounded in the air. The soldiers ran out of the house, one of them was lightly wounded, there was blood all over his face. I was standing at the house next to a tank, and my soldiers reported to me what had happened. I ordered them to toss hand-grenades through the windows, but then we changed our mind – we might also kill our own soldiers. We rushed into the house and opened fire with submachine-guns and illuminated it with flashlights. We found two men and a woman in the house: they were Poles, and we asked them who had fired. They answered that those were Schwabs, i.e., Germans, and pointed at the attic. We found two Germans there, they had both been killed in the exchange of fire. The Poles informed us that one of them was Lieutenant Colonel and the second was a Captain. The Lieutenant Colonel was the city's commandant, while the Captain was his deputy. The Poles told me that they were afraid to warn us, as the Germans threatened to execute them. The soldiers stayed in the house, while I went away and left them alone, especially as a 'mount the tanks' order came and we again moved on forward to the west.

In general, our battalion's and the Brigade's actions deep in German rear in winter 1945 were a military success. I do not know about the other companies, but our company did not have high casualties. The Brigade was moving forward at high speed and as a result we were at a significant distance from the Field Army's infantry units. We had certain difficulties because of this – in particular, it was harder to supply tanks with fuel and ammo.

We arrived at the Oder on 23 or 24 January, 1945, with only our company and the battalion commander with his deputies. Other companies of the battalion were at that time engaged in battles with German reserves that had arrived. By that time other units of our Corps – the 17th Guards Mechanized Brigade with some units of the 16th Guards Mechanized Brigade had already crossed the river after heavy fighting. As for us, we crossed the river relatively safely, on a small ferry, although under German bombs – finally, the German air force appeared again. The Germans were still putting up resistance on the other side, and the company, assaulting the German strongpoint jointly with units of the 17th Guards Mechanized Brigade, managed to throw the Germans back. By the way, the commander of our 4th Tank Army, General Lelyushenko, was already there at the crossing, and that was just two days after the 15th Guards Brigade had crossed the Oder!

The Advance to the Oder

We captured the German town of Keben together with a company from another Brigade. Having reached its western outskirts, we stopped. For some reason battalion commander Kozienko was also there. He was receiving orders for attack first from the commander of the 17th Guards Mechanized Brigade and several days later from the Chief of Staff of the 6th Guards Mechanized Corps, Colonel Koretski. Our company was defending the crossing and other dangerous approaches. We put ourselves in order in Keben, even getting our hair cut by the medic (they never shaved soldiers' heads at the front), somehow washed ourselves, mostly the upper parts of our bodies. It was a pity that from time to time we were disturbed by the German air force, but apart from that, it was almost paradise, even our kitchen drove up. Both our bodies and souls rested and we could even sleep in warm houses.

The main body of the Brigade caught up with us several days later; the 2nd and the 3rd companies of the battalion also joined us. They arrived quite depleted, but they were immediately thrown into battle to assist the 17th Guards Brigade that was trying to extend the bridgehead before strong German reinforcements arrived.

The battalion commander ordered me to report to the Corps Chief of Staff Colonel Koretski. When I arrived and reported, he looked at me and said: 'You know what, Bessonov, you have been in the Brigade for a long time. Kozienko sent you here on my order. Your task is to guard the crossing, the Corps staff as well as put out fires in the city. You take the mansion across the street from my Staff, and always be there at hand. Do not let any other units into the mansion.' This is how I got the mansion for my platoon and the 2nd platoon of the company, a total of not more than 30 men. Vyunov's and Guschenkov's platoons, in turn, followed the battalion together with the company commander.

The mansion was rich; it had everything one could imagine! There was enough food and the soldiers cooked it themselves. Soldiers would be cooking all day long, grilling something and drinking tea. We did not drink alcohol, except for some weak wine – anything could be found in the mansion's cellar. We slept on beds. I had a wide bed with rich linen and a satin blanket. I could take off my clothes before going to bed! We threw away our underwear and replaced it with German silk underwear. Everything would have been just perfect, if only Koretski did not send us to put out fires and on guard duty during air raids against the crossing. Soldiers of our arriving infantry units set the houses on fire as revenge for their houses burnt down by the Germans in the Soviet Union. We did not have any equipment to extinguish the fire, so we would just come and stand at a burning house, watching until it burnt to ashes. That's why the most effective measure was to send patrols and catch the arsonists. It helped, but not in all cases. Sometimes we were just pretending to be extinguishing the fire, so that Koretski did not rebuke us. I should say that that period was a rest for the platoon. Before that we had travelled at least 600 kilometres in 12 or 13 days from 12 to 25 January, 1945.

ON GERMAN SOIL

We were now on German territory and everything there was different from what we saw in Poland. Highways were covered with asphalt; roads to fields and barns were covered with cobblestone. We saw clean pine woods without any brushwood, rich houses and mansions, small roadside villages and farms with peaked red-tile roofs. However, there was not a single living soul in the city. The population had been evacuated westwards, far across the Oder, leaving all their belongings in the houses, including cattle and poultry. Some guys found two really old women in Keben when searching for German soldiers, but they did not find anyone else.

Our rest at the 'resort' did not last long. One day Colonel Koretski called me and ordered the battalion to depart, giving me a truck and explaining the route to me. We left the 'resort' with sadness. I found the battalion in a village, where it had stopped for a mid-day rest, and reported my arrival to both battalion commander Kozienko and company commander Chernyshov. I accommodated my soldiers and went to the house where some officers gathered for lunch. They greeted me with joy, almost shouting 'Hurrah' – the officers were a bit tipsy and were fooling around. They made me sit down at the table, and poured a *shtrafnaya* or punishment glass for me (*a punishment glass is an extra glass of wine or vodka that a person has to drink if he or she is late for a party – translator's comment*). I noticed that besides Vyunov, Kes, Guschenkov, Belyakov, Tsikanovski and Mochalov there was a strange Lieutenant in the house. I was introduced to him – this was Fedor Popov, with whom we fought till the end of the war. A brave, middle-sized, physically fit and modest person, he became a good comrade to me. Besides him,

Lieutenant Grigori Mikheev arrived in the company in those days to replace wounded Petr Shakulo as a platoon leader. A native of Siberia, he was a big and physically strong guy; later we became good friends. He came to us from the signal platoon. He was dismissed from that office for drunk driving, when he lost control over the truck of the signals platoon and the truck capsized. However, they put it back on wheels later, no one was hurt, but Mikheev was punished and appointed platoon leader in a motor rifle company.

On the evening of 4 February we started our tank raid. The battles that followed were bitter; the Germans resisted stubbornly, holding on to every village and hill. The enemy threw Vlasov's soldiers against us – we would defeat them as well, but I should say they fought better than the Germans. The Germans deployed *Panzerfaust* anti-tank missiles *en masse* against our tanks. It was a dreadful close-range weapon against our tanks and other vehicles. A *Panzerfaust* easily penetrated a T-34 tank, its explosive energy was enormous, and it could even penetrate a JS-2, if it hit the side.

As usual, I travelled on tanks with my platoon far ahead of the battalion. Once, before we could reach a small village at the road, we came under heavy fire. The soldiers quickly dismounted, while the tanks drove back a bit. I moved forward a little with my platoon, but had to lie down in a ditch because of heavy fire. Snipers were firing. Besides that, I saw anti-personnel '*spring*-mines' and anti-tank mines. If you touched the wire from a '*spring*-mine', it would jump up to 2 metres and explode, killing men with its contents. Anti-tank mines were placed on the highway.

Vyunov arrived with his platoon, but he acted smarter – he did not move along the asphalt highway, but moved a bit to the right and advanced through a young forest. Eventually his soldiers also had to lie down in front of the village. Chernyshov came running; I had not seen him for a long time. As always, he started to shout: 'Forward, Bessonov, forward!' I told him: 'Wait, Nikolai, look around. Can't you see the mines on the road and snipers firing? Vyunov's position is better now, he should attack the village.'

We shouted 'Forward!' to Vyunov, but either he did not hear us or was also pinned down by snipers, but at all events his soldiers remained on the ground. Chernyshov wanted to run there, and I tried to talk him out of it, putting it bluntly: 'They will kill you.' I recommended he go back and bring up the heavy JS-2 tanks, but Chernyshov did not listen to my advice: he jumped up and before he made two steps from the ditch, a shot sounded in the air and Nikolai fell down. We pulled him into the ditch and bandaged him. He was wounded in his chest. After that we carried him at the rear. All this time Chernyshov was unconscious. This incident happened around 8 or 10 February and he had to stay in hospital until 18 April, 1945.

A JS-2 tank drove up to us at that moment. The soldiers indicated targets to the tank commander and the tank fired its 122 mm gun. All of a sudden I saw three German self-propelled guns (we also called them assault guns) rushing out one by one from behind the houses several metres from us. Our tank opened fire on them, but they quickly disappeared behind a bend of the highway. I got my soldiers to attack, and shouting 'Forward, follow me, forward!' I ran along the ditch, jumping across the detonation wires of *spring*-mines (what an idiot!). The soldiers were smarter than me and ran on the field to the right and left from the highway, there were no mines there. We rushed into the village; Vyunov and his platoon also broke into the houses on the outskirts of the village. The enemy fled. My men searched the houses, but they were abandoned – not a single human soul was there. We waited for the battalion commander with his staff. He already knew about Chernyshov's wound. After that T-34 tanks with Major Stolyarov, commander of the tank regiment, arrived.

Battalion commander Major Kozienko called me up – political officer Gerstein and the battalion's chief of staff, Captain Grigoriev, were also there. Kozienko told me that they had decided to appoint Senior Lieutenant Grigori Vyunov the company commander in place of the wounded Chernyshov. Vyunov had arrived at the battalion as late as October 1944 and was five or six years older than me. I replied to Kozienko that I had been in the battalion from August 1943, that it was my fourth operation, and I was always the last officer to remain in the company, *de facto* leading the company and did not I deserve to become the company's commander? Major Kozienko told me that he made the decision jointly with Gerstein and Grigoriev and that it was not just his decision. So, I again remained platoon leader. Somehow I was not very lucky when it came to promotion.

The following battles were very hard for us and we were losing a lot of men. The Germans threw *Volkssturm (the German Home Guard –*

translator's note) against us — old guys and young boys armed with *Panzerfausts*, who resisted most stubbornly. Sometimes they fought to the last man. Every day we had losses in men and equipment. We could achieve almost no deep penetration into the German rear, as we had in the Ukraine and Poland. Battles took place day and night, and this really exhausted us. The battalion attacked as a concentrated task force with all three companies, or all that remained of them. The Germans, in turn, only retreated to consolidate their positions at another place that was prepared for defence.

The population fled from us. Traces of panic flight were everywhere — we saw cases, bicycles, pillows and other things in the ditches. All villages, both small and large, were abandoned, no one stayed behind. Cattle, poultry and other things were left behind, so we did not stay hungry. On the contrary, we ate as much as we could cook during short breaks. Once our column caught up with fleeing local civilians. It was a column of stiff old men, children and women of different ages. Some travelled on carts, some walked and pushed carriages with their belongings that they could carry, some had back-packs on their backs. We stopped all those people and in our broken German explained to them that they should go back to their homes. The battalion travelled on in order to complete the mission, and we do not know where the Germans went — we had other things on our minds.

We never harassed German civilians. We did not rob them, did not search them and did not take anything away. To be honest, I was very strict about this with my soldiers, and I think that other officers were also of the same opinion. We did not rape women, or at least, such things never happened in our company or battalion. The senior officers were also very strict about such things both in the battalion and the Brigade. Besides that, I personally warned many soldiers about my strictness in this respect. Not only in my company, but also in the other companies of the battalion they knew about my attitudes and even the most notorious soldiers were afraid of me. Why? I was the veteran of the battalion, I had been through it all, and there had been a lot of rumours, known as 'soldier's radio', about my strictness. Even the most undisciplined and impudent soldiers didn't mess with me. Many times I heard: 'Bessonov is coming!' — especially after a rumour that I almost executed a soldier for disgraceful behaviour.

This thing did not take place in reality, but there was a rumour, and some believed it.

It was a cloudy day, sleet was falling, and it was quite chilly on the tanks. Everyone was trying to get closer to the tank's radiator – bad weather for infantry. During 9 and 10 February the enemy put up stubborn resistance, throwing armour, infantry and *Volkssturm* into action, raining shot and shell on us. We had a hard time, but the enemy's resistance was broken and after taking losses the Germans had to withdraw, leaving heavy equipment and weapons behind – tanks without fuel, artillery and mortars. We were in the middle of a forest; sometimes one could not see where Fritzes' fire came from. Tanks moved forward carefully, following the tank riders – our task was to destroy German *Panzerfaust* teams with small arms or indicate Fritz targets to the tanks, so that they could destroy them with main guns. The enemy tried to stop our advance by all means, laying ambushes – sometimes with very small groups, which was almost a suicide mission with its only goal being to stop us and inflict casualties on us. One evening, just when it started to get dark, the three vanguard tanks approached the edge of a forest. My platoon and I were in the middle of the advancing tank column, while a group of soldiers from another company was in forward security. All of a sudden several artillery shots shook the air and the column stopped. I jumped off the tank and ran forward to find out what had happened. It got completely dark, but I saw a group of commanding officers, among them the commander of the tank regiment, Stolyarov, battalion commander Kozienko and others. Soldiers from the three first tanks ran back from the forest edge and brought a heavily wounded soldier on rain cape. The soldier died soon after the incident. According to the soldiers, at the forest edge they came under fire from German assault guns. One of our tanks was knocked out, almost an entire escorting tank rider squad died, and only a few wounded survived. Two other tanks tried to evade fire. One crew abandoned their vehicle, but the driver went into reverse, and the tank rolled backwards without the crew. The regiment commander ordered the tank to be stopped and brought back to the column. The order was carried out.

The commanders did not dare to mount a night attack, so the attack was shifted to the next morning. At dawn the battalion – all that was left of its three companies – started to advance through the forest to the left of the road. We did not know anything about the enemy. At first everything was nice and quiet, no shots were fired at us, the enemy did not see us, and we did not see the enemy. However, this did not last for long, as the enemy spotted us and opened rifle and machine-gun fire. We returned fire and advanced forward in short rushes.

The outnumbered German infantry retreated, or rather fled from our attack. However, we came under fire from three German assault guns, which turned out to be some 50 metres from us. We had to take cover behind trees, as the assault guns fired at almost every single soldier. My orderly and I were lying under a tree, which was hit by a shell, a metre from the ground. We were shell-shocked, the tree was cut down, but we remained unharmed and sneaked to another tree. We were lucky again, not for the first time. We did not know what to do, as the tanks did not support us, staying far behind, but the 3rd company commander, Kostenko, quickly came up with a solution. He brought a heavy JS-2 tank almost to our line and indicated targets – the assault guns – to the crew. The tank fired two shots from its heavy gun (122 mm), and one assault gun literally fell apart, while the second round penetrated two assault guns at once. I had never seen such a 'miracle' before. Our way was free. The battalion advanced a bit further through the forest and the enemy was nowhere to be seen. Our tanks caught up with us, we were ordered to mount the tanks, and we drove on.

Overcoming the stubborn resistance of the enemy, during the night of 11 February our battalion with the other battalions of the Brigade crossed the Bober river and then crossed the Neisse river on 16 February. We were already some 105 or 110 kilometres from Berlin. The Neisse was deep and wide in the place where we crossed it. There was a good multi-ton bridge across the river, but it was booby-trapped, and German battle engineers were waiting for the order to blow the bridge up. However, guys from the Brigade's scout company captured the bridge and killed all the battle engineers – they received help from a Russian girl that the Germans must have known – she worked at the farm next to the bridge. Thus we were able to cross the river on the bridge and set up defences on the left flank of the Brigade, no more than 100 metres from the river. The 2nd and the

3rd battalions of the Brigade were in defence to the right of us, some 250 metres from the river. We did not have enough forces to advance any further.

Our company had just ten or fifteen soldiers when it arrived at the bridgehead at Neisse. Guschenkov had probably just three or five soldiers with one Maxim machine-gun left. Besides this, the company had company commander Vyunov, platoon leaders Guschenkov and me, Sergeant Major Bratchenko, medic 'Brotherly Heart', clerk Chulkin and a company commander's orderly. The company's total strength was just 22 or 23 men: at the beginning of the operation on 12 January, 1945, the company had had up to 100 men. Our company's losses were up to 80% of personnel. The other companies were not in a better position. Company commander Nikolai Chernyshov was heavily wounded, platoon leaders Shakulo and Mikheev were lightly wounded. We earned our victory at a high price, a very high price. It was not only our battalion that suffered significant losses, but also the other two battalions of the Brigade, as well as the tank regiment. All tanks were out of action, just three or four tanks could still move, but they could not fire – their main guns were broken. However, even these tanks could make it to our bridgehead on the Neisse river, in order to make a show of armour. This contained the Germans to a certain extent – tanks are still tanks. Brigade commander Colonel Turkin was at that time recovering from a wound in a hospital. The Brigade was under the brigade chief of staff, Lieutenant Colonel Arkadi Arkhipov. Turkin was wounded in the following incident: in front of a village we were caught by German fire; tanks stopped, tank riders dismounted, and we moved forward a bit and lay down. I had to clarify the situation, find out where the enemy was and what forces opposed us. Some other officers were with me at that point. I sent several men to find out what was going on – I did not like to attack without knowing anything about the enemy. The scout party returned and reported that they did not see the enemy, but Germans had fired on them from basements and house windows. My three tanks bluntly refused to continue the attack, but the main body of the Brigade was about to arrive. While I was thinking whether I should attack the enemy, it drove up. Brigade commander Colonel Turkin and the Brigade's tank regiment commander, Major Stolyarov, arrived at the scene. I reported the reason for our stop, but they did not believe me. Turkin told me: 'You got scared by a single Fritz, there is no one there! You just thought you saw someone. Forward, Bessonov!' They got into their APC and as soon as they had driven some 100 metres, a *Panzerfaust* team knocked out their APC. Both Turkin and Stolyarov were wounded, while the APC crew was killed. Our tanks arrived and opened fire from main guns; the company went forward, firing on the move. The enemy fled.

The bridgehead at the Neisse river was very small; it was exposed even to machine-gun fire, while German artillery fired at us day and night. Soldiers talked about an armoured train firing at us, but I was not sure about that. We did not have sufficient force to extend the bridgehead, and although the Germans brought up reinforcements, their infantry was not numerous either. They did not bring any tanks, as they must have suffered too heavy losses. We stayed for some five or six days at the bridgehead, and the Germans gave us no respite day or night. The Germans were in bushes not more than 50 metres from our company, and threw themselves at us several times, day and night. But the soldiers of my platoon opened heavy fire every time, while Lieutenant Guschenkov's machine-gun cut them down without mercy and they had to fall back with losses. The air force bombed us during the day, dropping bombs at the bridge, but fortunately for us they all missed. The Germans even launched torpedoes down the river to hit the bridge. The torpedoes were quite powerful, but they all missed the bridge, hit the banks of the river and exploded not far from the bridge. The Germans used a new weapon against our infantry, at least I had not seen such a weapon before. They dropped boxes or containers from the planes: in mid-air the boxes opened into two halves and small bombs that resembled Russian F-1 grenades rained on us from there. They could cover quite a vast area. Again, fortunately for us they missed us, apparently they did not know exactly where we were. We could not dig in, as the the water table was too high, we only dug skirmisher's trenches, not deeper. Eventually, everything worked out fine and we did not have losses.

My orderly Andrey Drozd and I slept in turns; not far from the riverbank we found concrete rings for facing wells and they served us as a good shelter from shell and bomb splinters. This is where we rested when Germans did not attack. Our rest was a couple of hours of sleep, all the other time we were awake. Apparently, the Germans suffered hellishly from Guschenkov's machine-guns, which fired at them at point-blank range, cutting down the attacking soldiers. As a result, the Fritzes ceased their attacks on our company and it was quiet for a couple of days. Soldiers could calmly put themselves in order, at least, those who wanted to could shave or wash their faces. The battalion's field kitchen would come to us across the bridge before dawn and in twilight in the evening, and all day long we had to eat the remains of captured German food. When the Germans had calmed down, company's Sergeant Major Mikhail Bratchenko organized lunch during the day. They stayed in a small house together with company commander Grigori Vyunov not far from the front line, and set up kitchen there. The company's medic, clerk and orderly also stayed there, Alexander Guschenkov sometimes also visited there. He already had four or five wounds and this was the first operation in which he was not wounded.

ON TO BERLIN

On 24 February, 1945, rifle units replaced us, while our Brigade headed towards the town of Ober (Oberau) for replacements. The officers that took over our defence sector, said to us, after they heard we were from the 4th Tank Army: 'Aha, so you are the bandits of Lelyushenko's Army!' We did not get the joke. They had to explain to us. There had been a special broadcast to the German people on the German radio: 'Germans, save yourselves, bandits are coming – the tank crews of General Lelyushenko.' One can conclude that our 4th Tank Army, including our Brigade, had played an important role in destruction of the German troops, if we scared the Nazi top brass so much. We stayed in Ober until 11 or 12 April, 1945, when the Berlin operation, the last operation of the War, commenced. We were so exhausted that for the first two or three days we just slept and did not wake up. After breakfast we would sleep till lunch, and then sleep again till evening. In the evenings we would play cards or write letters home, and then sleep again till morning. It is interesting that the entire company stayed in one house. The soldiers took two rooms, while platoon leaders Guschenkov, Mikheev, Petr Shakulo, who had returned from the hospital, the company's Sergeant Major Bratchenko and I stayed in the third room on the second floor. I had a separate bed, above which I hung a German submachine-gun; Vyunov and Shakulo also had beds, while Mikheev and Guschenkov had to share a large sofa. All of us, including the soldiers, had feather beds and pillows.

Many officers and men were awarded with orders and medals for the Vistula–Oder Operation, including me – I got the Order of the Patriotic War 2nd degree. That was my third order in the war. They promised to recommend me for the Hero of the Soviet Union for battles in Poland and destruction of the German column – Major A. D. Stolyarov personally told me about that. However, as I later learned from Brigade's clerk Chulkin (he had been my soldier since 1943), the recommendation was later replaced with recommendation for the Order of the Red Banner. The staff of my 6th Guards Mechanized Corps in turn, returned the recommendation paper with instruction to recommend me for the Order of Great Patriotic War 2nd degree. Well, God is their judge. I personally tried to recommend as many soldiers of my platoon as possible for decoration, and most of my recommendations worked, especially given the fact that Brigade Commander was authorized to award medals and the Order of the Red Star.

After an Order of the People's Commissar of Defence of the USSR of 17 March, 1945, our Tank Army became part of the Guards – it was renamed the 4th Guards Tank Army. Our 49th Mechanized Brigade was renamed into 35th Guards Kamenets-Podolsk Mechanized Brigade, and we started to get higher wages (my wage, for instance, from that time on was 1,200 roubles, out of them 600 roubles as Lieutenant's wage, 300 roubles for service at the front, and 300 roubles for being part of Guards). Money was not the main thing, though. It is prestigious to be a part of the Guards. We were all young at that time and we all had human needs. We wanted to do many things – have a nice dinner, sometimes have a drink, have a talk and recall things that we had experienced in peacetime and during the war, pay our honour to the dead and wounded.

The battalion commander and *zampolit* came to us one sunny day and told us that it was time to stop sleeping and start doing business – train the soldiers. We also had to be on alert, as there were groups of stray Germans roaming the area, who tried to go to the west, having come out of different encirclements. Alex Belyakov took prisoner several stray Fritzes, and some Germans were killed when trying to resist. We started to go to a nearby field for tactical training, but we did that as a pure formality, mostly resting – the replacements had not arrived yet. The real training was still ahead, after the replacements arrived – that was when we had to train the newcomers to fight the war. So far, there were very few of us – the battalion was almost completely wiped out. It was already March and it was nice warm weather in Germany; soon afterwards we received summer uniforms, throwing away the old winter uniforms, which we had worn for over four months, since November 1944. Despite that, we would change underwear more often, mostly we had German silk underwear, as there was plenty of it in abandoned German houses. Nevertheless, on pictures taken at Prague upon my return from the hospital (May 1945) I am dressed in winter woollen trousers and a *gimnastyorka* tunic. Apparently, I had not changed into summer uniform – I could afford it, but the battalion's commander tolerated this, knowing my love of warm clothes. Just like many others, in Ober I ordered leather jackboots and a woollen garrison cap for myself, although during the summer we would all normally wear field caps.

Soldiers and sergeants, who had already fought the war in the battalion, started to come back to the battalion from hospitals, and finally we were fully manned. Many soldiers were Russians who had been taken from the USSR into Germany and had worked in Germany on farms or in German industries. We had to train them a lot – we had to teach them how to fight the war. In my platoon I only had soldiers who had fought in the platoons of the company before being wounded. I was glad to see them, they knew me, and I also knew them from previous battles.

My orderly Drozd with his companion showed initiative and brought a cheese (it was of size of a car wheel), chicken and other poultry, spirits, flour, butter, sugar and even two cows. We had around 40 chickens, not to mention the other things. We organized cooking by the soldiers of the company who knew how to cook, and soon most of the soldiers of our depleted company stopped going to the battalion's kitchen. One would come back from the training for lunch, have a bit of alcohol, a snack and then eat *borscht* or chicken soup, fried potatoes and roast meat of chicken, followed by tea or stewed fruits and *pirogi* or doughnuts. We were already sick and tired of the battalion's kitchen with its *schi* (cabbage soup) or pork fat soup. In the mornings soldiers had milk with fresh white bread and cheese and something else. I was even scolded by the battalion's commanders, because my soldiers were not eating anything from the battalion's kitchen – for some reason they called me, not the company commander or the company's Sergeant Major, and told me to stop the 'mess' and feed soldiers only from the kitchen. After that they told me that though my platoon had experienced soldiers that had seen the war, many of them were to go to other platoons and companies as squad leaders in order to bolster the green soldiers. Then they asked me: 'Do you know why the soldiers want to be in your platoon?' I answered, that they would probably want to be under command of battalion's and company's veteran. They answered: 'No, not because of that. The soldiers say that no one gets killed in your platoon!' After that they showed me statistics, that my platoon did not lose anyone in the previous two or three months, just had wounded that returned to the platoon later. I had not paid attention to the fact that my platoon only had old hands. The soldiers had noticed that and asked to transfer to my platoon. Actually, travelling from the Vistula to the Neisse as a vanguard of the Brigade and not having a single soldier killed was a miracle. I was unable to save my soldiers and myself from enemy fire, I just could not do it, but we escaped without fatalities. It just means that we were all extremely lucky, that's it. Others were less lucky in the operation. On 19 March the commander of our 6th Guards Lvov Mechanized Corps, Colonel V. F. Orlov, was killed. Colonel N. D. Shuprov, commander of the 10th Guards Tank Corps, was also killed in March; the commanders of the 16th Guards Mechanized Brigade, Colonels L. D. Churilov and Ryvis, were heavily wounded. No one is insured against death at the front.

In March and April we did intensive training, preparing the men for the coming battles. We knew that it would be the last battle, the last operation for the ultimate destruction of Nazi troops, and then peace would finally come. We did not know when exactly the all-out offensive would start, but some time around April 12 we left Ober and concentrated for the offensive closer to the front line, in a waiting area. We marched on foot to the waiting area. Normally we would only march at night, and in daytime all traffic died out. The enemy must not know where the main strike would come. All the personal equipment that we had in the company, we gave to the deputy battalion commander for logistics, Zaitsev, who had a small support unit – cooks with a kitchen, several soldiers, supply trucks, drivers and so on. We could not just leave it all for someone else!

We did not do any training in the waiting area, and we were given time for rest. Most of the time we slept; many officers played cards, the simple 'score' game. I was extremely unlucky in cards, and since that time I have never played cards for money. We followed camouflage procedures, as it was strictly required, and this is why the soldiers did not hang around the forest. It was quiet. During the night from 15 to 16 April we moved from the waiting area (some 3 to 5 kilometres from the front line) to the jump-off area, just 1 or 1.5 kilometres from the enemy. Tanks had already been distributed between the platoons and we were just waiting for the signal to start the offensive.

Many books have been written about this operation – the encirclement and especially the assault of Berlin – both fiction and in memoirs. I will try to describe the battle through the eyes of a junior officer, platoon leader and company commander, who was personally in action together with tank riders and tanks of the 56th Tank Regiment of our Corps. I assaulted the enemy together with my men, and I knew what it cost us to drive the enemy out from his positions.

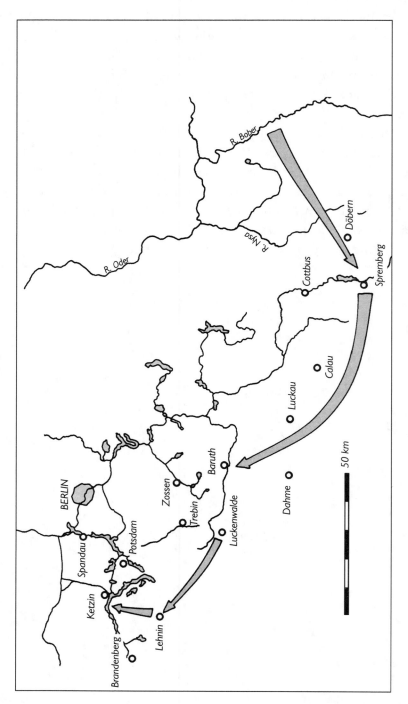

Map to show the advance on Berlin, April 1945.

THE BERLIN–PRAGUE
OPERATION

T he artillery barrage opened early on the morning of 16 April, 1945. Then bombers and ground attack planes delivered strong strikes on the enemy's defences. After the infantry units had broken through, it was our Tank Army's turn to go into battle. Tanks with tank riders had already lined up in a column on a road that ran along the edge of a wood. For some reason a heavy silence hung in the air; we could not see the enemy and it was a bit scary. It is always hard to get used again to combat operations conditions after a break, especially given the fact that many of the soldiers had not been in action before and did not feel confident. That is why there was some chaos: when we started to mount our tanks after the battalion commander's order, the Germans opened artillery fire on us. It was extremely unexpected, and the barrage was short, but concentrated and 'juicy'. We were all gone from the tanks in a twinkle of an eye, and our entire battalion ran into the wood. However, after we had covered some 100 metres, we stopped and came back to our senses, especially now that the barrage had ceased. We ran back to the tanks. It was silent again. The only casualty in our company was the Senior Lieutenant, Grigori Vyunov, who was wounded in the head. He was quickly sent to a hospital and I never saw him again and did not hear anything about him. The battalion commander ordered me to take over the company. We quickly debriefed the situation, received our portion of obscene curses, calmed down and received an order not to leave the tanks. After some time our column moved forward, to the west. Again I was the only officer remaining in the company – Shakulo was wounded again and was hanging around the administrative platoon of the battalion, Guschenkov was apparently also in hospital, while Grigori Mikheev stayed with the damaged tanks. But I was once more unlucky with promotion; several days later Senior Lieutenant Chernyshov came back from hospital. He came running into my shelter during a fast-paced battle for a village and told me that following the battalion commander's decision he had been appointed company commander.

We were conducting the offensive in difficult forest terrain that abounded with rivers, channels and swampy areas. We had to stick to the roads, which crippled our manoeuvres. The enemy put up stubborn resistance, bullets often ricocheted like rain from the armour of our tanks. We could not abandon tanks on the move, and only by a miracle were we without fatalities. The enemy's air force bombed the battalion's column, acting especially boldly in the absence of our fighter aircraft. I have already written that they very rarely covered us.

The roads were covered with mines, blocked with barricades and heaps of rubbish, especially in built up areas and in front of them, as well as under railway and road bridges, which had high embankments. They used *Panzerfausts* against our tanks. Battles raged during day and night without any break and this was seriously exhausting.

The Germans were afraid of us Russian soldiers. Sometimes we saw unfinished hot meals in houses, cattle was abandoned in barns. There were cases when entire families – two or three persons – would commit suicide and hang themselves, afraid of Russian revenge. Most of the villages that we captured were empty; we swept through some of them without combat, as the Germans had quickly abandoned them, but sometimes they would leave *Panzerfaust* teams behind to destroy our tanks. I prohibited my soldiers from eating the food that was left on the tables, as I was afraid that it had been poisoned. Whenever possible, we cooked our food ourselves – there was enough food left in German houses, or we ate pickled and preserved food that we found in cellars – one could find a lot of food there. In general, we didn't starve. We were quite cautious with wine, vodka and other spirits; for a joke we first asked Alexander Guschenkov to drink it, and when we saw that he was all right, we would drink it too. My orderly Drozd always had alcohol in his canteen instead of water – I tried to prevent him many times, but it was useless. Both Petr Shakulo and I were not big fans of alcohol, and generally there were few hard drinkers in the battalion, but there were some – Alexander Guschenkov, Yuri Grigoriev and Grigori Shtokolov.

Alexander Guschenkov was a good comrade of mine, he was almost ten years older than me. He did not have a better attitude than anyone else, but he always shared all things he had with me and never forgot about me. He was just the right type of comrade. It was he who hoped I would be lightly wounded – to stay for some time in a hospital on a bed with white linen, not in trenches on the ground next to the fire.

Despite the German resistance, our battalion's and the Brigade's advance was successful. The newcomers fought well, although their training had been short. I did not have anything to complain about. Pre-empting the events that followed, I note that from 16 to 25 April, 1945, we advanced some 450 kilometres through Germany in nine days. The Germans definitely had fewer tanks – they must have lost them in previous heated battles against our troops. However, their shortage of tanks was to some extent compensated for by *Panzerfausts* and assault guns – the self-propelled artillery pieces with weak armour. However, the enemy's air force was active, and it remained so for some time and we were hit hard many times.

On 18 April my platoon, three tanks and Lieutenant Fedor Popov with his machine-gun platoon were in the Brigade's vanguard and were crossing the Spree river in a narrow and shallow place. The other shore was very steep and the tanks stopped at the shore, unable to drive further. I walked up the steep bank with my soldiers and walked forward a bit, but we were pinned down by intensive machine-gun fire from Fritzes. All of a sudden I heard a rude commanding voice from a ditch or a trench: 'Lieutenant, why the hell are you lying here, go forward, get the men to assault!' I looked and saw that it was Colonel Koretski – at that time he was commander of the 6th Mechanized Corps. How on earth did he end up in front of our troops? He must have just got lost. Apparently, I was more scared of Vasily Ignatievich Koretski than the Germans – I jumped up like crazy and literally threw myself forward with a cry 'Get up, follow me, assault, forward!' The platoon's soldiers opened fire; all stood up like one and assaulted the enemy.

Assault, assault… Many things have been written about this in literature, but an assault can be of many kinds, and the worst one among them is assaulting across an open field. First you walk, then you move forward in short rushes and as you get close to the enemy – you run as fast as you can! And the fear you go through during all this time – bullets whistling in the air, German shells and mines exploding all around. Assaulting an enemy's position is a horrible thing for a person to do, no one knows his psychological condition during an assault and cannot honestly describe it – it would be a lie or something made up. But regardless of how scared you are, no one will fulfil your orders for you. You just run and think: 'Will they get me or not?' But more often you forget this as well, thinking just one thing: 'Where is the enemy?' If we encountered the enemy at short distance, say at 50 metres, we would cover this distance in a rush and capture the position. A platoon leader's task is to lead this rush: 'Forward run, open fire! Kill Fritzes!' But if the enemy stopped us by fire at a longer distance, then the company would deploy in a line and we would only start the assault after the company or battalion commander's order, with tanks or without them. Such an assault is scarier and there are more losses, as sometimes we did not have enough breath to run. The platoon leader's task in such a situation is not to allow the soldiers to lie down; this is why you run shouting 'Forward!'. The enemy would normally flee and we would jump in his trenches, barely catching our breath or continued to pursue the enemy, if we had energy for it.

The enemy fled this time too, reluctant to take us on in hand-to-hand fighting, but I decided to run as far as possible from Koretski and we ran almost to the houses of the village, where we were again stopped by intensive machine-gun fire. The platoon was pinned down. Popov was at our right flank with his platoon. There were thick bushes there, while in front of my platoon there was an open field with grass. I was lying there and saw the grass being cut down by the concentrated fire. It was good that we were lying behind a small elevation; it was very important, but some gloomy thoughts were revolving in my head: 'They can kill me here...' All of a sudden the machine-gun on our right ceased fire; Popov's machine-gunners had suppressed it. The second machine-gun went silent soon afterwards. We rushed into the village; the Germans fled from it. It grew silent. Fedor did a great job and helped us out at the right moment, otherwise how long would we have to lie on the ground and listen to the grass growing? The German MG34 machine-gun was a fearsome weapon, we could not lift our heads from the ground when it fired. But thank goodness everything went well and we did not have casualties. Both Fedor Popov and I decided not to go to Colonel Koretski, and neither did he call us; apparently he had left the riverbank and carried on with his business. This is how we accidentally rescued our Corps commander – but that went unnoticed, some forgot about the case while the others simply did not know about it. A runner from the battalion commander found us and passed on the order to come back to the river and advance along it, to a place that had a convenient crossing, where the tanks and the battalion would be crossing.

On 20 April the battalion received new orders to attack in a north-western direction towards Potsdam (a suburb of Berlin) and Brandenburg, and further towards Ketzin, thus enveloping Berlin from the west and completing the encirclement of the enemy's troops in that city. That was the Brigade's and the Corps' objective. The 4th Guards Tank Army had been advancing due west, to the south of Berlin, towards the Elbe river. But the first Belorussian front under G. K. Zhukov had a hard time capturing Berlin, and Stavka redirected our Army and General Rybalko's Army towards Berlin, or more precisely against its southern and western outskirts.

The terrain on this new direction of advance was drier; there were fewer natural water obstacles, but there were more villages and tidy German forests. We would not get more than three or four hours of sleep a day. It was already warm in Germany, so we slept not far from the roads in the grass. They fired on our column very frequently, either from woods or from any village that was next to the road. If this fire frustrated our further advance, we would as a rule dismount tanks, engage the enemy and force the enemy to retreat or destroy him. In most cases the Germans fled, leaving small arms, machine-guns and *Panzerfausts* behind. Such actions slowed down our advance, but on the other hand, we had to free the road from the enemy.

In one such battle Drozd and I almost kicked the bucket. They fired on us from a wood, and we immediately dismounted the tank. The 3rd company of the battalion assaulted the enemy together with my platoon (or rather, company). Everything became confused; the soldiers of our company were mixed with the soldiers of the 3rd company. I tried to restore some order, but it did not work; the platoon leaders from the 3rd company had just arrived in the battalion and I did not even know their names. We drove the enemy out of his well-dug trenches and stopped there for a brief halt, trying to see the situation and work out where the Fritzes had fled. We could see some buildings in front of us, which meant that the Germans had run there and we would have to drive them out. At that moment the enemy opened artillery fire on the trenches, but their shots so far exceeded the target. I pointed out a place some 100 metres from us, closer to the houses, to my orderly Drozd and ordered the men to dig skirmisher's trenches there, in order to close in with the Germans for the next assault. The soldiers of my platoon and then the whole company ran forward on my command. The other company, the 3rd one, stayed where it was. Why did I decide to leave the trenches? The enemy knew the location of those trenches; the first salvo went over the target, which meant that the second salvo would definitely hit us. I advised the Lieutenant from the 3rd company to leave the trenches, but he stayed behind and even took my trench, when I left it and ran to Drozd, who was already digging the dirt. It was my turn to dig deeper, so he could have a rest – it was hard to dig with a small entrenching tool while lying on the ground, but it was impossible to stand up. The Germans were firing their small arms and would immediately send anyone who stood up to his grave. Our entire company was digging in, in military terms – concentrating for an assault. Just as I expected, the Germans opened concentrated artillery fire on the trenches – apparently, they had an excellent artillery observer. The 3rd company had casualties, but we had left the dangerous spot in the right time. The orderly of that Lieutenant ran up to the skirmisher's trench that I shared with Drozd and informed us that their trench had been hit by a shell or a mine and the platoon leader was dead, while he himself had been lying next to the trench and escaped unscathed. Again my company soldiers and I were lucky. We captured the village, but did not pursue the enemy. There were plenty of such fast-paced clashes, the Germans held on to every village, hill, road crossing, a highway or railway embankment, a river or channel, even with small forces. This is why our advance was delayed every time we had to drive the enemy away.

This is exactly how it happened on one occasion: the column was stopped by small arms fire from a forest. The tank crews were afraid of the *Panzerfaust* teams attacks and did not advance further. The battalion commander ordered us to attack the enemy, and the battalion's companies together with the machine-gun platoons of Guschenkov and Greg Kes went into the forest. I do not know where company commanders Kostenko, Chernyshov and Belyakov were – the battalion commander led us. We deployed in a line and started our cautious advance through the forest. We did not see the Germans – thick bushes blocked our view. Then, I do not remember on whose command, we rushed forward shouting, firing our submachine-guns and light machine-guns. The enemy fled, abandoning his trenches; in some places there were *Panzerfaust* missiles and other weapons on the ground. Our company mixed with men of the 2nd company during the assault. Company's Sergeant Major Michael Bratchenko somehow ended up next to me; apparently the battalion commander had sent everyone who could carry weapons into action, as some men fell behind because their tanks had broken down. We walked out to the edge of the forest and I proposed moving a bit further – the forest edge was an excellent reference point for German artillery. However, the 2nd company's officers and Guschenkov and Kes disagreed with me. Before we could finish our argument, the enemy opened up with heavy artillery and mortar fire. It all happened very suddenly, and only during the barrage did the soldiers start to duck for cover. It is interesting that we did not have losses. I stood there as if I was dumbfounded, and for some time did not have any idea where I should lie down. A mine exploded at my feet. I was enveloped in smoke, finally came to my senses and threw myself under a tank that had driven up to us. Then Bratchenko and I ran a bit further on, as we were afraid that the tank would squash us. The firing quickly ceased and it became silent again. Bratchenko and I stood up and went to find out about the losses in the company. It turned out that there were no casualties, and it was quite amazing – I had not been under such an intensive strike for a long time. Guschenkov, Kes and two more officers were unharmed. I do not remember the names of those two officers as they did not stay in the battalion for long, they left soon afterwards. They had already calmed down and were about to deal with the stress with a good shot of vodka, but they did not make it, as Bratchenko and I arrived. It turned out that they were raising a glass (in fact, it was a mess lid) for the resting in peace of Evgeni Bessonov and the Sergeant Major. They had to revise the toast and raise the glass for our health when we showed up. They told me that they saw that a mine hit me, and when smoke cleared, I was not there. This is why they thought that Bratchenko had been killed and I had been blown into pieces. However, my jackboots were torn by splinters and greatcoat was also full of holes, but time and again I was unhurt, just like the rest of the company. It turned out that they ducked for cover in the German trenches. It is good that everything ended well. A runner from the battalion commander found us and passed on an order to come out of the forest and mount the tanks to continue our advance.

The Germans abandoned their positions and fled from the village. I do not remember the names of all those villages; there were many such villages along the route of our advance. If they had fled, that meant that they would put up a more stubborn resistance elsewhere. The closer we came to Berlin, the stiffer German resistance became, but they had fewer heavy Tiger and Panther tanks. They started to use more of the weak assault guns and *Panzerfausts*.

On 21 April our Brigade came up to the town of Zauhvitz and the action that followed lasted all day long. The Germans found a perfect defensive position. The terrain in front of the town was swampy and impassable for tanks; it was also impossible to dig in and hard to assault across the swamp – it was a quagmire. This swamp stretched some 300 or 400 metres before the town. The Germans placed tanks behind houses, set guns to fire over open sights, built up machine-gun nests and carefully placed snipers – they hit us hard. We were already used to going into battle with tanks and felt quite uncomfortable without them. It was one thing when a tank, a huge machine, was advancing toward the Germans, firing its main gun and machine-guns, and the enemy already felt uncomfortable, but it was quite another when we assaulted only with infantry. The Germans had machine-guns, mortars and all this was against lightly armed Soviet soldiers. We assaulted the small town of Zauhvitz straight from the march, without any clear directions – the order was just to go and capture it. Such things often happened. We deployed in an attacking line and moved towards the German defences as quickly as possible, running, before the Germans opened fire. We tried to run forward, as it is harder to hit moving targets. All of a sudden all the enemy's weapons opened fire, and the snipers started their work. In such moment a soldier wants to lie down, but I ordered 'Forward! Don't stop!' and myself advanced forward in short rushes. We had our first casualties. The soldiers moved forward in short rushes, but as the firing intensified, they just lay down, seeking cover and a more or less dry spot, where you could dig in. I saw the 2nd and the 3rd companies also ceasing their attack on our right flank; we did not have anyone on our left flank. The 'Slavs' were pinned down, and it would be hard to get them up and attack. Even more so now the snipers were active – they fired at any move in our line. You could not stand up so we had to sneak on the ground. Drozd and I crept to some house and dug in behind it. I wanted to go into the house, but they warned me not to do it – the whole ground had been pre-sighted by the Germans. I exchanged opinions with my squad leaders, and they proposed that we stayed put. I also decided to take my time and wait for artillery support from our side, a Katyusha salvo. These were not old men of the *Volkssturm* defending the ground in front of us, but experienced German troops, probably even Vlasov's troops, with whom we had already had encounters. I ordered the evacuation of the wounded and they were carried by men crawling to the forest behind us. The medical platoon's vehicle with Dr. Pankova and the medics were somewhere over there. The enemy turned out to have more forces than our command thought. It was impossible to capture the town on an important road junction with just infantry without artillery support – this was exactly what I said in my report to the battalion commander's orderly and then to the deputy chief of staff of our battalion Senior Lieutenant Michael Romanov. He sneaked out to us, and then Drozd and I were barely able to send him back safely – German fire was intensive, but we knew safe routes of retreat. I showed Romanov what a daytime assault would be like. Of course we could assault and all get killed there, but what would be the point? Who would go on to Berlin?

Why on earth did I have to attack without any support, send my guys to a certain death and be killed myself before the end of the war? Why the hell did I need this? Where were the artillery, mortars, Katyushas – they had been silent for a long time, it was time for them to act! There was no artillery support, but I was supposed to have it! Tanks did not support us either, they were cowering from enemy fire. An instruction from the battalion commander came a bit later. It said that I should stay put and wait for further orders. They had finally understood that one had to fight the war skilfully using all the resources at one's disposal. Where were company commander Chernyshov and platoon leaders Mikheev and Guschenkov? Again I had to lead the whole company, not just my platoon. There was absolutely no co-ordination between the companies of our battalion in that battle. I cannot say anything about the other battalions.

They brought the battalion's artillery to us – two 57 mm guns that the crews man-handled forwards. They put their guns behind the company, in a small forest. Then an SU-85 self-propelled gun arrived; apparently it was from the Corps' armour regiment, but I did not know the guys in its crew. However, the gun did not manage to fire a single shot, as a spare fuel tank on its back part caught fire. The vehicle could have been saved by merely dumping the fuel tank on the ground, but the gun crew did not even try to do it. Our battalion's artillery crews fired several rounds on targets in the town and even knocked something out. I was observing the enemy when a mine exploded on the breastwork of my foxhole and the edge of the foxhole even collapsed. I was buried in it, and who knows where the mine splinters flew. Everything was all right, although the mine fell only a foot short of the foxhole. I was not killed – again I was lucky, which happened time and again in that war. My orderly Drozd, who had been in another foxhole, crawled up to me, dug me out, checked if I was wounded by splinters and told me that I was lucky. I had bells ringing in my head for several days, but later the ringing disappeared.

In this manner we spent almost the whole day. Finally, in the late afternoon our artillery opened heavy fire and the Katyushas fired several salvos. We also received an order to go into action. I got my company up and the neighbouring units also joined our assault. The enemy did not fire so intensively any more, and under the cover of our artillery we quickly reached the outskirts of the place. It was already growing dark. We quickly walked through the town and reached the opposite side of it; the enemy was retreating, returning fire at us. It was hard to walk in the streets, as they were barricaded with heaps of roof tiling that fell from the roofs. Artillery and mortar crews did a great job, the enemy suffered significant losses. They should have done this a long time before, then we would not have had to lie the whole day hungry in a swamp under enemy fire.

The soldiers, excited by the battle, shared their joys. We felt like having a snack, but the 'Mount the tanks!' order came and we moved on forward to finish off the enemy. A dark night fell. We had a snack with what we had managed to grab from the houses. There was no time to relax, we had been delayed in front of Zauhvitz, but after we captured it, the roads to west and north-west were open.

The night march from Zauhvitz went well, we just drove through some villages without dismounting tanks, sometimes opening fire from the tanks, and sometimes merely kicking the Germans out of our way, and rushed forward, without delaying and engaging the enemy.

Before that, from 22 to 24 April, the Brigade and the battalion captured Spremberg, Velzov and other towns. In late April the Brigade captured Calau, Luckau, Dahme, Belzig, Luckenwalde, Lehnin, Brandenburg, Ketzin and Potsdam in three or four days.

At dawn on 22 April we approached a high railway embankment and were stopped by intensive fire. We could have quickly destroyed the German delaying force and moved on forward, but the problem was that the passage under the railway bridge was filled with sand and fortified with big logs, connected with metal girders. We did not manage to destroy that barricade. The tanks turned to the right and drove to look for a place to cross the railway, while we, the tank riders, were thrown off so we could break through the defences on the embankment. That time it was the 2nd and the 3rd companies and Lieutenant Popov's machine-gunners that captured the embankment. I crossed the embankment after the 3rd company. Lehnin village was behind the embankment; the 2nd and the 3rd companies assaulted the village right from the embankment, while I moved a bit to the right with my company, on the road that went out from that village. Three or four T-34 tanks arrived at the scene in that moment, and sitting on one of them was our political officer Captain Gerstein. The tanks stopped, Gerstein jumped off the tank and for some reason shouted: 'Bessonov, quickly get on the tanks, quickly!' We 'saddled' the tanks and moved forward. I was on the first tank with some of my men, while Captain Gerstein and the rest of the company were on the other tanks. I do not remember where the battalion commander and company commander were at that time. We rode on tanks for some time and all of a sudden came under fire from trenches on the right side of the road. The tanks stopped, I ordered: 'Dismount! Fire! Fire!' and the whole company ran towards those trenches, firing non-stop from our submachine-guns. Right in front of me there was a Fritz in a trench. I tried to cut him down with my German submachine-gun, the one that used to hang over my bed during training, but apparently during the skirmish at the embankment some sand had got into the bolt. I jerked the bolt, pulled the trigger, but it did not fire. The German did not think long, grabbed his rifle and aimed at me. I had a thought flashing in my head: 'This is the end, Bessonov, your life is over.' Right at that time a submachine-gun burst sounded in the air and the German dropped dead to the bottom of his trench. It turned out that it was Drozd who cut him down with a Soviet PPSh submachine-gun, which never jammed in battle, in any situation. Why the hell did I carry that German submachine-gun? We jumped across the trenches, some Germans fled, while the rest were killed. Andrey took away my submachine-gun, took out the clip and threw the submachine-gun away. He gave me the clip, as its ammo could be used in my Walther pistol. We lay down after capturing the trenches, as we were too exhausted to run, but then Gerstein arrived at the scene and ordered: 'Forward, Bessonov, don't stop, we must capture those houses! Come on, get soldiers up and attack. Faster!' I had never seen him in the attacking line before that.

I got my soldiers up and we rushed into those houses, which were some 250 or 300 metres away. There were just three or four houses there. The Germans fled; even their two self-propelled guns drove away at high speed on a road that had trees planted on its sides. The alley went to the village, which we could see at some 300 metres.

One self-propelled gun managed to knock out one of our T-34 tanks in an ambush. The tank was burnt out and the whole crew was killed. All these things happened before our eyes – it was so horrible that I do not even want to write about it. We moved forward a bit and dug in by a hedge that edged an open field that stretched to the next village. I sent one squad down the lane to check out where the Fritzes were, but the squad came under fire and dug in on both sides of the lane. The 2nd and 3rd companies of the battalion arrived and dug in on our left flank. We did not have any further orders. We had time to feed the soldiers. We found some food, cooked it and satisfied our hunger.

At midday a regiment of 37 mm anti-aircraft guns, eight guns and eight trucks, quickly rushed pass our positions. I have no idea why the regiment commander sent them there. The trucks stopped in the open, the guns turned their barrels towards the enemy and opened fire on the village. They did not fire for long, as the Germans returned fire with artillery and all the crews were killed or wounded, and almost all the guns were destroyed. Then the commander of the regiment arrived on the scene – he was drunk and could barely stand on his feet. An orderly soldier was with him. This Colonel behaved in a strange manner: first he ran out into the field, but the Germans fired on him and he had to return to the gardens. After that he started to run back and forth along our line and try to get the battalion to attack. As we did not have any orders from our command for attack, I ran off to get out of harm's way, to the combat outpost and lay down there. The Colonel was getting more and more angry, waving his pistol in the air, cursing and shouting, but no one from our battalion reacted and no one was going to obey him. The Colonel got so mad that he grabbed the submachine-gun from his orderly and executed 3rd platoon leader Lieutenant Antipov on the spot in his foxhole. Antipov was around 35 years old. He was a calm and slow person who had just recently arrived in the battalion. He was a quiet and regular officer. I wanted to kill that Colonel or at least wound him; I even ran forward, a bit closer to the enemy, so that my shot could be perceived as a German one, especially given the fact that they continued firing at us. But my hand did not lift against my countryman. I could not do it; I just did not have the stomach for it. The deputy chief of staff, Senior Lieutenant Mikhail Romanov, also wanted to shoot the Colonel, but, apparently, he also did not have the stomach to shoot a Soviet citizen, even such a filthy one. Soon after that officers from the anti-aircraft regiment staff came running and took the Colonel away by force to their HQ. I never saw him again, but our comrade was killed, not in battle, but by a drunken bastard. This Colonel also destroyed his regiment by being drunk – a sober person just could not do such a stupid thing. There are really some bastards in this world... I heard later that the Colonel was eventually brought before a court-martial.

After the Colonel was taken away by his staff officers, a female medic came along with a wounded soldier from an anti-aircraft gun crew. She ran several more times to the destroyed guns, each time coming back with a wounded soldier, carrying him on a raincoat or on her back. She was creeping there under enemy fire and apparently got tired, or maybe she was scared. Anyway, she sat on the bottom of my foxhole and burst into tears. After she calmed down a bit, she asked for a smoke and then for a drink. She stayed in the foxhole for a little while and then again went on to rescue more wounded, saying farewell with: 'Lieutenant, wish me luck, so that I might survive this bloodbath.' A brave girl.

Soon afterwards the battalion left that area, and again we drove on tanks in the night to complete our tasks. However, that night march ended up with a comedy, as people say, enough to make a cat laugh – we were driving almost the whole night (the tank riders were dozing off) and came back to exactly the same place from which we had started our march in the evening. I do not remember such an embarrassment for the Brigade's or the tank regiment's staffs in other operations. It is quite impossible to get lost in Germany: all roads have road signs with names of localities, directions and distances. This was how we again lost time, again falling behind our schedule. Then we had to speed up and complete the mission. That time I was not in front of the Brigade – another company was the Brigade's vanguard. War is war, all kinds of things happened, even funny things. Regardless of how hard it was for us, junior officers and privates, we had our sense of humour. As soon as we had a break from fighting, one could hear laughter, jokes and stories – Lieutenant Grigori Kes, the machine-gun platoon leader from the battalion's machine-gun company, was especially skilful in that. A happy and cheerful person, he was respected by all.

The enemy's air force rarely raided our column any more. The Red Army captured most of their airfields, and only a few airfields or highway strips remained in German hands. We mostly had to fight the ground troops of the enemy, but on 23 April the German air force did deliver a horrible strike on the Brigade's column. Apparently, it was the Luftwaffe's last strike, their swan song. We thought that the Germans could not employ their air force any more, but it did happen, and we suffered significant losses. The entire Brigade's column was on the move in daytime, some companies were on tanks, others were on Studebaker trucks. The Brigade's staff with the Brigade's commander Colonel Turkin and his deputy (political officer) Lieutenant Colonel Skryago were also there in the column. As soon as the column entered a small forest, enemy aircraft appeared in the air. These were fighter-bombers, some ten or twelve aircraft. The planes dived, dropped their bombs and prepared for the second dive. Even before the planes appeared, an air raid alarm sounded, but it was a bit too late. The tank column stopped and we quickly dismounted the tanks, but almost no one made it away from the road. We were lucky that the Germans dropped their bombs without aiming; the bombs fell far from the road way over their target.

I had time to run just several metres from the road, when I bumped into Lieutenant-Colonel Skryago. He was also running from the road, but he apparently got exhausted and was short of breath, as he was a fat guy with a big belly. He asked me: 'Help me, Bessonov, I do not know where my orderly is.' Before we could make a step, a Fritz plane appeared. It flew along the road at extremely low altitude, almost hitting the treetops, and fired its machine-guns. Skryago and I just froze, we were standing there as if we were dumbstruck. We were just standing and looking at the bullets kicking up mud, and we saw those bullets hitting the dust closer and closer to us. We both thought that this was the end for us, as the fire was very dense, but a miracle happened again – the burst stopped just a few metres short. The plane soared upwards to take another dive. Yes, we were extremely lucky just before the end of the war! The Lieutenant-Colonel and I regained our senses and ran further from the road. I literally had to pull him, as he could barely move his feet. I saw two or three more or less thick trees and we lay down behind them. The air raid ended soon, but the battalion had losses. Lieutenant Colonel Skryago went to the staff, while I went to my battalion. It was good that my company did not have losses. As soon as we were about to mount the tanks, another air-raid warning sounded in the air, and numerous enemy aircraft appeared in the air. Soldiers scattered running in the forest, while I with Senior Lieutenant Anatoly Kashintsev, commander of the mortar company of the battalion, jumped into a trench right on the road. Then we ran in short rushes further and hid in another trench (apparently, the Germans had dug them even before our arrival). Suddenly a big bullet fell from the breastwork to the bottom of the trench. When I picked it up, it was still hot. We were again lucky that the bullet did not hit us; because of the noise of the air raid we had not even heard the bullet's whistling. We decided to leave that trench as well, ran further from the road and lay down behind a tree. The soldiers also scattered in the forest. I lost my men from sight; everyone saved their lives by themselves. The air raid was awful. The planes continued their assault, dropping bombs and firing incendiary shells at tanks. German pilots dived almost to the very ground and fired their machine-guns. They fired not only at the highway, but also at the forest at the road. Planes dived in groups of three and five, firing long machine-gun bursts not only at the tanks, but also at the pinned-down infantry. I had not seen such an air raid since the Lvov battles. It is hard to say how long the raid was, but apparently it lasted at least two or three hours. Our fighters were not there, we only had one 37 mm anti-aircraft gun, but it did not help much. After the air raid we went back to our units. Both Kashintsev and I and the soldiers went to the road. We saw people standing around the bomb crater, which was on the trench where we had previously hidden and heard them talking about us. We arrived at the scene, both safe and sound. Then they started to guess who had been killed in that trench and decided that it was a truck driver. I was again lucky – intuition and luck saved my life.

We started to check the casualties. Casualties were significant, both in personnel and equipment: over ten trucks were burnt out, and several tanks were destroyed. A bomb exploded next to a T-34 tank, the tank was lifted up and crashed down with all its weight on the men that were hiding under it, while the main gun was almost torn away from the turret. After the explosion it stood vertically up from the turret. It must have been a large bomb if it had enough explosive energy to lift and move a 30-ton tank. There were dead and wounded among the tank riders, truck drivers and tank crews, and we searched the forest for the remaining dead and wounded. Luckily, in our company and in the battalion just a few were killed. Wounded were gathered next to the medical truck in order to send them to the rear – there were more wounded than dead. When we put ourselves in order and could continue the march, the column left the ill-fated forest. There was an open field in front of us, and we tried to drive across it as quickly as possible, fearing another air raid. Indeed, three Messerschmidt fighters appeared. However, the 37 mm anti-aircraft automatic gun crew set an example of courage and bravery in that situation. The crew quickly prepared the gun for fire, and when the Germans started to dive on us, they opened fire with tracer shells. The first Messer could not stand the fire and turned to the side, the other two planes also ceased their attacks. I was standing behind a Studebaker truck and saw the tracer shells flying accurately towards their target. Fighters tried to dive two or three more times, but could not take the fire from the anti-aircraft gun and flew away. Our guys did a great job; they were not afraid of the air raid and forced the German pilots to cease their attacks on the column. I should mention that during that assault the tank riders did not scatter, but stood behind the tanks and trucks, observing the duel. It was the Germans that did not have nerves or courage against our anti-aircraft crew. When the planes left, we moved forward, as we had to catch up with the schedule. I was not in the vanguard with my platoon or rather company. Sometimes the battalion commander Major Kozienko would order: 'Bessonov – forward!' and show me the route of advance on the map, pointing at the place for a stop and where I should wait for the main body of the battalion and the Brigade, but it happened more rarely than before.

That time company commander Nikolai Chernyshov again was absent from the company. The battalion commander called me up and gave me an order to move forward on three tanks with the company and Fedor Popov's machine-gun platoon from battalion's machine-gun company. Tank regiment commander Stolyarov and the Brigade's commander Colonel Turkin were also there – Turkin was back from the hospital after being wounded in February 1945 when a *Panzerfaust* team destroyed his APC. I really did not want to go first: I had only few soldiers let and I wanted to spare at least them till the end of the war, but I had my orders and I had to fulfil them.

We were moving forward successfully, everything was quiet, and as always 'all of a sudden' we were caught by enemy fire before we could reach the forest. Our tanks stopped, the tank riders dismounted. Everyone stood behind the tanks – we had to find out what was going on. The enemy was firing, mostly from small arms, from the forest on the right of the highway. We had to drive the enemy out of his positions, as the whole Brigade was about to arrive. Lieutenant Popov also dismounted his platoon, took his two Maxim machine-guns from the tanks and we prepared to assault the Germans, but their positions could not be seen in the forest. We made a deal with the tank crews that they would slowly move forward, while the tank riders would use them for cover. Two soldiers were to sit on each tank in order to have a better view of the terrain and guard the tanks from *Panzerfaust* teams.

This was the manner in which we started our slow advance towards the enemy. We reached a fruit garden, the fruit trees were in full blossom – it was late April and the weather in Germany was warm. Behind the garden there was an open field, which continued all the way to a village. Popov's platoon and our company did not go further but lay down in the orchard. The enemy's snipers were delivering aimed rifle fire. The tanks also stopped, fearing *Panzerfaust* attack. They did not want to die, but did we, the infantry, want to? As it turned out later, there were no *Panzerfausts* there, just eight or twelve snipers. Popov's machine-gun platoon opened fire on the forest edge, and half of the company, some twelve or fourteen soldiers rushed to assault on my command, while approximately the same number of men gave them fire support. There was an open field up to the forest. The soldiers ran into the German trenches, and killed some of them; others fled, while one Fritz was taken prisoner. The Fritz was a stubborn one; when my soldier ran up to his trench, he fired at him at point-blank range, but luckily, only lightly wounded him in his forearm. They pulled the Fritz out of his foxhole and brought him to me; he was armed with a sniper rifle. I was stressed and angry after the assault and shouted at the German, mostly in Russian, and then hit him twice on his ear. They bandaged our wounded soldier. This was a strong and brave soldier, a former Ukrainian partisan. He would normally fire from his RPD (the Degtyarev infantry machine-gun) on the move during an assault. Normally we fired from that machine-gun lying on the ground, as it weighed 12.5 kilograms with the ammo drum. It is a pity that I forgot the name of the guy.

I started to interrogate the Fritz, as I knew a bit of German. He had fourteen decorations, and had received one decoration, the Iron Cross, personally from the hands of Adolf Hitler. He had been fighting against the Red Army for a long time – a pure Nazi, member of the German Nazi party. He got another box on the ears from me. In general, I never beat up or harmed prisoners, but in this case I lost my self-control.

The main body of the Brigade arrived, including our battalion. I reported the results of the battle and the captured Fritz to the company and battalion commanders. Guys from the Brigade's intelligence section came running to take the prisoner away, I told them to go to hell, but the battalion commander ordered me to give the prisoner to the intelligence officers, saying that it was Turkin's order.

The Brigade did not go deeper into the forest, as it received a new order – to continue its attack in a different direction. As soon as the Brigade's column formed on the road, Il-2 Shturmoviks appeared in the air. Apparently, they mistook us for Germans and started to deploy for attack, and they were at least 20 to 25 planes. Soldiers ran out into the field from the highway, waved their hats, hands and even shouted. We did not have recognition flares to show them that we were Russian. Finally, someone fired a green flare, then some more, and this saved us from big trouble. The group leader realized that we were friendly troops and stopped its dive, followed by other pilots. They formed their group, waved their wingtips at us and flew away. All is well that ends well.

The Brigade also moved on. It was probably the other battalion of the Brigade that was in the vanguard, not us. I do not know anything about the combat operations of the other two battalions of the Brigade, which is why I do not write about them. I had the impression that our battalion was always the first in battles, as well as my company. The only thing I know about the other battalions is that they also had losses. In the following battles we went into battle in turns: one battalion was in action, the second would be in reserve, while the third one would be resting, waiting for its turn to go into battle.

On one of those days our battalion was resting and the 2nd and the 3rd battalions were in action. We were staying at several houses at a roadside. The soldiers went to sleep after dinner, while I got under a truck, put some straw on the ground and also fell asleep. In the evening, or rather in the night, Alexander Guschenkov, the machine-gun platoon leader of our company, found me, woke me up and dragged me into a house for a snack. The party was in full swing. Some seven to nine men sat around the table: Tolya Kashintsev, Alexei Belyakov and others. There were many snacks on the table and a whole battery of vodka and wine bottles. The officers were happy to see me, made me sit down, poured vodka and gave me some snacks. They wouldn't let me go from the table. It had been a long time since we had all gathered for such a party. I wanted to go to sleep, as we had to go into action the next morning, but they did not let me go. Alexander Guschenkov showed me the door of a safe in the wall. He tried to open it, but it did not work. I proposed blowing up the safe's door with a hand-grenade, but it was impossible to set it there – the door was straight and there were no hinges. We started to break the brick wall with crowbars and finally broke the safe's door open. There were no valuables in the safe, just two or three shares of Saint-Petersburg-Moscow Railway, which each cost 100 thousand Tsar's roubles. The shares dated back to the beginning of the century. That was the first time in my life that I saw shares, I had not even heard of them in those times. I don't know where those shares ended up – either someone of those who were at the table took them or just threw them away.

As our forward battalions were far away and our company did not have wheeled vehicles, in the morning my soldiers found some horses with carriages, mostly coaches, and we travelled on in them. Some soldiers had the great idea of putting on tuxedos and high hats and some other funny stuff. I was laughing together with them, looking at this masquerade. Some cars bypassed us, then they stopped, and a General escorted by several Colonels from the Staff of our Tank Army emerged from them. They called me up (company commander Chernyshov was not there), scolded me and ordered me to stop the 'masquerade', but permitted us to use the coaches. We threw the fancy clothes away and travelled in the coaches before we reached the other battalions. It was our turn to go into battle. In a village we stopped for a break to refuel the tanks, have a meal and replace ammo in tanks. After a brief rest, during which the soldiers stocked themselves with butter, cheese and fried poultry, and we moved on forward.

I was standing behind a tank turret, while right behind me was the company's medic 'Brotherly Heart'. The Germans launched an artillery strike on us. A shell exploded behind our tank and the medic was wounded in his back with its splinters. No one else was hurt. I stopped the tank, we took the medic into a house and bandaged him with bandages from first-aid kits. I left a soldier behind just in case so that he could send the medic to our medical platoon and catch up with us later. Sometimes I allowed such things. Had it not been for 'Brotherly Heart', the splinters would have ended up in my back. I was lucky again.

We waded a shallow and narrow river, probably the Spree, and rushed into a small village, but were stopped by small arms fire from basements of houses. The soldiers pointed out targets to the tank crew, and after several shots from main guns the German fire ceased. The company walked to the edge of the village. The battalion commander arrived in the company and shouted: 'Come on, Bessonov, forward, don't linger!' We mounted our tanks and continued our journey. Clashes with Germans were unceasing, we only had short breaks. We again ran into some Germans, but as soon as they saw our attacking line supported by tanks, they all threw their arms in the air. I formed up this fearsome army of 80-100 men and ordered them to lay down their weapons. These were *Volkssturm* – old unshaven men with grey hair, who were shouting '*Hitler kaputt!*' The battalion's political officer, Gerstein, arrived in the meantime, and shouted to me: 'Do not execute them, do not execute them, Bessonov!' As if I had been executing prisoners the whole war! I did not have a slightest thought of harming those old men – I have never been a fiend! On my command, the Germans picked up their bag packs and I sent them '*nach Haus*' – home. I did not have time for them. The old Germans were very happy to hear the order and quickly disappeared.

In general, the battles were heavy and the Germans put up stubborn resistance. That was the only case when such a large number of soldiers surrendered. Even in this case it was only privates and recruits that surrendered, while officers and NCOs slipped away, they were afraid of us. I also saw boys of 14 or 15 years old from the Western Ukraine, dressed in German uniform. They served in anti-aircraft artillery, which was in action against the Russian, and American air force. They also served as telephone and radio operators and observers.

In early April 1945 they sent a Major to our battalion to be the deputy battalion commander for personnel. General Lelyushenko, commander of our Tank Army, sent this Major to our battalion as a punishment for some wrongdoing at the office of the head of cultural section of the Army. He did not fight the war for long with us. Once we rushed storming into a village, where Germans put up insig-nificant resistance, firing *Panzerfaust* missiles. Our tanks were waiting for the company to drive the Germans out of the houses. Again my soldiers and I were the vanguard of the battalion and the Major somehow happened to be with us. He ordered us to move forward in that village, but I told him that we had to look around, spot the enemy's weapon emplacements and only after that we could start an assault. We entered a house with him and my men; I walked up to a window and started to look at the nearby houses. I did not like the feel of it, I don't know why, but I ordered: 'Quickly out of this room, go to the other room, that one!' The Major first tried to resist, but then followed us, and then an explosion, followed by another one, shook the air. It grew quiet again. We peeped into the room that we had just left and saw that *Panzerfaust* rounds had destroyed the wall at which we had just stood. What rescued me? Intuition? Luck? The Major again started to hurry me with the assault, but I tried to talk him out of it, saying that first we had to fire on the house windows at least with submachine-guns. The Germans had not yet abandoned those houses. He did not believe me and decided to capture the nearest house with several soldiers, telling me that the house was empty. As soon as he walked into an open spot from behind our house, the Germans fired on him; he was wounded and lay down in a ditch, calling for us to come to his rescue. We pulled him into a safe place, bandaged him and I ordered my soldiers to carry him into our rear. The Major was lightly wounded in the buttocks. He thanked me as he said good-bye and acknowledged that he had been wrong.

After his departure we fired on the German ambush with machine-guns and kicked the Fritzes out of that village. Some of them fled, others were killed during the battle, while some were taken prisoners. Under cover from one team of soldiers, the other assault team would reach a building and toss hand-grenades in its windows. It was not an easy task and took a great deal of courage and bravery! Tanks also helped us with fire from their main guns; my soldiers pointed out targets for them. I had casualties, but I fulfilled the order. The battalion commander walked up to us. We laughed at the wound of the deputy battalion commander in his buttocks. With everyone laughing, I told the story of Major's wound and how he groaned, being scratched in his ass and almost dying from fright. The battalion commander gave us a new mission. We were briefed and again moved forward, in front of the Brigade.

The end of the war was drawing near, but while the Berlin operation continued, we were in battle every day, breaking the enemy's resistance and losing men and equipment in battles. Most of the population had left the houses around Berlin. Those who stayed in their houses and apartments hung white linen out of their windows, showing that they surrendered and were at the winners' mercy. Some German civilians informed us about where German soldiers had dug in, who was a Nazi, who had tortured Russian prisoners of war or those who were sent to Germany for forced labour. All kinds of things happened.

The offensive continued successfully. Sometimes we drove forward in one column, which had the Brigade's staff, medical vehicles and the battalion's field kitchens in it. To be honest, I did not like such a concentration of vehicles, as it only frustrated the combat companies. We also did not need the kitchens, as we mostly fed on the German cattle and poultry. The soldiers had a great time in that respect, they cooked what they wanted. We mostly ate poultry – geese, ducks and turkeys. We ate pork more rarely. In battles we continued to guard the tanks from the *Panzerfaust* teams and point out targets for them. I was again ahead on three tanks with my company, while the main body of the Brigade was setting a rest place. No one would tell me what to do, no one threatened me or advised me – it was nice!

During the day of 24 April, 1945, we rushed into Schmergov. The Fritzes fled and we captured the village straight away. We moved forward a bit and stopped in front of a water obstacle – the Havel channel. There was no bridge, while the channel was up to 150 metres wide and was deep and navigable. Before that channel we had already crossed the Bober, Spree, Neisse, channels Teltov, Hogenzoller, Hute and other water obstacles. Parez and Ketzin towns were on the other side – these were our last towns on the route of our Brigade. The Brigade was supposed to join up with units of the first Belorussian front at Ketzin, thus completing the encirclement of Berlin. The main body of the battalion, the artillery battalion and the remaining tanks of the tank regiment drove up. The 2nd and the 3rd battalions were sent to Brandenburg in the meantime. There they encountered strong resistance from the enemy – the Germans had plenty of infantry and even Tiger tanks, but united the battalions drove the Germans out of the city. The battle for the city was intense; the enemy had numerical superiority, but Brandenburg was captured and the enemy suffered heavy losses. I learnt about all those things from the stories of my friends from these battalions.

Colonel Turkin, Majors Kozienko and Stolyarov and other officers walked up to the channel. All was silent. The battalion commander called me up and asked me where Chernyshov was. I answered that I did not know and I was the only officer in the company. Major Kozienko ordered me to find several good swimmers, volunteers, cross the channel and bring a ferry on the other side of a channel in order to transport the rest of the company. The Germans were nowhere to be seen; no one was firing at us. Three or four brave guys volunteered, they swam across the channel; no one fired on them on the other bank and they were able to bring the ferry to our side.

Kozienko sent me across with a dozen soldiers. We did not know the capacity of the ferry, but eventually we crossed the channel safely. We went up to a mound, lay down behind it and spotted four Tiger tanks ahead of us. They were standing in a garden some 60 or 80 metres from us. The gardens were in full blossom and we could not see the tanks clearly. I sent a soldier back across the channel to report about the tanks to the battalion commander. The tanks were standing there quietly and did not show any signs of life. The entire company crossed the channel and we lay down behind this natural shelter. The battalion's battery – two 57 mm guns under the command of Lieutenants Kharmakulov and Isaev – also crossed the channel. Company commander Chernyshov also finally came running to us, he looked around and told me: 'Let's assault, not towards the tanks, but to the right, towards the city.' I objected, saying that the tanks would kill us there and squash us all with their tracks. I told him that we had to wait for our artillery to knock the tanks out first. The problem was that the tank crews of our tank regiment were really bad shooters. The Tigers, in contrast, first damaged one tank on the other side and then knocked out the second one. Lieutenants Shakulo, Mikheev and Guschenkov were away in hospitals, and Chernyshov and I were the only officers that remained in the company. Chernyshov ran to the right flank of the company and got Shakulo's platoon up to attack. Soldiers started to advance in short rushes towards Ketzin between the ugly houses and structures, closer to the road. He should not have done it, he could have lost his soldiers and have died himself, but he did not even listen to me, just cursed at me, while I could not stop him. I did not send my soldiers to attack in such a careless manner – the war was about to be over, why should I have shown such bravado? Chernyshov, however, was out of control and would often make a show.

The events that followed were even more horrible than I could imagine. I had not seen such a thing before at the front. A German APC arrived and at first we did not pay attention to it, as they normally had a machine-gun mounted on them. But all of a sudden the APC started to shoot fireballs and flame and I realized that this was a flame-thrower — a horrible weapon that burnt people to ashes and could even burn a tank. The temperature of the flame was very high, if I am not mistaken, it was around 1,000 degrees Celsius. The APC threw flame several times. It was good that it was at first behind a house and the company's soldiers were out of its sight. When the APC emerged from behind the house, we were extremely lucky. Before it could throw flame at the soldiers who had not yet made to follow Chernyshov's command and at my platoon, two shots sounded from the other side of the channel, and the APC's flame liquid container exploded, killing all of its crew. The APC was knocked out by the battalion's artillery battery. They did a great job by not missing with the first shot, otherwise we would have been in big trouble. The enemy's tanks fired several rounds against the other side of the channel, turned and departed from our sight. Chernyshov again gave us the 'Forward!' order; we all stood up and entered the town. With no enemy armour in sight it was a different story. There was no enemy infantry there. As we were passing by the spot at which the flame-thrower fired, we saw the burnt bodies of our soldiers, mere ashes. It was an awful sight, although I had seen a lot of sights in the course of the war. Luckily, there were only three to five burnt soldiers, but they died because of the stupidity of one foolish commander, following an idiotic order. Later the incident was forgotten and no one recalled it. But I still recall that battle and those soldiers burnt by the flame-thrower even 60 years later…

At first I wanted to move forward through the gardens, not in the streets, just in case, but it did not work. Every garden with a mansion was separated from the next one by a fence, a high and strong metal mesh. We had to move forward along the street, and we did not even check the houses, which were locked — so much was Chernyshov hurrying us. It was late, but it was still light. In some places we had to fire on individual targets. Some random Fritzes were still there sometimes. I have already written that the town of Ketzin was part of our combat mission, and we were supposed to meet the troops of the first Belorussian front in the town. The town was captured by practically a single company without tanks, because they were only just starting to cross the channel on the ferries that were brought up.

The Berlin–Prague Operation

Late in the evening of 24 April, 1945, my platoon and company established contact with cavalry reconnaissance and the tanks of the first Belorussian front. Thus, Berlin was fully encircled by Soviet troops. That was the day when I was wounded.

THE END OF THE WAR

We were standing in a group by a house, such things happened in built-up areas, although one should never do that. Company commander Chernyshov and telephone or radio operators for communication with battalion commander were also there. I sent the company's men forward – we should not have stood in such a big group. I was rescued by the fact that I had walked several steps from the house in order to follow the company's men and had not hung around Chernyshov. In that very moment a random shell hit the house's wall – whether German or Russian, its explosion cut many men down. I was wounded by its splinters along with several other men from signals platoon; several men were killed. Again, I believe that I was lucky, which happened time and again in that war. My belt buckle saved my life. The splinter went through it and got stuck in it, severely tearing the skin on my stomach. The blow was so strong that it bent me double. The other splinter hit my leg; the third one seriously damaged three fingers on my left hand, almost tearing them off. Some other smaller splinters hit me was well.

They bandaged me on the spot, and the battalion's doctor Pankova sent me in a truck to a hospital along with the other wounded. First they sent me to a transit hospital in Luckenwalde, which was in the building of a former German hospital. I should say that we were lucky in our journey to the hospital, too: Germans, who were wandering in forests, abandoning Berlin in small groups, could have caught us. The Germans would merely execute the wounded; they were angry enough to do that. There was a rumour in Luckenwalde that some trucks with wounded were under fire or were even destroyed, but our vehicle made it safely either before Germans appeared on the highway or after they had left the highway and disappeared into the forest. There were many wounded in Luckenwalde and we all sat in an underground corridor, from which we were transported to the other hospitals by trucks. I sat on the floor with my back against the wall, sometimes sleeping or dozing off, as it was already almost morning. The medical inspection was under way; depending on the wound we were distributed among different hospitals and that set the order of evacuation. Several doctors walked up to me as well. A female doctor, a Major of the Medical Corps, asked me about my wound and how long I had been at the front. I answered her and she gave an instruction to another doctor to evacuate me immediately with the first truck available.

During the night of 26 April I was sent to the stationary hospital of the 4th Guards Tank Army in Sarau, also in Germany, but deep in our rear. We arrived there around noon. I met several soldiers from my company and my platoon; some of then had been in the hospital from the very first day of the offensive, 16 April, while others had arrived earlier. I gave my pistol and map case to one of the soldiers. I unclipped my decorations from my tunic and wrapped them in a handkerchief together with my party membership card and other papers. First the girls washed the others and me in a steam bath – it was hard to wash myself with one hand. They took my uniforms (tunic, trousers, field cap and probably greatcoat) for fumigation to kill all the insects and threw away all my underwear and foot wrappings, giving me new underwear after the steam bath.

They put me on a table in a dressing room. A surgeon, Major of Medical Corps, started to inspect me and gave nurses instructions about the bandages. One of the nurses asked my permission to have a look at my decorations in the handkerchief, and told the Major: 'Look how many decorations he has.' The Major asked me how long I had been at the front, and I answered that I started in 1943, was lightly wounded but never went further than the Brigade's medical platoon. 'Yeah, ' he said, 'For the first time in this war I see a Lieutenant, a platoon leader and a company commander, also a tank rider, who was seriously wounded for the first time after two years at the front.' They bandaged me and the Major said that I should again come and see him at lunch, and then they took me to my room. I put on my old uniform that had already been 'fried'. They put me in a hospital room that had three beds. The hospital was located in a three- or four-storey building. I think that it had been an apartment house before, but the German inhabitants had abandoned it with the approach of the Soviet troops. The beds had linen, a pillow and a blanket. As Lieutenant Guschenkov would tell me, it would be good if I was lightly wounded, go into a hospital to sleep on a clean bed with clean sheets! This was exactly the place that he wished for me.

I picked up my pistol and map case from the soldier. I went to my soldiers, we had a talk, and I was invited to celebrate our meeting in the evening at dinner. I went to lunch with the Major – the head of the hospital's department, who had received me. We walked into a room, where the hospital's doctors were eating, and he introduced me and said that I would eat there together with them and pointed me at my place at the table. Doctors in officers' ranks, up to Lieutenant Colonel, mostly ladies, were sitting at the table. They were all much older than I was. The doctors did not object and started to ask questions. I had to briefly tell them my life story, it was quite brief – at that time I was not even 22 years old. This is how I started attending the doctors' canteen, not the ordinary canteen for wounded men and officers. I do not know why they gave me such a privilege. The ladies were very friendly with me; they treated me as an equal and only called me by my first name. They were always busy – the war was still going on and wounded kept on coming in, thus we rarely met in the canteen. But when I met them, I was very embarrassed by their attention, I was not used to such things. I had become alien to people, especially ladies. I slept a lot, enjoying my soft bed. I would hang around the town of Sarau with my soldiers; the town was small, there were few German inhabitants, but there were many Russian women, who were gathered from the whole of Germany in order to go back to Motherland, to the Soviet Union. In the evenings we would watch films in the hospital's cinema theatre, both Russian and German films. It is interesting that a few days later my wounded orderly Drozd arrived at the same hospital. He told me that if I got wounded, he would also be either killed or wounded by the Germans. He got off with a wound. I was glad to see him. I remembered Sarafanov, Ishmuhammetov and Chechin from the other company. Five to seven men from our battalion were there. Sometimes we would hang around the town together. On one of those days I met the Major, the one that had been wounded in his buttocks. He had recovered from the wound and was again leading the Army's song and dance ensemble. The Major started to complain to me that some of the singers in the ensemble were giving him a hard time; he was afraid of being beaten up and asked for my help. We walked into a room where the ensemble stayed. Drozd, Chechin and some others were there with me. There was a scandal there again, artists were cursing the Major, I do not remember why, probably because of his affairs with women in the ensemble. The Major addressed me with a request to appease the men in the ensemble. I intimidated them and said that if they continued their disrespectful behaviour, they would have to face my guys and me. It became quiet and we left. I think they took our threats seriously and there were no more complaints.

I am paying so much attention to my stay in the hospital because I would like to emphasize the good care of doctors and nurses and how well they treated the wounded, regardless of their rank. For the first time after long years of military service and war I was in an environment that I had not seen for a long time – quiet, peaceful and slow-paced hospital life. No enemy air force. No bullets whistling in the air, no mines or shells were exploding around. You could sleep as much as you wanted; the only thing to remember was not to miss breakfast, lunch and dinner. You could watch films in the evenings. After a film I would come to my room, take off my jackboots and uniform and lie down on my bed with linen sheets, feather mattress and a pillow. I would receive a new bandage at a specially specified time from young and attentive nurses. It was bliss, real paradise. But I, a fool, wanted to go back to my unit as soon as possible, as if the war would not end without me. But the Major was not in a hurry to let me go, telling me that he would only discharge me when my wounds were fully healed. He would say: 'Why are you in such a hurry, you have fought enough, the war would be over soon, and you deserve your rest.' Actually, I do not know myself why I was in such a hurry. Later, when I arrived at the battalion and reported my arrival to

Captain Grigoriev, battalion's chief of staff, he was very amazed and said that they were not expecting me, as they thought I would be sent to another unit from the hospital. They had also deleted me from the personnel lists of the battalion. Battalion commander Major Kozienko and his deputy in political affairs Captain Gerstein also reacted to my return quite indifferently. I was not even recommended for a decoration for the Berlin operation; they either forgot it, or did it on purpose, I have no idea. It's like that.

Berlin's garrison surrendered on 2 May. The unconditional surrender of Nazi Germany was signed in Karlhorst, a suburb of Berlin, on 9 May. The Presidium of the Supreme Soviet of the USSR declared the day of 9 May VICTORY DAY.

The Major of the Medical Corps, the head of one of the hospital's departments, did release me from the hospital before the end of the war. Finally, on 12 May, I was officially discharged from the hospital along with several other soldiers from our company, including my orderly Drozd. On all kinds of transport, sometimes by train, sometimes on bicycles, or hitchhiking, we started our journey to Prague. In Dresden we stole a car. The cars were gathered in a square under guard of the local Soviet command, and we stole a car from under their noses. We did not enjoy the car ride for long, as we ran out of fuel, and we had to abandon it on the highway. We travelled, hitchhiking on a truck almost all the way to Prague and arrived at the battalion on 13 or 14 May, 1945.

Most of the battalion's officers were happy to see me, except for the battalion's command, as if I had not fought under their command for almost two years. I managed to obtain by request spirits from the logistics platoon leader and we organized a small party to celebrate both Victory and my return. Lieutenants Guschenkov, Mikheev, Tsikanovski, Popov, Kes, Zemtsev, Senior Lieutenants Chernyshov and Kashintsev, platoon leader Lieutenant Ivan Akazin (he arrived in the company after I was wounded) and others, including the company's Sergeant Major Mikhail Bratchenko, were present. Lieutenant Petr Shakulo was still recovering from his wounds in a hospital. By the way, the first ones to be transferred to the reserve because of wounds in September and October 1945, were Alexander Guschenkov and Ivan Akazin. Alexander was already 31 years old in 1945 and he had some seven or eight wounds, so he tried his best to leave the army, while Ivan's right wrist did not function properly again after his wound.

We partied for a long time; someone made a trip to a Czech village and brought more wine, vodka and snacks. I think we partied till dawn – some people were coming, some were leaving, while some were sobering up and coming back to the table. For some reason they had not had a party without me, they were always busy in battles. The war for the battalion was over on 11 May – they had to finish some Germans off after 9 May. Most of the battalion's soldiers were liberated prisoners of war, Soviet people from concentration camps that abounded around Berlin. We were all happy that we survived, but at the same time we grieved about the dead. As they told me, after my wound at Ketzin the battalion had an order to capture Potsdam; on 27 April, together with the 2nd and the 3rd battalions, they took part in capturing Brandenburg and then had to repel attacks of German units, that were trying to break out of Berlin. Besides that, they also had to repel attacks from the west, from Wenck's 12th Army, which abandoned its positions against the English and American forces and had been ordered to break through to Berlin to relieve its garrison. After capturing Brandenburg on 6 May, 1945, the Brigade as a part of the 4th Guards Tank Army, carried out a forced march to Czechoslovakia, to Prague, which our Army liberated on 9 May. It was there, in a forest in vicinity of Prague that I found my battalion after my return from hospital.

Our Brigade travelled 450 kilometres during the Berlin operation in the nine days of the offensive, from 16 to 24 April from the Neisse to the western outskirts of Berlin, at an average speed of 40 or 50 kilometres a day. We suffered significant casualties in those battles, but destroyed the German units that stood in our way. Many Soviet prisoners of war that we liberated took an active part in those last battles, replacing our casualties. My cousin, the son of my father's sister, Alexander Georgievich Fedorov, was in the prisoner-of-war camp at Luckenwalde. In early spring of 1941 he was drafted into the Red Army as a construction officer in the rank of a Technical-Intendant, a rank equivalent to Lieutenant. In autumn of 1941 he was taken prisoner at Vyazma, where three Soviet armies, around 300,000 men, were surrounded. I have already mentioned that we, our battalion, rushed through Luckenwalde at night and did not stop there. After the war he served for some time in the 16th Guards Mechanized Brigade of our 6th Guards Corps, and in June he visited our battalion, but did not meet me, as I was away doing something on the battalion commander's order. I also went to visit him in his unit, but did not find him there – he had already been sent to the USSR. There were no complaints about Alexander's behaviour in German captivity, and in September 1945 he went back home to Smolensk, where he had lived before the war.

The war was over. My unending session of active service at the front, officially as a motor rifle platoon leader, and in reality mostly as a company commander, lasted from August 1943 to May 1945 – a total of 650 days or 22 months, which makes it almost two years. Every day the Germans fired at me, not only with small arms, but also with their artillery, mortars, tanks, air force and anti-tank teams with *Panzerfausts*, snipers and flame-throwers. They missed. They planted anti-personnel and anti-tank mines in my way. All these things were designed to kill me, wound me, hurt me and make me a cripple. The enemy was professionally trained, possessed modern military equipment and was expert in using it. The enemy was harsh, mean and brave. The enemy had the typical German punctual discipline. However, I survived. They could not kill me during daytime or night time, in winter or summer, in good or bad weather, in field or forest, in villages or cities. They did not manage to kill me or make me a cripple, but they did with many others. What helped me to survive? It is hard to answer this question. It was not just me who survived. Take, for example, my soldier Nikolai Chulkin – he did not even get wounded. But how many good, young and healthy men were killed in battle! Some were my subordinates, many others were just my brothers in arms. So many died when liberating our Motherland – the Union of Soviet Socialist Republics – from Nazi invasion, and later when crushing the enemy in Poland, Germany and Czechoslovakia... From the summer of 1943, when I came to the battalion, to May 1945, only one third of the officers remained – just 14 out of 45. The rest were wounded and never came back to the battalion or were killed. I bow my head before all those who died and I bow my head before their heroic deeds. May eternal glory be with them! Their heroic deeds will live for centuries and the memory of them will stay with me till the last day of my life.

EPILOGUE

In May of 1945 we were stationed near Prague, and in June the Brigade relocated to the Hungarian and Austrian border. I do not remember the name of the village. We built some temporary dwellings out of wooden planks for all the personnel of the battalion. Tsikanovski and I got the boards from a timber mill, we paid for it, but it was still cheap. Guschenkov, Shakulo, Mikheev and I also managed to get beds for ourselves, the company's officers. Besides that, Drozd also got a feather bed, pillow, blanket and even sheets for me. Many officers envied me because of this. We went through medical inspection there, apparently, there was an order to check the health of the officers. My height was 182 cm, weight 76 kg, age 22. They said I was healthy.

We stayed there for about a month. We did sports, such as cross-country running, climbing ropes, we even organized the Brigade's soccer championship. I was in the battalion's team. Later we were ordered to move out from that place and on to Vienna. On the way, during one of the breaks the battalion stayed for several days, while I was resting in a house on a feather bed with a pillow. The owners of the house were not there. Battalion commander Kozienko, his deputy, Gerstein, deputy chief of staff Romanov and machine-gun platoon leader Tsikanovski walked in. They woke me up. The battalion commander told me: 'You've had enough sleep. You and Tsikanovski are to get some wine. Take a car and go.' Someone added: 'Do not come back without wine.' We brought a decent barrel of some 600 litres of wine. All personnel got this dry wine during lunch in normal doses. No one was drunk.

Several days later the battalion reached Vienna. We were stationed near Wiener-Neustadt in Hitenberg village some 30 km from Vienna. I went on vacation to Moscow from there on 15 August, 1945.

In November we left Austria and moved to Vesprem in Hungary. My wife also arrived there. I had married my classmate on 5 September, 1945, during my vacation in Moscow. The barracks were large, there were several storeys, and all personnel of the Brigade stayed there. Officers lived in separate houses, some two or four men in a room. My wife and I stayed in Vesprem in the town's outskirts, with a Hungarian. We stayed in one room with a small stove, on which we cooked food and warmed tea.

We regularly held tactical training, but it was more for show. Everyone was tired of this tactical stuff, assaults of dummy enemy and so on. Older soldiers started to retire. Then the officers started to retire as well.

Between June and November Dr. Pankova, Guschenkov, Kashintsev, Mikheev, Oplesnin, Tsikanovski, Kes, Kostenko and a few other officers retired.

A military school had been established, which had two companies: one for training sergeants and the second for training officers. There were approximately 200 to 250 men in that school. I was appointed commander of this motley crew in late October 1945. Battalion commander Kozienko was against my appointment and was all the time demanding my return to the battalion, in which I was a company commander after the end of the war. Finally, after his recommendation I was relieved of my command of this school. The training was almost complete – cadets were promoted to sergeants, while drivers were still in the process of examination for driving licences. This all happened in Bernau, where the 4th Guards Tank Army, including our Brigade, was relocated in June 1946.

My wife and I received a two-room apartment in Bernau. The apartment was heated with stoves. The German stoves with tiling were really good! The stoves were heated with briquette coal. Gas, running water and a bathtub and gas heating were also there. Some furniture was also provided: a metal bed, table, sofa, wardrobe, a Telefunken radio set, silverware and even an iron. We lived in the city, next to some former barracks. The Brigade commander, his deputies and battalion commanders all lived in mansions for one or two families. All officers were there with families, children and wives.

They issued food rations both for me and for my wife, and when our son was born, they also provided rations for him, except for the cigarettes! In Hungary it was possible to exchange 'stuff' for food, but in Germany it was quite a problem, as the local population did not have any food. It was only in Berlin on the black market that one could exchange cigarettes for food, or rather delicacies – sausage, smoked fish and other things that were not available in the rations. In principle, the rations were sufficient, so we even fed the orderly, when he did not go to the canteen.

After I came back to the battalion, I was sent with my company to Friedrichagen to guard the former German centre for development of V missiles. At that time we did not know what kind of centre it was. We only knew that our experts were working there, some of them were Colonels and were holders of Stalin's Award (they had those small Stalin Award badges). We stayed there for three or four months, and then, in late November I think, we came back to our base.

In October 1946 they introduced wages depending on the military rank and office. Because of this my wage grew from 1200 roubles to 1500 or even 1700 roubles, I do not remember exactly. Besides that, we were issued German marks. However, one could not buy anything with them, and there was actually nothing to buy. One could go to a barber's shop – they had already opened again. One could pay with just cigarettes.

By 1947 there were only three veterans left in the battalion – commander T. G. Kozienko, his deputy, Gerstein, and me. By that time the battalion consisted of just eight officers and five soldiers. We prepared guns for long-term storage and helped the tank crews to prepare tanks for long-term storage. We did not do anything else, except for going on guard duty in the city, as there were almost no soldiers left in our Brigade.

In late December 1947 I went to the USSR, to Tbilisi. This was the end of my service in the 1st motor rifle company, 1st motor rifle battalion, 35th Guards Mechanized Kamenets-Podolsk Brigade.

BROTHERS IN ARMS

The Company

The company commander's staff consisted of the company commander himself, the company's Sergeant Major, the clerk, the medic, the orderly and the runners from the platoons. It is impossible to remember all the names of all soldiers, and there is no point in listing all the names. However, I will provide several names.

Vasily Blokhin, the company's Sergeant Major. He was older than me. He had been in the war for a long time, even taking part in the battle of Stalingrad. He was strong and tough, a former seaman of the Pacific Fleet. We became good friends. In March 1944, in the town of Skalat he was heavily wounded. After Blokhin Mikhail Karpovich Bratchenko, born in 1916, was appointed the company's Sergeant Major in September 1943. He was a veteran; in Kursk he was a machine-gun crew leader in the machine-gun company. A tall and strong person, he was a brave and demanding NCO, but also caring for his subordinates. He was with the company in action all the time. He treated me as a friend, but did not allow for any familiar manners. He was in the company from 1943 till the end of war. I met him in Moscow in 1995.

Barakovski, the company's clerk. A big guy, but not strong physically. He suffered from night-blindness – could not see anything in the evening. Took good care of his responsibilities. Soldiers often asked him for help. As a rule, he was with the company. I think that he went missing in action in January 1945 – I cannot remember where and how he disappeared.

Safronov, medic. He was approximately 45 years old, the company's veteran. He was a big and physically strong person. He took care of us well. He was kind-hearted and soft, a good comrade, he sometimes called us younger officers by our first names 'Zhenya', 'Pete'. It was only the company commander that he addressed with full title. He was killed in August 1944 at the Sandomir bridgehead by a shell from our Russian tank.

Jambul, sniper. A strong and muscular man. He was a Kazakh. He was expert in handling his rifle. Went missing in action in March 1944. He was very quiet as he did not speak good Russian.

Sabaev, assistant platoon leader. I took part in battles at Kursk together with him. He was of medium height, some five years older than I was. He was a cunning guy. After those battles he was appointed Sergeant Major of the 2nd company. I rarely saw him after that. He survived the war – I met him by accident after the war in Germany (in May 1945), when I was on my way back from hospital.

Andrey Ulianovich Drozd, my orderly from January 1945. Born 1925. In general, he was supposed to be called runner, but I would call him orderly. A tall guy, of the same height as me, he was fast, brave and always an optimistic person. He was very enduring, a wiry kind of guy. He saved my life during an assault, when he cut down a Fritz that had been aiming his rifle at me. He is still alive, living in Korosten (Ukraine). Worked as a driver after the war. Now retired.

Nikolai Ilyich Chulkin, clerk. Born in 1925. He arrived in the battalion in October 1943. He was of average height, not very strong physically, but enduring and brave. He was very modest. He would often go on reconnaissance missions with the squad, and many times was in hard situations, but managed to get out from them due to his bravery and cleverness. He had good handwriting and was appointed the company's and then battalion's clerk for his diligence, eagerness for work, as well as modesty and literacy. He served in the personnel section of the Brigade for a long time after the war (Bernau, Eastern Germany). He was awarded several times during the war. He worked as an operator of harvesting machine and was awarded with Order of

Lenin already in peace time. He lives in Vinnitsa area (Ukraine).

Nikolai Mikhailovich Savkin, Sergeant. Born in 1925. He arrived at the battalion in October 1943 with a replacement of almost untrained soldiers. He quickly won a good reputation. In almost every operation he was acting platoon leader, replacing wounded Lieutenant Petr Shakulo. Savkin was tall, quick and enduring. He was extremely brave. Always followed order. I liked him a lot. He went missing in action in January 1945 together with his squad and a tank that had broken down and had to stop for repairs. They later said that retreating German units that ended up in our rear, attacked the village where the tank had to stop. After a short battle Germans burnt the broken tank, destroyed the crew and executed the squad from main guns of their tanks. This is how Sergeant Nikolai Mikhailovich Savkin died, being 19 years old.

'Brotherly Heart', medic. He arrived after Safronov's death. He appeared in the company in October 1944. For some reason I only remember this nickname, not his last name or even his first name. He knew his job well, bandaging soldiers on the battlefield, sending wounded to the hospitals and burying the dead. He was quite old already, he was around 40 years old. He was a real fan of card games and made many officers addict to cards, but never cheated during card games. He was tall and slim, physically strong. When we were stationed on Sandomir bridgehead (autumn 1944), he was quite good at making moonshine. In April 1945 he was wounded in his back, when he was standing behind me on a tank and all splinters hit him, not me. I left a soldier together with him to send him to a hospital. I have not heard anything about him since that time.

Karabai Tajidaev, Sergeant. Born in 1925, a heavy machine-gun (Maxim) leader from the company's MG platoon. A Kazakh, he fought the war from 1943 to 1945. He survived the war. He was a great guy. He was of medium height, enduring and brave person. He arrived in the company in October 1943. At first he did not speak good Russian, but later learnt the language very well. I was always relying on the fire support of his Maxim machine-gun. He distinguished himself among other soldiers of his age with his outstanding bravery. Both the battalion and the company loved him, he was awarded with several decorations. He left the Brigade in 1947 (from Bernau, Germany).

Ivan Egorovich Karnaukhov, Sergeant. Born in 1925. He was short and not very strong physically, but fast and enduring. He was fast and mean in battle. He came back into the company after being wounded. He was the battalion's veteran, soldiers respected him and were not afraid to fight the war by his side. He was a good comrade and could find common language with everyone. He survived the war. In recent times (around 1995) he lived close to Samara. Until 1991 he worked as a chairman of his village soviet. Now retired.

Ivan Zakharovich Chechin, Maxim heavy machine gun crew leader. Born in 1925, a tall and physically strong person. In battle he was brave and smart. He provided fire support for our company in the battles in Lvov. He survived the war. In April and May 1945, we were in the same hospital with him. He had several decorations. He did not come back to the battalion after the hospital. Apparently, he left the service.

Konstantin Mikhailovich Efron, Private. Born in 1921, a tall, physically strong and enduring soldier. He was also brave. He arrived in the company in June 1944. Wounded in August 1944. Was treated in hospital in Kopychintsy. He survived the war and found me after the war. He lives in Moscow.

Anatoly Nikolaevich Danilyuk. Born in 1923. He arrived in the company in August 1944. He was part of partisan movement in Ukraine. It was he that swam across Havel channel in front of Ketzin together with several other soldiers and brought the ferry to our side, so that the company could cross the channel and assault the German positions. For this heroic deed, a real act of heroism, no one received an award. Danilyuk survived the war. He lives in Kiev. He used to work as a surgeon. We met in Moscow in 1995.

Mikhail Vladimirovich Sarafanov, Sergeant, rifle squad leader. Born in 1925. He was short and enduring, but not very strong physically. He was modest, but brave and stoic. One could rely on him, especially in reconnaissance missions. He had a sailor's gait – he would rock from side to side when walking and then step firmly on the ground. He was the first one to stand up during the assault, and the whole squad, and sometimes even platoon and company followed him. He was expert in handing his weapon. He cut down quite a few Fritzes with his submachine-gun. He survived the war. He passed away in 1977.

Pavel Nazarovich Poddubny, Sergeant, rifle squad leader. Born in 1925, he was quite tall. He was well-built, physically strong and enduring. One rarely meets a braver guy than him. He always assaulted the enemy at his full height, pressing forward. He was not afraid of Fritzes, on the contrary, they were scared of him. He never used a submachine-gun, he fought the war with his carbine. During an assault in April 1944 (in the vicinity of Dobropolie) a German machine-gun crew fled after seeing Poddubny, leaving their MG34, submachine-gun and lunch behind. His bravery was a good support and example for his soldiers. His soldiers felt confident and fit next to him. He had several decorations. I cannot say anything else about him or his life after the war.

Shamrai, Junior Sergeant. Arrived in October 1944 at Sandomir bridge-head. He fought the war well and had several decorations. But I do not remember what happened to him. When I came back from the hospital, he was no longer there.

Ishmuhametov, RPD machine gun crew member. Born in 1925. He was a tall, slim and enduring guy. Survived the war. He was brave and his machine-gun always worked. However, during battles around Sambor (Lvov operation) he screwed up, which was really not like him, leaving his machine-gun behind, so that it would be easier to flee the Germans. That was his only act of cowardice in the whole war. He fought till the end of the war and retired from service.

Alexei Pavlovich Kolesnikov, Sergeant, assistant platoon leader. Born in 1925. He was of medium height, slim, physically strong and quick (an important feature in combat). He distinguished himself with bravery. He would be the first one to stand up during the assault, carrying the rest of the platoon behind. Was also tenacious in defence. He easily took all hardships of life at the front. He would never lose heart and was always cheerful. He was awarded with the Order of Glory 2nd and 3rd degree. He was wounded in the end of the war and went to the hospital.

The Women of the Battalion

I also still remember several names of women that fought the war in the battalions of our Brigade.

Praskovia Mikhailovna Pankova, Senior Lieutenant of Medical Corps, doctor of our 1st battalion. Born in 1920, she arrived at the battalion in June 1944. She survived the war. Dismissed from service in June 1945 on the grounds of pregnancy. She was married to deputy battalion commander M. T. Burkov, who was killed in January 1945. Her ambulance vehicle was in the same column with us, with tanks. She provided timely treatment to the wounded. I remember two or three occasions when their ambulance was destroyed by the enemy. Guri Borisovich Yaranski, her medical assistant, was killed. She must have had a hard time to be the only woman among hundreds of soldiers, but she stood up to the test. Everyone respected her a lot. She had several awards from the government.

Cook. The second woman in our battalion, I do not remember her last name, but everyone called her Lelka (apparently her full name was Elena). She survived the war and was dismissed from service after the war. She was no more than 25 years old. She was quite chubby and short. She arrived in the battalion most probably in November 1944. I saw her after the war, she left service in 1945.

Alexandra Grigorieva. (We called her Shurka) After the war she married the battalion's chief of staff, Grigoriev. I do not remember how she ended up in the battalion, she was some kind of a medic. I think she arrived in March or April 1945. I rarely saw her and can say almost nothing about her. She survived the war and stayed in the Brigade as Yuri Grigoriev's wife.

Brothers in Arms

Maria Ivanovna Chernomorets, doctor of the 2nd battalion, Lieutenant of Medical Corps. She went through the war and survived. She married 2nd battalion commander Major Grigori Afanasievich Chernomorets. I kept correspondence with them after the war, but after Grigori's death the correspondence stopped. They lived in Stryi, Western Ukraine.

Nina Arkhipovna Vasiltsova, doctor of the Brigade's medical platoon. She went through the whole war as Captain of the Medical Corps. She was a fragile woman, but everything worked out fine. After the war she married to tank regiment commander Major Alexander Danilovich Stolyarov. I maintain contact with her, she lives in Gomel (Belorussia).

Evdokia Alexandrovna Chuyah, medic of the Brigade's medical platoon. Born 1921. She had been at the front from the battle for Stalingrad (from 1942). She survived the war. After the war she married to the 3rd motor rifle battalion commander of the Brigade, Major Alexander Grigorievich Chuyah. They had three sons, now already grown up, they have their own families. However, one of their sons died, and Evdokia herself also died (in 1998). Alexander, her husband, died in 1988. They lived in Dnepropetrovsk. I stayed in touch with them until their deaths.

I remember that there was also *Anastasia Mikhailovna Turchenko*, born in 1921, in the medical platoon. She lives in Dnepropetrovsk. Sukacheva, another female medic, also served in that platoon. After the war she married to deputy Brigade commander (technical support) Leonid Timofeevich Sukachev. She lives in Saint Petersburg.

Officers of the Brigade

I would like to add few final lines about the fate of my brother officers from the Brigade, about their lives after the war. Some of them continued their service in the army:

Tank Rider

Colonel Petr Nikitovich Turkin, Brigade commander. He stayed in the army after the war and served for some seven to ten years. Before his retirement he served in Kaliningrad (former Koenigsberg). This is where he settled with his wife, Alla Alexeevna. When he passed away in the spring of 1987, he was over 80 years old.

Colonel Grigori Vasilievich Starovoit, Deputy Brigade commander. Born in 1915. Apparently he served in the army until 1965 and settled down in Kiev. I met him at the Brigade's veterans meeting in Kiev (as he left for Kiev for the office of Brigade commander in 1946). Passed away in 1985.

Lieutenant-Colonel Afanasi Grigorievich Skryago. Born in 1906. Settled down in Kiev after retirement. Passed away in 1966. I did not have any contact with him.

Major-General Vasili Ignatievich Koretski, Chief of Staff of the 6th Guards Mechanized Corps. Born in 1913, retired from the office of chief of staff of the 5th Guards Tank Army. He lived in Dnepropetrovsk. Passed away on 23 August, 1986.

Lieutenant-Colonel Terenti Grigorievich Kozienko, battalion commander. Born in 1914. Served in the army until 1955. Retired as deputy regiment commander and settled down in Cherkassy. He passed away on 30 January, 1995 after a prolonged illness. Our families stayed in touch with him and often visited each other.

Major Abram Efimovich Gerstein. Born in 1912, former political officer of the battalion. He was in the army until 1955. After his retirement he lived in Moscow. He died in 1995. I used to meet him often at the veteran meetings. I visited him when S. N. Kostenko and I. S. Tsikanovski visited Moscow.

Major Petr Sergeevich Shakulo. Born in 1923, served in the army until 1971. He did not have any higher military education, this is why his career was so slow. He served in the local army recruitment office in town of Essentuki. This is where he died on 6 July, 1986 after a serious illness.

Colonel Fedor Grigorievich Popov. Born in 1925. He was in the army for over 40 years, until 1985. He retired at the age of 60. Together with him I served in the head personnel section of the Defence Ministry. After that he was transferred to the office of head of personnel department of the Engineer department of the State Committee of external relations (there was such a body during the soviet times). Fedor died on 10 April, 1994.

Lieutenant-Colonel Nikolai Danilovich, mortar platoon leader. Born in 1923. Retired in 1947 and joined the service again in 1957 – he entered the military institute of conductors (there was such a college, later it was reformed and made the military faculty at Moscow Conservatoire). After graduation he served in the Baltic Military district. Later, in 1957, he was transferred to the Ministry of the Interior and appointed the military conductor of Irkutsk military academy of the Ministry of the Interior. He died in February 1996 after a prolonged illness.

Colonel Alexander Danilovich Stolyarov, Commander of the tank regiment of the Brigade. Born in 1914, served in the army in different offices after the war. After his retirement from the army he settled down in Gomel (Belorussia). He passed away on 4 December, 1999.

Colonel Vladimir Dmitrievich Belyakov, Company commander. Born in 1924. Retired from the office of military commissar of Chimkent (Kazakhstan). Passed away on 24 June, 1989. He lived in town of Troitsy, Moscow region.

Colonel Alexander Ivanovich Traiduk, deputy chief of staff of the battalion. Born in 1923. Was the deputy chief of staff of the battalion. Later served as military prosecutor in Nizhni Tagil, Sverdlovsk region. He passed away in 1990.

Colonel Nikolai Dmitrievich Tsygankov, the Brigade's HQ commandant. Born in 1923. After the war he served as the military commissar of Timiryazevo district in Moscow. Passed away on 22 October, 1991.

Nikolai Konstantinovich Chernyshov, Senior Lieutenant, 1st company commander of the battalion. Born in 1924. They said that he drank himself to death, selling all his war decorations. He died in 1978.

Lieutenant Alexei Kuzmich Belyakov, commander of the 2nd company of the battalion. He lived in Podolsk. Passed away in 1987.

Lieutenant Israel Solomonovich Tsikanovski, machine-gun platoon leader of the 3rd company of the battalion. Died in Tashkent in 1990.

Senior Lieutenant Anatoly Anatolievich Kashintsev, commander of the battalion's mortar company. Passed away on 9 July, 1992.

Classmates

I think that now it is time to recall my classmates and friends from school. The guys with whom I graduated from high school in June 1941. I will mention the guys of my age, the ones that went into the war in 1941 and many of whom did not make it back. Dozens of years have passed since the end of the Great Patriotic War, and now I am writing about the guys that I grew up with, the ones I studied with and with whom I was good friends. First I will mention my classmates. There were 31 children in my class, 15 girls and 16 boys. Of these boys 9 survived and 7 died.

German Gavrilov. Born in 1923. I studied with him from the 1st grade. He looked quite sickly. He was physically weak and I think he did not even do physical education. He studied quite well, even very well in the last classes. He was modest, silent and quiet. He was good friend of everyone, did not have any best friends. Killed in action.

Vasily Zolotukhin. Born in 1922. I started to study in the same class with him in the 8th grade. He was a very successful student. He was also physically fit – he was a good soccer player and was even part of Lokomotiv youth team. A very ambitious guy. Was slightly arrogant with the rest of the guys. I did not make good friends with him. He was the school's Komsomol secretary in the 10th grade. It was only Nikolai Kaminin that was at friendly terms with him – Zolotukhin helped him in his studies. Zolotukhin was killed in 1941 during battle of Moscow.

Nikolai Kaminin. Born in 1923. A short and physically strong guy, he was a fast, happy and kind-hearted person. He was a good friend of everyone, but especially with Zolotukhin. He was quite bad in his studies. Everyone in the class loved him. For some time I helped him in mathematics, as we lived on the same street. He was killed in battle of Kursk in 1943. I studied with him from the 8th grade.

Yuri Novitski. Born in 1923. He was a tall and slim guy. He did not have a sense of humour and was always offended with our jokes. He was an athletic guy and a successful student. He did not have any good friends, I do not know why. He was killed in 1944. I studied together with him from the 1st grade.

Vladimir Popov. Born in 1923. He was a good comrade and a calm person. He could study better. I was friends with him. He was physically strong. He left school before graduation. He completed a course in pilot club and entered a military school of junior specialists. During the war he was a tail gunner and a radioman of a bomber crew. He was killed in 1943. I studied with him from the 8th grade. Everyone in the class respected him.

Leonid Fetisov. Born in 1923. A good guy. I studied with him from the 1st grade. He was tall and calm. He did not do any sports. He had the best grades in the 10th grade, especially in mathematics. We were good friends with him. He was modest and timid. He was the first guy in our class to be killed – on 8 August, 1941 he was killed by a German bomb next to his house at Bolshaya Pochtovaya street.

Alexander Fokin. Born in 1923. He was a tall and athletic guy. He was good at volleyball and taught me to play volleyball, too. He was calm and the most beautiful guy in the whole class. He was quite respected in the class. He had good grades. He, Zolotokhin and I had the best results in high jumps in the whole class during the 10th grade. He studied with us from the 8th grade. He was a sociable and humorous guy. We were good friends and also had another friend from another class – Andrey Otryganiev. That guy survived the war and died in 1955 from stomach cancer. Alexander and I were drafted on the same day; the only difference was that I went into infantry, while he went into artillery academy. He was killed during the battle of Kursk in 1943.

Nikolai Balabanov. Born in 1923. He was of average height, physically weak. He was calm, but he deserved his last name – he was an awful *balaban* (chatterbox), he could lie very well. He was not a very good student, as he was awfully lazy. He would often copy homework from the others. I studied with him from the 7th grade. I met him after the war, he said that he had been at the front, but I did not understand where he was and what he we was. I have not heard anything about him later.

Vladimir Grivnin. Born in 1923. He came to our class in the 8th grade. He had top grades. He was of average height and a physically fit, calm and modest person. I was a good friend of his. We prepared for the final exams in the 10th grade together at his place. He helped me a lot. We heard the news of the war together with him at retro film theatre. In 1941 he entered the Military Institute of oriental studies and graduated it. He did not go to the front. Some twenty years ago he was a professor in Moscow University, as they told me. I did not meet him after the war.

Viktor Kasatikov. Born in 1923. He was a strong and average sized guy. From the 1st grade he only had excellent grades. He was especially strong in mathematics. He was modest and timid, somehow he did not make friends with anyone. He fought the war and survived. I met him after the war, but did not quite understand what he did at the front and where he was. I did not have any contact with him. They said that he joined the Ministry of Interior.

Boris Kopchenov. Born in 1923. I studied together with him from the 1st grade. He was shy and timid, he would blush all the time. He studied well and in the 10th grade he started to study *very* well. He was a company commander in the war. I met him in 1949 after the war, but the meeting was short. I have not heard anything about him since that time.

Alexander Lapin. Born in 1923. He was a short, but strong guy. I studied together with him from the 8th grade. He was silent and modest. He had top grades in the 10th grade. He did not have any good friends, but I was at friendly terms with him. He had a good sense of humour. He fought the war and survived. He graduated from college after the war and worked in a factory as an engineer. I met him between 1949 and 1952, although quite rarely. I did not have any close contact with him. I do not know where he is now.

Mark Popov. Born in 1923. He studied in our class from the 8th grade. An excellent student, a decent and clever guy. Of small height. He had weak health, something went wrong with his leg and he was incapacitated. He did not serve in the army. I met him in 1943, he lived with his parents somewhere in Siberia. I have not heard anything from him since that time.

Ivan Sedov, Born in 1922. I knew him from the 1st grade. He was very diligent student. He was quite well built, but did not do any sports. He did not have friends. He was modest. He fought the war. Actually, in 1941 he entered the Military Institute of oriental studies (together with Grivnin), but in 1942 he asked the Institute to let him go to the front. He went through the war. For some time he served in the army. Retired from service in 1955. Later he worked as a professor in Moscow University. He lives in Moscow. Sometimes we call each other, but never meet.

Viktor Selvanovich, Born in 1923. We studied together from the 1st grade. He had weak health and was modest. He was calm and did not have friends. He studied quite well. We were friends with him; he did not make friends with anyone else. We were also neighbours, our houses were facing each other. We were drafted on the same day, on 11 August, 1941. He fought the war, was heavily wounded and retired from service. He lived in Perm together with his wife. I met him when he came to Moscow to visit his mother. After that I lost contact with him.

I have already written about myself during my school years. I was skinny, but sports helped me: bar, soccer, volleyball, wrestling, skiing and skating – well, I was quite bad at skating. I did not obtain any significant results, but became stronger, especially after starting wrestling sessions at Lokomotiv stadium. For some reason I was a bad student before 6th and 7th grades. In the 9th and 10th grades I started to make progress. I did not become a distinguished student and never was one. I was good friends with everyone. As someone said: 'we only deserve respect to the extent that we can appreciate the others.'

INDEX

Index